REVOLUTIONISTS IN LONDON

REVOLUTIONISTS IN LONDON

A STUDY OF
FIVE UNORTHODOX SOCIALISTS

BY

JAMES W. HULSE

CLARENDON PRESS · OXFORD

1970

Oxford University Press, Ely House, London W.1

GLASGOW NEW YORK TORONTO MELBOURNE WELLINGTON
CAPE TOWN SALISBURY IBADAN NAIROBI DAR ES SALAAM LUSAKA
ADDIS ABABA BOMBAY CALCUTTA MADRAS KARACHI LAHORE
DACCA KUALA LUMPUR SINGAPORE HONG KONG TOKYO

PRINTED IN GREAT BRITAIN
BY BUTLER AND TANNER LTD
FROME AND LONDON

TO
BETTY

60865

FOREWORD

FOR several years I have had an interest in left-wing political movements and the men who guided them, but the conventional histories of Socialism, Communism, and Anarchism have often been disappointing. They are usually so technical, so preoccupied with institutional and doctrinal disputes, and so narrow in scope that they tell little of the personalities involved. Finding people more interesting than petty factional struggles and men of integrity more fascinating than men of power, I began to concentrate on some of the Socialists and Anarchists of the late nineteenth and early twentieth centuries who were oddities within their own movement as well as critics of the larger society. This interest led, of course, to a number of dead-ends, but eventually it did produce some observations that seemed to be interesting enough to offer to my colleagues.

Much of the work for this manuscript was possible because the Desert Research Institute of the University of Nevada provided a grant which enabled me to spend several months at the Library of Congress in 1966, and subsequently a sabbatical leave allowed me to complete the project at Oxford. In addition, I was privileged to use the collections of the British Museum, the International Institute of Social History in Amsterdam, the New York Public Library, and the Berkeley Library of the University of California. I have relied regularly upon the resources of the Stanford University Library and the Hoover Institution for more than a decade, and I have called most frequently upon the helpful librarians at the University of Nevada in Reno. My intellectual debt and gratitude to the personnel of these institutions is constantly growing.

Fellow historians at Nevada—particularly Russell R. Elliott, Wilbur S. Shepperson, and Paul H. Smith—often encouraged me and shielded me from distracting pressures. Robert Armstrong kindly lent me volumes from his admirable collection on Bernard Shaw. Mrs. Rose Tollefson has been a most conscientious, patient, and efficient typist; her contributions to this effort were substantial. R. Harré of Linacre College, Oxford, gave valued advice and encouragement at an important point in the evolution of the manuscript. The staff of The Clarendon Press have been generous with assistance and efficient in their handling of the work.

I am grateful to the Society of Authors of London for permission to quote from the works of Bernard Shaw, to the Society of Antiquaries of London for permission to quote from unpublished writings of William Morris, and to Basil Blackwell and Mott Ltd. for permission to use certain passages from May Morris, *William Morris: Artist, Writer, Socialist.*

Above all, I acknowledge the devotion and patience of my wife, to whom this volume is dedicated. She has handled her duties as critic and editor almost as naturally as those of home-maker and mother. My two small children, while not exactly contributors to a project that required hours of quiet concentration, have seemed to make the study of idealistic reformers of the past more pertinent for the future, so they too have had a part in pushing the effort along. It would have been much less meaningful without them.

J. W. H.

Oxford, *March,* 1969

CONTENTS

I

FIVE SOCIAL REFORMERS IN LONDON

In the summer of 1876, a distinguished Russian aristocrat escaped from a prison hospital in St. Petersburg and hid for a few days from the imperial gendarmes of Tsar Alexander II. Aware that the police were diligently searching for him throughout the city and that he was too well known to escape arrest, he fled across Finland and Sweden, in a few days reaching the port of Christiania. Still apparently pursued by Tsarist spies or others who might betray him, he sought a ship that would take him to England. Informed that a vessel was available for passage to Hull, the refugee proceeded to the place of embarkment:

. . . As I went to the steamer, I asked myself with anxiety, 'Under which flag does she sail,—Norwegian, German, English?' Then I saw floating above the stern the union jack,—the flag under which so many refugees, Russian, Italian, French, Hungarian and of all nations, have found an asylum. I greeted that flag from the depth of my heart.[1]

This refugee was Prince Peter Kropotkin, by birth a member of Russia's most privileged aristocracy but by choice a revolutionary propagandist. That he should have fled to Britain under the circumstances was logical, for as his words imply, that island and its people had the reputation for accepting the human flotsam and jetsam from other shores and giving them a home. Since the early eighteenth century, London and her sister cities had seen a parade of outcasts and misfits from foreign lands, and they had provided not only relative safety but in some cases instruction and opportunities to carry on the intellectual activities that had been forbidden at home. A century and a half earlier Voltaire had retreated from the threat of punishment at Versailles, where his wit was not appreciated, and his three-year exile provided the material for his *Lettres sur les Anglais*, which was promptly banned and burned after its appearance in France in 1733.

Although Britain had produced its own substantial contingent

[1] Peter Kropotkin, *Memoirs of a Revolutionist* (Boston, New York, 1899), p. 377.

of expatriates who sought refuge on the continent in the seventeenth century, the number and importance of these people declined in the eighteenth century, and by the early nineteenth century she was well established as a haven for political outcasts. The press was relatively freer there and the police institutions less restrictive. And the British showed no special preference for either the rebels of the Left or the would-be monarchs of the Right. To these shores came Étienne Cabet, the French Socialist, in 1834, and he used the British Museum as he wrote his *Voyage en Icarie*. A few years later Louis Napoleon, the pretender to his uncle's imperial heritage, was able to use the island as a base for his planning and his pleasures. When Prince Clemens Metternich fled from the Vienna revolutionaries in 1848, it was to England that he went to spend the dangerous weeks, and when the revolutionary forces within the Austrian Empire were crushed, it was in England that many of the threatened rebels chose to seek safety. In the 1850s, one might have encountered there, among others, Louis Kossuth, Giuseppi Mazzini, Karl Marx, and Alexander Herzen. Many of such men published and proselytized, and a few of them were welcomed as heroes by small contingents of admirers.

England, of course, was not the only place that a renegade politician or rebel might go for safety, but it was the country most willing to accept the whole spectrum of exiles over a long period of time. Switzerland, which was also relatively receptive to foreign outcasts, became less tolerant to Russian revolutionaries after the assassination of Alexander II in 1881, and it discouraged the German Socialists from operating there after 1888. Belgium and France were even more inconsistent in their policies, and the United States was too distant to satisfy most men who had aspirations to return to their homelands in triumph in a relatively short time.

In addition to the advantages of proximity and tolerance, Britain offered its visitors a cosmopolitan audience on which to test their various ideas. The hub of the Victorian empire, London had assembled representatives from scores of principalities and provinces beyond the seas, and it Anglicized non-Britishers by the thousands, enabling them to share ideas and impressions more readily than in any other place in the world. In the process of embracing the expatriates, the British often brainwashed them; Voltaire is only one of the most prominent beneficiaries—or, if you will, victims—of this unconscious, unplanned process. The Anglicized American Henry James was expansive on the subject in 1888:

London is indeed an epitome of the round world, and just as it is a commonplace to say that there is nothing one can't 'get' there, so it is equally true that there is nothing one may not study at first hand.

. . . once in a while the best believer recognises the impulse to set his religion in order, to sweep the temple of his thoughts and trim the sacred lamp. It is at such hours as this that he reflects with elation that the British capital is the particular spot in the world which communicates the greatest sense of life.[1]

Ford Madox Ford, in his perceptive description of the city written shortly after the turn of the century, represented it as essentially democratic (James had also applied such an adjective to it), assimilating and gently erasing the intellectual differences of those who came from abroad.

If in its tolerance it finds a place for all eccentricities of physiognomy, of costume, of cult, it does so because it crushes out and floods over the significance of those eccentricities.

. . . it destroys all race characteristics, insensibly and, as it were, anaesthetically.[2]

This is exaggeration, of course, but it is not a serious misrepresentation of London of that time. Not only the metropolis but also the British generation of the late nineteenth century was tolerant of novelty. In every section of London there were debating clubs, societies, and periodicals with which a foreigner might identify and to which he could occasionally pour forth his ideas. Even the pages of the sedate and prestigious *Times* often carried the news and the compositions of the more notable renegades. The presence of such a receptive environment obviously caused some of the foreigners to adjust their messages to it. This era in England was characterized by an attitude of 'social earnestness' —to use the term that Holbrook Jackson applied to the 1880s,[3] a condition that was encouraging for many of those who had fled

---

[1] Henry James, *English Hours* (Boston, New York, 1905), pp. 11, 12.
[2] Ford Madox Ford, *The Soul of London: A Survey of a Modern City* (London, 1911), pp. 11–12.
[3] Holbrook Jackson, *The Eighteen Nineties: A Review of Art and Ideas at the Close of the Nineteenth Century* (London, 1913), p. 28.

from their homelands because their social and political ideals had got them into trouble. So it was with Kropotkin and some of his fellow Russians.

TWO NARODNIKS

Because of his prestigious ancestry and his family traditions, Kropotkin belonged to the high ranks of the Russian aristocracy. Few families in Russia had better credentials of nobility than the Kropotkins, and no one had better claim to the positions and honours that the Tsar could bestow on the well-born. As a boy, Peter had been a member of the select corps of pages in the imperial palace, and for a time had been a personal attendant of the Tsar himself. This could have been a stepping-stone to special privileges and opportunities in the political hierarchy of St. Petersburg, but by gradual steps the young Prince turned away from his heritage and embraced the cause that made him an outlaw, racing across Europe to avoid the wrath of his royal master's agents.

Kropotkin brought to England substantial scientific training as well as revolutionary zeal. He was one of the better educated of Russia's aristocratic young men and one of his country's most promising scholars. He was only thirty-four years of age when he made his famous flight to England, but he had already established himself as a leading geographer by his scholarly papers and books. In his early twenties, he had explored Siberia and Manchuria with military and scientific expeditions and had produced a new—and correct—thesis about the geographical structure of northern Asia. His fertile imagination and his study of Arctic Ocean currents enabled him to speculate on the existence of the Franz Joseph Islands north of the heartland of Russia several years before they were discovered. His fruitful hypotheses on the ice age of Europe and on the changing climate of Eurasian land mass invigorated geographical studies in Russia and elsewhere for several years. For a period of nearly forty years after 1880, Kropotkin's main scientific writings were published in English journals for Anglo-Saxon readers.

It was his second reputation, however, that was most striking to the average Englishman. Kropotkin had become a Communist-Anarchist during his first visit to Europe in 1872, accepting some of the objectives—but not necessarily the methods—of Bakunin. Deeply influenced by his exile contacts in Switzerland and with the watchmakers of the Jura Federation, he had returned to Russia convinced that anarchistic principles could be used to refashion society. He had joined the famous Chaikovsky circle of St. Petersburg, and when some of its members decided to carry a message of reform to the people, Kropotkin was among them. He was one of those *narodniki* arrested in 1874 when the imperial authorities strangled the movement, and he spent two years in prison before his dramatic escape in the summer of 1876.

The flight to England in that year was only the preliminary to his eventual settlement there. Ten more years of revolutionary adventure were to intervene before Kropotkin, in 1886, became a permanent resident of London. In the interim, he went to Switzerland where he edited a small newspaper, *Le Révolté*, and published his first hopes and projections for the rebuilt anarchistic society. He also issued pamphlets and worked with Geneva revolutionaries until Swiss authorities expelled him in 1881—an after-effect of the assassination of Tsar Alexander II. He went to England in the fall of that year and made an unfruitful effort to stimulate a revolutionary movement there; England's Left Wing had not yet awakened from the lethargy that had immobilized it for two decades, and Kropotkin became increasingly frustrated. Moving to France in 1882 during a time of industrial tension, he was arrested with a group of other anarchists, taken to Lyons, accused of criminal membership in the outlawed International Workingmen's Association, and sentenced to prison after a widely publicized trial. He spent nearly three years in prison, while his case and his recurring illnesses were widely discussed by intellectuals and left-wing agitators in England and on the Continent. Finally, after many strong protests on his behalf in France and elsewhere, he was released early in 1886 from the prison at Clairvaux, and he went once more to England. Here he was to remain, except for brief trips, for more than thirty years, until his return to Russia in 1917, in the evening of his life.

Kropotkin had an unusual place among the Russian *émigrés* in the final quarter of the nineteenth century. In a short time he became the most famous of the Russian exiles in Western Europe and the senior member of that restless fraternity. He was a link between the generation of the sixties and that of the nineties, not belonging quite to either. The writings of Herzen had helped enlist his sympathies for the reformist cause when the young prince was in the Tsar's corps of pages in the late 1850s. Kropotkin recalled in later years how avidly he had read the prose of *Poliarnaia Zvezda* (The Polar Star):

> The beauty of the style of Hérzen,—of whom Turguéneff has truly said that he wrote in tears and blood, and that no other Russian had ever so written,—the breadth of his ideas, and his deep love of Russia took possession of me, and I used to read and re-read those pages, even more full of heart than of brain.[1]

The gentle scholar never quite escaped the influence of Herzen, while most of those who followed him into exile were nourished on harsher fare.

Herzen had been dead for six years when Kropotkin reached England in 1876, and Herzen's generation was quickly passing from the scene. Michael Bakunin, from whom Kropotkin borrowed some of his anarchist ideas, had died in Berne during the same summer that Kropotkin escaped from the prison hospital in St. Petersburg. The two men never met. Nikolai Ogarev, the friend and associate of Herzen who worked for a time in London on *Kolokol* (The Bell) and who was regarded as one of the leaders of the movement in the early 1870s, became mentally unreliable in the middle of the decade and died in 1877. Peter Lavrov, the author of the much discussed *Historical Letters* of 1868–9 and the hero of a vigorous circle of gradualist reformers in the middle 1870s, ran into troubles with some of his disciples. His periodical *Vperiod* floundered, and after 1877, he was semi-retired. Although he lived until 1900 in various parts of Europe and wrote some propaganda, he was, in the words of Richard Hare, 'nearly an extinct volcano, a lonely and rather pathetic figure . . .'

The new generation of notable expatriates, including such persons as Georgi Plekhanov and Vera Zasulich, began to arrive in substantial numbers in the late 1870s. There was, of course, a good deal of illicit moving across the Russian frontier, but we are here concerned with the long-term exiles who were more or less permanently separated from their homeland. In short order Kropotkin had the questionable distinction of being an 'old exile', long removed from the internal struggles.

Kropotkin had relatively little contact with the revolutionary

[1] Kropotkin, *Memoirs of a Revolutionist*, p. 127.

movements after they became terroristic, and he had strong reservations about this kind of activity. In his *narodnik* days he had been an opponent of Nechayevism—the policy of cynical, amoral revolutionary action which embraced a programme of reckless terror—and he advocated rigid limits for this weapon from his exile. As editor of *Le Révolté*, he preferred to discuss the ills of society and the arrangements that would follow the revolutionary transformation, rather than to advocate violence. When he proposed 'propaganda by deed', he was not referring exclusively or even primarily to assassination or other social outrage; he was more interested in propaganda and education, with acts of violence to be reserved for cases when self-defence was involved. He found the Russian revolutionary activities of the late 1870s and early 1880s incompatible with his personal objectives. One of his Russian friends wrote of him in 1882:

He is too exclusive, and rigid in his theoretical convictions. He admits no departure from the ultra-anarchical programme, and has always considered it impossible, therefore, to contribute to any of the revolutionary newspapers in the Russian language, published abroad and in St. Petersburg. He has always found in them some point of divergence, and, in fact, has never written a line in any of them.

It may be doubted whether he could ever be the leader, or even the organiser of a party, with conspiracy as its sole means of action. For conspiracy, in the great Revolutionary struggle, is like guerrilla fighting in military warfare. . . .

Krapotkine's natural element is war on a grand scale, and not guerrilla fighting. He might become the founder of a vast Social movement, if the condition of the country permitted.[1]

The author of these lines was Sergei Mikhailovich Kravchinskii, better known to his contemporaries by his revolutionary pseudonym 'Stepniak'. When he wrote these lines, he was living in Italy, but within a few months he too would be settled in London, and for the remainder of his life he would be in close contact with the anarchist prince, with British Socialists, and with members of the English exile community. He took up permanent residence in London in 1883—nearly three years before Kropotkin's final arrival there, and for a dozen years he did more than any other individual to convince the English-reading public that there was

[1] Stepniak, *Underground Russia: Revolutionary Profiles and Sketches from Life*, with a Preface by Peter Lavroff. Translated from the Italian (London, 1883), pp. 98–9.

some merit in the cause of the Russian revolutionary movement and some justification for the policy of assassination.

Like Kropotkin, Stepniak had blossomed as a revolutionary agitator in the Chaikovsky circle between 1871 and 1874. He was ten years younger than Kropotkin and undoubtedly more dramatic and daring. During his youthful years of training in a military academy, he had been fired by the writings of Bakunin and had helped to distribute the periodical *Narodnoe Delo* among his colleagues. As a member of the Chaikovsky circle, he had proved to be zealous and fearless. With an extensive knowledge of the Bible, he had adapted scriptural texts to his revolutionary message and had become interested in the anti-Orthodox groups as potential centres for rebellion. When the imperial regime stifled the *narodnik* movement in 1874—putting Kropotkin among others in prison— Stepniak escaped.

For a few years, he was a Garibaldi-like adventurer. He went to Herzegovina in 1875 to participate with Serbian insurgents against the Turks. According to some accounts, he had a role in Kropotkin's escape from prison in 1876. In 1877, he was involved in the ill-fated Benevento uprising in the vicinity of Naples and was one of the insurgents condemned to death. Escaping once more, he appeared in Switzerland in revolutionary circles in 1878, and there he heard of the dramatic act of Vera Zasulich—the attempted assassination of General Trepov. Returning once more to St. Petersburg to throw himself into the intensified conspiratorial movement, he became an editor of the underground periodical *Zemlia i Volia*.

On 16 August 1878, he performed the most spectacular deed of a spectacular life. In a St. Petersburg street, he walked up to the chief of the Imperial Third Section, Adjutant General Mezentsev, and assassinated him in the full light of day. With characteristic skill and good fortune, he eluded the authorities once more and immediately published an explanation of his act, a provocative pamphlet entitled *Smert' za smert'*—a death for a death. He continued to operate in the underground for more than two years and then went into exile again.[1] In 1881 he was in Geneva, in close

---

[1] Not all biographical accounts are in agreement on this point. According to an article written by Stepniak's friend Felix Volkhovsky for *Free Russia* (London), VII (February 1, 1896), p. 14, Stepniak left Russia in the autumn of 1878 and never returned. According to most accounts, his last departure was a year or two later.

contact with his friend Kropotkin, and by 1882 he was contributing articles to Italian newspapers, describing the oppressions of the Tsarist regime and the struggles against it. From these articles—as from Kropotkin's journalistic pieces published in *Le Révolté*— came a book that was to receive considerable attention and to give Stepniak new opportunities for revolutionary work.

This book, published initially in Italian as *La Russia Sotterranea*, appeared in English as *Underground Russia* in 1883 and introduced Stepniak to the Anglo-Saxon countries. During the same year, Stepniak moved to London, determined to exploit the interest that his book had aroused. He called himself a nihilist and undertook a crusade of ambitious scope. In the course of the next twelve years, he produced several more books and many articles on the 'Russian inquisition' and won an extensive reputation. He became one of the important participants in the social reform movements that took form in England in the last years of the century, but he did not live to see the new century begin. The man who had proved so adept at evading the Tsar's police network was struck and killed by a train in London in December 1895.

These two men—Russia's most famous anarchist and her most outspoken nihilist—found the English-speaking world remarkably receptive to their respective messages. In effect, they resumed in Great Britain the *narodnik* programme that they had been forced to suspend in Russia a decade earlier. Both of them became active in groups that resembled the Chaikovsky circle in their general objectives. They were regarded with suspicion and fear by some English people who came in contact with them, but they won many admirers beyond the ranks of the revolutionary circles, and by the middle of the 1890s, England had done much to tame their revolutionary impulses. They were both moderates, and they were both dedicated to a more noble standard of morality than most of their revolutionary colleagues. They gave prestige to the Russian revolutionary cause perhaps as much by their personal conduct as by their propaganda, and they lent support to the idea that the revolutionary could be a man of honour.

A GERMAN REBEL

The man whom later generations have come to regard as Victorian London's most important resident exile—Karl Marx—was gone from the scene by the time Stepniak and Kropotkin took up their work there, and he did not quite belong to their *genre* in any event. Marx had not thrown himself into the midst of English life and controversy; he was a recluse, working erratically at his theoretical and economic treatises, keeping his circle of English friends rather small. His colleague and benefactor, Friedrich Engels, was somewhat more involved in English life as a Manchester manufacturer and, in his later years, as a resident of London, but he too preferred a rather limited contact with the variety of revolutionaries in the city.

After the death of Marx in 1883, Engels constituted a kind of pope for the Marxian orthodox for a dozen years. He devoted himself to carrying forward Marx's unfinished work on *Das Kapital* and tried to guide the Social Democratic movement in Germany through his contacts with younger disciples of the Marxian doctrine. Engels had been urged after the death of Marx to move to Zurich, but he had declined. England offered more security and a better opportunity to carry on the research and organizational work that Marx's papers required, and residence on the continent might have required his participation in agitation. For this, he did not feel suited in the 1880s.[1]

Although Engels has become famous for some of his brief comments on the English working class, he had little contact with it and no marked influence on it. He feuded intermittently with Henry M. Hyndman, the founder and leader of the Social Democratic movement in Britain and the Englishman most committed to Marxian ideology. He had only a few English friends who belonged to the reform movements; we shall have occasion to refer to some of them later. He did make his home on Regent's Park Road the centre of a lively circle of exiles from the continent, most of them Germans. It remained for some of his younger colleagues to establish meaningful intellectual contact with cosmopolitan London exiles of the 1880s and 1890s.

The German *émigré* who was most receptive to London's intellectual offerings at this time was Eduard Bernstein. Although he did not begin his exile in London until 1888 and was for several years closely identified with the work of Engels, he emerged in the late 1890s as one of the outstanding theoreticians and mave-

---

[1] Gustav Mayer, *Friedrich Engels: A Biography*, with an introduction by G. D. H. Cole (London, 1936), p. 234.

ricks of the Socialist movement. His Revisionist theories shook the German Social Democratic Party (SPD) severely at the turn of the century and eventually prevailed as party policy, and the crucial years for the formation of his ideology were those he spent in London.

Bernstein had known the German Social Democratic party during its infancy and during the so-called 'heroic years'. He had joined the Eisenachers—the Marxist-oriented group that helped to found a Social Democratic Labour Party—in 1872 when he was twenty-two years of age. Although he had little schooling and no university training, he managed to make his mark as a vigorous orator and industrious party worker. He attended the Gotha conference of 1875 which brought about a union of the Eisenachers and the disciples of Ferdinand Lassalle in the single party. In 1878, after having gone to Switzerland as secretary to a prominent Socialist, he found himself involuntarily exiled there when Bismarck's anti-Socialist law was invoked. Since the party's main newspaper, the *Sozialdemokrat*, was published in Zurich and smuggled into Germany during the next decade, a unique opportunity for journalistic agitation offered itself; he became editor, and therefore one of the most influential men in the party in 1881. Thus at the beginning of the 1880s Bernstein was engaged in much the same kind of propaganda work as his future friends Stepniak and Kropotkin.

Bernstein was a controversial figure in his party during most of the 1880s. Identified with the Radical faction of Social Democrats under the leadership of August Bebel, he was often involved in disputes with the Moderates who predominated in the party's Reichstag delegation during the middle 1880s. At least twice his fellow party members in the Reichstag tried to restrain his provocative editorial policies and to put the *Sozialdemokrat* under more rigid party control, but he succeeded in avoiding any such restrictions. Bernstein often took belligerent stands in German politics that caused trouble for his comrades in Germany. Some of them eventually went to jail as Bismarck's anti-Socialist measures became more severe in the late eighties.[1]

---

[1] An excellent survey of this period and Bernstein's role in it is Vernon L. Lidtke, *The Outlawed Party: Social Democracy in Germany, 1878–1890* (Princeton, 1966). For discussions of challenges to Bernstein's authority on the *Sozialdemokrat*, see pp. 131–4 and 204–10. For an orthodox Marxian account, see Franz Mehring, *Geschichte der deutschen Sozialdemokratie* (Berlin, 1960), 2 vols.

Bernstein served his Socialist apprenticeship with only minimum guidance from the authors of Marxism. He had met Marx only once, and he had only two additional brief meetings with Engels in London during the years of his editorship of the *Sozialdemokrat* in Zurich. Although there was a great deal of correspondence between Engels and Bernstein before 1888 and although Bernstein acknowledged the pre-eminence of Engels in the movement, he was obliged to make his own decisions about the day-to-day editorial problems, and he found himself once or twice in disagreement with the master on tactical questions. On practical matters, Bernstein charted his own course in the largely uncharted Socialist waters even after 1888 when his editorial duties were suppressed in Switzerland and he moved to London.

Bernstein's good friend and sometime fellow-exile in Zurich and London, Karl Kautsky, had a different kind of background and different set of experiences. He had been to university and was interested in economic theory, and he spent more time in his formative years under the direct guidance of Engels. As editor of *Die Neue Zeit* in London in the middle 1880s, he concentrated on the explanation of Marxian economic theory and elaborated on Scientific Socialism generally. This experience made him more deterministic and less flexible than Bernstein, and less interested in practical policies.[1] Kautsky and Bernstein were both loyal Marxists in 1890 and had both identified themselves consistently with the Radicals, but the decade of the 1890s was to emphasize their differences. As Bernstein became more flexible in his attitude, Kautsky became more rigid, and they came to represent conflicting wings of the SPD, until the crisis of world war united them again.

The often-discussed Erfurt programme of 1891 embraced the dichotomy that these two men personified. The Gotha programme of 1875 had brought about the unification of the Lassalleans and the Eisenachers, but it had greatly displeased Marx himself because it seemed too Lassallean. When the anti-Socialist laws lapsed in 1890, the party leadership was emboldened to write a new statement of principles. The Erfurt programme has often been cited as a blend of revolutionary theory and short-range practical objectives. The first part of the programme reiterated the basic premises of Marxism: monopoly capital will increase as capitalism expands, exploitation of the working-class will become ever greater,

[1] For an excellent discussion of these points, see Lidtke, op. cit., pp. 279–82.

economic crises will become more frequent and more damaging, and the class struggle between the bourgeoisie and proletariat will become increasingly bitter. In the end, the working classes will have to take the lead, engage in a political struggle, and transfer the means of production from private hands to social ownership. It was the assertion of these ideas that gave the SPD its Marxian character during the subsequent period. Kautsky, who by this time had removed *Die Neue Zeit* back to Germany, was largely responsible for the formulation of this part of the statement.

There is disagreement about the extent to which Bernstein—with the aid of Engels—influenced the second part of the programme. Gustav Mayer gave much of the credit to them,[1] but Engels did have some misgivings about the final product because it did not categorically call for the creation of a republic. In any case, both men had a hand in defining the demands that were incorporated. They proposed universal and equalized voting privileges for adults —both male and female, for regular legislative sessions with regular re-apportionment of legislative seats, for arrangements that would permit legislation by petition and plebiscite, for annual tax measures and progressive income, inheritance, and property taxes, for parliamentary decisions on questions of war and peace, and for expanded social welfare programmes for labouring men. It was a programme, in short, that had much in common with liberal reform proposals in other parts of the world, including those of the American Populists and Russian constitutionalists. As long as one accepted both parts of the programme, one encountered no problems. Bernstein created a crisis when he embraced the second part exclusively and argued—in the last years of the 1890s—that developments had proved the first part inaccurate.

The fact that Engels was ambiguous and that Bernstein was softened in his militancy by 1891 was due partly to the fact that the German Social Democrats were doing so well within the constitutional framework of the German Empire. In 1878, the year of the enactment of the first Socialist Law, party candidates for the Reichstag had received 437,147 votes and had won nine mandates. After twelve years of the restriction of nearly all political rights except voting and office holding, the Social Democrats received nearly a million and a half votes and thirty-five seats. The party had become a major political force in spite of its handicaps, and

[1] Gustav Mayer, op. cit., p. 277.

Bismarck had been removed by the Kaiser partly because he adhered too stubbornly to the anti-Socialist policy. So there was strong reason for hoping that the German government would evolve towards more representative forms and practices.

Bernstein lived in England for a decade after 1890, engaging in publishing work and writing for the party and reviewing his own political theories. When he finally returned to Germany he found it difficult to leave London, where he had discovered an intellectual home:

For a long time political and personal associations made my exile from home and Fatherland hard to endure, and for these reasons it was years before my wife and I became acclimatised in London. But when one day I was told: 'You are free to return to Germany'—and owing to the nature of my political situation the permit was in itself a categorical imperative—the first emotion that came over us was less joy than dismay, and the subsequent farewell to London was truly grievous to both of us.[1]

Obviously England had given Bernstein the leisure and freedom to refine his social ideas, and the opportunity to make many valued friendships.

BRITISH SOCIALISM

Perhaps one reason for Bernstein's deviation from conventional Marxism was the animosity that some of the leading British Social Democrats expressed towards him. Almost from the beginning of his sojourn in London, he incurred the hostility of Hyndman, that contentious would-be patriarch of British Socialism.

Hyndman did not have the qualities of leadership that would have been required to make Marxism palatable to a large number of Englishmen. Perhaps no one did, but in retrospect it appears that Hyndman was particularly ill-equipped to guide England towards a Socialist millennium. Not that he was intellectually unequal to the challenge of interpreting Marx for Englishmen; he won praise from the master himself for some of the articles he wrote immediately after his conversion to Marxism in 1880. But Hyndman's almost legendary conceit and tactlessness took him into one quarrel after another with his prospective colleagues. He founded the Democratic Federation in 1881 to undertake the propaganda

[1] Bernstein, *Aus den Jahren meines Exils* (Berlin, 1918), pp. 303–4; *My Years of Exile* (London, 1921), p. 280.

that Marx and Engels were neglecting in England, but almost immediately he incurred the wrath of Marx by the publication of *England for All*, the book that borrowed Marxian ideas and arguments without acknowledging their source. Hyndman later argued that Engels, because of jealousy, poisoned the mind of Marx against him in this instance. In any case, Hyndman's efforts on behalf of Marxism were repeatedly disparaged after 1881 by the authors of the movement.[1]

Hyndman looked upon himself as a natural leader, whom others must follow loyally and completely; perhaps he was too much like Marx in this to have retained his friendship for long in any case. The descendant of a wealthy middle-class family that had made its fortune in the West Indies, the product of a gentlemanly but non-academic education at Trinity College, Cambridge, the beneficiary of extensive travel to Italy, Asia, Australia and America as a young man, Hyndman could never regard himself as one of the working-men whom he was undertaking to liberate. He had begun his career as a Tory Radical, and the fact that he continued to wear his top hat and frock coat as a Socialist propagandist struck many of his colleagues as symbolic. There is some exaggeration—but not a great deal—in Bernard Shaw's statement written in 1911: '. . . Hyndman has charming manners and is the worst leader that ever drove his followers into every other camp—even into the Cabinet—to escape from his leadership.'[2]

When Hyndman began his work as champion of Socialism, he was nearly alone in the enterprise. There had been no dynamic Socialist movement in England since the Owenites and the Chartists had foundered in mid-century. Although the political strength of the labouring class had increased, partly as a result of franchise reform and because of the relative improvement of the real wages of the workers, they had no effective political instrument or philosophy. Hyndman, then, recognized a real opportunity when he mastered Marxian doctrine and established his Federation.[3] It did not call itself the Social Democratic Federation until

---

[1] The standard biography of Hyndman is Chushichi Tsuzuki, *H. M. Hyndman and British Socialism*, edited by Henry Pelling (London, 1961). It is also revealing to consult Hyndman's *The Record of an Adventurous Life* (New York, 1911), for confirmation of his monumental vanity.

[2] Bernard Shaw, *Pen Portraits and Reviews*, Vol. XXIX, *The Collected Works of Bernard Shaw* (New York, 1932), p. 133.

[3] See Henry Pelling, *The Origins of the Labour Party: 1880–1900* (London,

about two years after its founding, but Hyndman's Socialist intention seems to have existed from the beginning. He established the newspaper *Justice* and thus gave the Socialists their first important publication in a generation.

Hyndman gathered around himself some of the old Owenites and Chartists and a few discontented radicals and intellectuals, but he could not enlist the support of the Christian Socialists who were showing new life in England at the same time.[1] Nor could he win or keep the allegiance of many of the Socialist exiles who had assembled in Britain. Despite the fact that he read and apparently admired much of the revolutionary literature from the continent, he was suspicious of foreigners. He translated Kropotkin's *An Appeal to the Young* from the French and saw to its publication in England, and he offered to translate Stepniak's *La Russia sotterranea* from the Italian, but he was much less receptive to new ideas than this interest would suggest. When Henry George, the American single-taxer, made his successful tour of the British Isles in the early 1880s, Hyndman was characteristically condescending while many other Socialist sympathizers were enthusiastic. Little wonder that a man like Bernstein, sympathetic to English life and culture, should have found the leader of the English Marxists one of the more difficult people in London. Perhaps the English Socialist movement was too heterogeneous to remain united in any event, but Hyndman's personality made the fragmentation of the movement virtually inevitable.

The splintering of the Socialist movement in England during the 1880s has been well described by participants and scholars. When the Socialist revival was in its infancy in the early 1880s, they could overlook differences in policy and emphasis, but by the middle of the decade, the anarchistic Socialist League had broken away from Hyndman's Social Democrats, and the Fabian Society was beginning to define its moderate programme, frequently expressing distaste for the Social Democrats in the process. From time to time, representatives of the rival groups would share a speaker's platform or would unite in opposition to the civil authori-

---

1965), pp. 1–21, and G. D. H. Cole, *Socialist Thought: Marxism and Anarchism, 1850–1890*, Vol. II of *A History of Socialist Thought* (London, 1957), pp. 379–96.

[1] On the Christian Socialist movement, see Peter d'A. Jones, *The Christian Socialist Revival, 1877–1914: Religion, Class and Social Conscience in Late-Victorian England* (Princeton, 1968).

ties who were harassing them, but more often they filled the columns of their respective periodicals with criticisms of the other organizations. The hours of crisis—such as 'Bloody Sunday' in Trafalgar Square on 13 November 1887, when thousands of marchers tried to defy a government order against assembling at the base of Nelson's statue for political protest—produced only superficial unity. Hyndman alone, of course, was not responsible for this state of affairs. A number of his left-wing contemporaries were at least as intransigent as he.

THE IRISH PURITAN

G. K. Chesterton, Shaw's long time friend and intellectual adversary, pointed out as effectively as any critic has ever done the importance of Shaw's foreign background to his English experience. Although he was not an expatriate in the sense that his German and Russian friends were, he was emotionally as uprooted as most of his colleagues from abroad—and considerably more belligerent towards his chosen place of exile. 'Bernard Shaw entered England as an alien, as an invader, as a conqueror,' Chesterton wrote. 'In other words, he entered England as an Irishman.'[1]

Shaw was only twenty when he reached London in 1876, the child of an emotionally unhappy but intellectually stimulating home. His unaffectionate mother had preceded him to the metropolis to pursue a musical career; his father remained behind in Dublin, the victim of social humiliation and alcohol. Shaw had no clear purpose or obvious talent when he followed his mother across the Irish Sea; Chesterton even went so far as to say that he had no traditions, except a kind of negative Puritanism, emptied of its religious content. Being an Irishman of Protestant descent made him instinctively rebellious.

In the half-dozen years that were to expire before Shaw discovered his role in Socialism, his life was relatively uneventful. The Reading Room of the British Museum was more nearly a home than his mother's residence, although the latter did afford

[1] G. K. Chesterton, *George Bernard Shaw* (London, 1935), p. 23. This is one of the most important books of criticism on Shaw, despite its age (the first edition appeared in 1909) and its loquacious, often tedious arguments. Occasional insights continue to be of interest.

him an opportunity to continue his interest and education in music. He was ghost writer of occasional pieces of musical criticism and a visitor at art galleries, activities which prepared him for the art and music criticism that he wrote about a decade later. His reading during these formative years was extensive and crucial, and it was paralleled by his early experiments with creative writing. The five unsuccessful novels that came from his pen between 1877 and 1883 are a monument not only to his slowly blossoming literary ability but also to his free time and his tenacity—both, apparently, the results of his unsocial and un-English attitudes. Shaw had no strong commitment to anything other than his own talent until he was swept up by the Socialist revival of the early 1880s. He was, however, able to develop the techniques in dialogue and debate that were to become the distinctive feature of his plays while exploring London during these formative years. The many debating societies and literary groups that flourished during the late Victorian years gave him extensive training on platform tactics as well as on social and aesthetic questions. When he finally discovered the importance of economics and the prospects of Socialism by hearing Henry George and reading Karl Marx, his forensic equipment was well developed.[1]

Shaw attended meetings of the Social Democratic Federation, discovered the writings of Marx, and briefly became a convert to that doctrine. But he obviously did not feel at home with Hyndman and his associates, and he did not unite with them. It was in the early part of 1884 that he discovered the fledgling Fabian Society and joined it. In short order he had become one of its leaders.

The Fabian Society did much to give an English shape to Shaw's Irish instinct for rebellion. It never quite tamed him, and London certainly did not 'anaesthetically' eliminate his national characteristics—Ford Madox Ford notwithstanding. But the Society and the city did enable him to enter the mainstream of English reformist thought. The Fabian Society was the intellectual heir of the utilitarianism of Jeremy Bentham and John Stuart Mill, and Shaw acquiesced in its moderation by 1887. As the Society took up its programme of 'permeation', seeking to insinuate its reform

---

[1] This phase of Shaw's career is most adequately discussed in Henderson, *George Bernard Shaw: Man of the Century* (New York, 1956), pp. 132–60. For a more succinct but excellent summary, see William Irvine, *The Universe of G.B.S.* (New York, 1949), pp. 35–44.

programme into existence through other social and political organizations, Shaw was one of the most dedicated practitioners of the
policy. He put a permanent stamp on the movement with his early
editing and writing for it, the most notable example of which
appeared in the *Fabian Essays* of 1889.[1]
Yet he was too eclectic to remain comfortable within the Fabian
format. He became restless in the late 1890s and searched for new
approaches to the social disorders of his time. Discovering his
talent for the drama and the essay, he engaged in provocative
experiments with the literature of the theatre, sometimes playing
with the various Socialist ideas of his contemporaries in dramatic
form and sometimes subjecting Socialism itself to intensive
scrutiny. Late in his long life, his drama gave abundant testimony
to his indebtedness to his Socialist colleagues of the 1880s and
1890s.

THE CRAFTSMAN-POET

   William Morris was not an exile, but emotionally he had more in
common with some of these foreigners than he did with most of
his fellow bourgeois Englishmen. He was a man born out of his
'due time', who had found his artistic sensitivity as foreign to
Victorian England as Kropotkin's anarchistic sentiments were
foreign to Tsarist Russia. He was nearly fifty years old when he
entered the Socialist movement, but he had been struggling against
the prevailing system of values for most of his adult life.
   Morris's own tastes had their genesis in the Epping Forest of his
childhood ramblings, in the Gothic architectural monuments of
England and the continent that he studied in his youth, and in the
poetry of Chaucer, Malory, and Keats. His juvenile imagination
had enabled him to fashion his own half-medieval world, and the
contacts with the Pre-Raphaelites in young manhood had fortified
his preferences for artistic and imaginative forms that were foreign

---

[1] The classic account of the Fabian Society's early years is E. R. Pease, *The
History of the Fabian Society*, Third Edition (London, 1963), written a half
century ago by its long-time secretary. Of the more recent treatments, the best
chronological survey is Margaret Cole, *The Story of Fabian Socialism* (Stanford,
1961), and the best interpretative study of the society's policies is A. M. McBriar,
Fabian Socialism and English Politics: 1884–1918 (Cambridge, England, 1962).
A popular and less satisfactory summary is Anne Fremantle's *This Little Band of
Prophets* (London, 1960).

to the prevailing patterns of his day. For the first half of his productive life, however, he did not express his discontent in political activity. In a famous letter written while he was a student at Oxford in 1856, he said: ' . . . I can't enter into politico-social subjects with any interest, for on the whole I see that things are in a muddle, and I have no power or vocation to set them right in ever so little a degree. My work is the embodiment of dreams in one form or another. . . .'[1]

Morris's early poetry was the 'embodiment' of some of his youthful dreams. The *Defence of Guenevere, and Other Poems*, published in 1858 when Morris was only twenty-four years old, is a visit to the Arthurian past. The long verse-epics of a decade later on which his reputation as a poet was founded—*The Life and Death of Jason* (1867) and *The Earthly Paradise* (1868–70)—explored further realms of dream and folklore and found a reading public responsive to the aesthetic retreat which they offered. In the meantime he had explored—in imagination and in verse—the scenes of ancient Troy, and in the early 1870s he visited—in the flesh as well as in imagination—the rugged landscape of Iceland. *Sigurd the Volsung* (1877) was the poetic product of his discovery of the northern mythology. Twenty years had passed since he had written his letter, and the 'embodiment of dreams' remained his foremost preoccupation.

The 'embodiment' involved more than verse-making. Morris's well-known experiments with the visual and plastic arts were efforts to substitute an imaginary world for the often crass and sordid scenes of industrializing England. His involvement with the pre-Raphaelites, his experiment with painting under the influence of Rossetti, and his participation in the establishment of the firm for the manufacture of stained glass, tapestries, furniture and the like were progressive steps in his work of 'embodiment'. Tangible objects of handicraft and decoration came from Morris's own hands and those of his colleagues in the company that he organized and directed during the last half of his life. Appalled by the growing ugliness of British homes and communities, alarmed by the decline of art and fine individual workmanship, Morris spent part of his time in his middle years struggling for the restoration of arts and skills that he believed to have flourished in an earlier era and

---

[1] Quoted in J. W. Mackail, *The Life of William Morris* (London, 1899), I, p. 107.

another part of his time exploring the misty-world of the poetic sagas. He read and embraced the novels of Walter Scott, the poignant poetry of Keats, the ideas of John Ruskin on the values of art, and the arguments of Thomas Carlyle on the virtues of work.[1] From each of these men Morris drew confirmations for his aesthetic and social dissatisfaction. Only after this discontent was well developed did he turn to politics as a means of fulfilling his hopes for changing the world.

Even when he did begin to participate in politics in the late 1870s his first objectives were very limited. He took part in the protest against the Disraeli government's support of the Ottoman Empire in the Eastern Question crisis of 1876–8, and gradually became identified with the Liberal Party and Gladstone's programme. This provided occasions for further disenchantment with English society, specifically with its political institutions; by the 1880s he was thoroughly disgusted with the machinations of the politicians of the established parties. This is also the period of Morris's involvement in the 'Anti-Scrape' movement—the fight to preserve medieval British cathedrals and other buildings from 'restoration'. Such projects more often defaced and destroyed, Morris argued, when they were carried out by those who lacked the aesthetic sense of earlier generations. These controversies gave Morris overwhelming evidence that the existing political and social system was bankrupt and made him eager for an alternative. He joined Hyndman's Social Democratic Federation in January 1883.

It is not surprising that the poet who had taken refuge in the epics and in the Middle Ages should have found himself often in the company of refugees from abroad when he began to search for an acceptable forum for his new political conscience. The ideas of men like Stepniak, Kropotkin, and Marx—representing not only challenges to the existing order but also voices of rebellion in a modern struggle of epic proportions—had special attractions for a man of Morris's background and temperament. In a word, they introduced him to a new kind of dream, the response to which invited participation in the modern revolutionary movement.

[1] For the influence of Keats, Carlyle, and Ruskin on Morris, see the perceptive comments by E. P. Thompson, *William Morris: Romantic to Revolutionary* (London, 1955; New York, 1961), pp. 36–69.

THE FIVE DISSENTERS

Historians of European Socialism have a challenging task when they undertake to describe that vigorous movement in the late nineteenth and early twentieth centuries. The impressive works of people like Carl Landauer and G. D. H. Cole become virtual encylopedias, carefully categorizing the leading Socialists according to nationality, faction, and ideology. Less ambitious and less well informed scholars usually content themselves with the organizational machinations of the Socialists or anarchists in a single country or resort to some form of biographical account, the number and quality of which has improved in recent years. Yet the subject is far from exhausted, and the relationships of the various reformers and revolutionaries with one another is generally understood only when some close affinity or some well-publicized conflict has existed.

The present work is an experiment in synthesis. The five social reformers who are the primary subjects of this study belonged to different schools of thought and in most cases their allegiances were to different organizations and to different short-range causes. I believe, however, that it is possible to understand each of them better by looking at them together, comparing them as it were with one another rather than describing each of them against a more generalized background.

There are some obvious reasons for considering these men in the same context. Stepniak, Kropotkin, Bernstein, Morris and Shaw all participated vigorously in the London Socialists circles for an extended period of time between the early 1880s and the late 1890s. They all knew one another and occasionally two or more of them would share a lecture platform or engage in a debate in person or in print. They all had rather distinctive views of the Socialist-anarchist tendency, but they shared certain values and interests. Contrary to most orthodox Marxists, they did not confine their energies and their interests to narrow political or economic problems. While many of their colleagues became more dogmatic and more thoroughly committed to their various policies and organizations, each of these five retained an independence of mind and spirit during most of his life. Each became a dissident within his own group. Stepniak was a revolutionary in the tradition of Mazzini and Garibaldi, but he made exploratory contact with the orthodox Socialists and the Fabians and ended his career with experiments in creative writing. Kropotkin underwent a metamorphosis from Communist anarchism of the purest form to a kind of modified federalist republicanism, and closed his life near the threshold of existentialism. Bernstein began as a radical, made his mark with his attempted revision of Marx, and finished by becoming the voice of conscience for his party and his country. Morris and Shaw adhered to different Socialist ideas at different times of their respective lives, and they brought to the movement their artistic interests and talents, which coloured their Socialism substantially.

None of these men can accurately be placed in traditional Socialist or reformist categories without the risk of distortion. It is easy to label Stepniak as a nihilist, Kropotkin as an anarchist, Bernstein as a Revisionist, Morris as a Marxist, and Shaw as a Fabian, but to do so without substantial modification or reservation is to oversimplify.

These men lived in a golden age for revolutionary theory. It was not merely that London was singularly open to their work. Although the modern revolutionary tradition was nearly a century old by the 1880s, its literature was still young and its dogmas were not yet crystallized. The Marxist school was emerging as the predominant Socialist movement on the continent by the end of the century, the anarchist movement was gradually becoming more negative and uncompromising, and a young Labour Party was giving the distinctive character to Left-Wing British politics at about the same time, but Stepniak, Kropotkin, Morris, Shaw and Bernstein all experimented with ideas and speculated about reform and revolution before this process had gone very far. There were many others, of course, of whom this can be said, but these five were among the most versatile of their fraternity.

Each of the five is worthy of continuing study. Stepniak has never been given his due by English scholars; Kropotkin and Bernstein have too often been stereotyped as leaders of their respective movements; Morris's Socialism was ignored or underemphasized by his earlier biographers and misconstrued as devoted Marxism by more recent scholars; and in his basic works Shaw's Socialism has usually—and understandably—been overshadowed by his drama. Beyond this, for each man, Socialism—and they each applied this word to their own ideas and works—had a broad meaning. There was a strong ethical content to the propaganda of each of them. They all held the view—contrary to most Marxists —that moral philosophy was important in its own right, and not merely as a reflection of the material conditions of production. Each tried to be a moral philosopher for a time during his life, believing that it was not simply economic exploitation or political oppression that caused the existing problems. Stepniak was less interested in moral philosophy than the others; he was generally content to accept the liberal values. But even his work touches on this field. London of the late nineteenth century saw the appearance of a dozen or so books on the subject of post-Christian ethics, and some Socialists were engaged in the quest for new guidelines in this field. Our subjects were all, in greater or lesser degree, engaged in the search. Thus Socialism was for them an avenue to more esoteric fields, and their varied thoughts continue to be intriguing.

BIBLIOGRAPHICAL AND BIOGRAPHICAL NOTES

Prince Kropotkin's biography and his basic ideas have been recounted often enough to be relatively well known, but most treatments do not show the subtle changes that occurred in his anarchistic theories, and little has been written about his intellectual interchanges with the English-speaking world. His own *Memoirs* provide the basic information on the first two-thirds of his life, but one learns very little about his anarchistic philosophy there. The only important biography published in recent years is George Woodcock and Ivan Avakumović, *The Anarchist Prince: A Biographical Study of Peter Kropotkin* (London, New York, 1950). The authors were highly sympathetic to their subject and his cause. They made a diligent search of Kropotkin material and apparently saw most of the extant documentation in Western Europe. The book unfortunately lacks scholarly footnotes, however, and the bibliographical essay is a disappointment to students who would like to pursue further some of the leads they offer. Their admiration for their subject shows on virtually every page of the volume, and their critical judgement was occasionally coloured by their affection. A valuable pamphlet by one of Kropotkin's disciples is Camillo Berneri, *Peter Kropotkin: His Federalist Ideas* (London, 1942). There is a mediocre French-language biography by Fernand Planche and Jean Delphy, *Kropotkine* (Paris, 1948). See also the collection of tributes edited by G. P. Maksimov, *Internatsional'nyi Sbornik Posviashchennyi Desiatoi Godovshchine Smerti P. A. Kropotkina* (Chicago, 1931), and A. A.

Borovoi and N. K. Lebedev (eds.), *Sbornik Statei Posviashchennyi Pamiati P. A. Kropotkina* (Moscow, 1922). Kropotkin's ideas have been treated briefly in works on anarchism, the best of which is James Joll, *The Anarchists* (Boston, Toronto, 1964). Richard Hare's *Portraits of Russian Personalities Between Reform and Revolution* (London, 1959) devotes its final chapter to him, and Barbara Tuchman has helped to familiarize the present generation with him in *The Proud Tower: A Portrait of the World before the War, 1890–1914* (New York, 1966). In the Soviet Union, significantly, Kropotkin's social and philosophical works have largely been ignored and neglected since the 1920s. Soviet presses have reissued volumes dealing with his travels and his scientific work in Siberia as a young man, but presumably his anarchistic thought is still too sensitive for extensive distribution.

There is relatively little biographical information available on Stepniak. The essay by D. Iuferev in S. Stepniak–Kravchinskii, *Sochineniia v Dvukh Tomakh*, I (Moscow, 1958), pp. v–xliv, seems to be reliable. There are also helpful essays on each of the individual works in this collection. Also valuable is Peter Kropotkin's essay written in 1907 for the earliest collection of Stepniak's writings: S. M. Stepniak'–Kravchinskii, *Sobranie Sochinenii*, I, *Shtundist Pavel Rudenko* (St. Petersburg, 1907), pp. xi–xxxi. This is the first volume of a six volume set issued in 1907 and 1908. Other notable short tributes and biographical sketches are L. E. Shishko, *Sergei Mikhailovich' Kravchinskii i Kruzhok' Chaikovtsev'* (St. Petersburg, 1906); Lev' Deich' (Deutsch), *Sergei Mikhailovich' Kravchinskii-Stepniak'* (Petrograd, 1919); and K. N. Berkova, *S. M. Kravchinskii* (Moscow, 1925).

The most helpful of Bernstein's autobiographical works is *Aus den Jahren meines Exils* (Berlin, 1918), which is available in translation as *My Years of Exile: Reminiscences of a Socialist*, translated by Bernard Maill (London, 1921); and 'Entwicklungsgang eines Sozialisten', in *Die Volkswirtschaftslehre der Gegenwart in Selbstdarstellungen*, I (Leipzig, 1924), pp. 1–58. For an account of his youth, one may consult his *Von 1850 bis 1872: Kindheit und Jugendjahre* (Berlin, 1926). There are a number of competent summaries of Bernstein's Revisionism. Peter Gay's *The Dilemma of Democratic Socialism: Eduard Bernstein's Challenge to Marx* (New York, 1952) remains the standard work in English, but it has been superseded in some respects by Pierre Angel, *Eduard Bernstein et l'évolution du socialisme allemand* (Paris, 1961). Other valuable studies are Carl E. Schorske, *German Social Democracy, 1905–1917: The Development of the Great Schism* (Cambridge, Mass., 1955), pp. 16–20, and Christian Gneuss, 'The Precursor: Eduard Bernstein', in Leopold Labedz, ed., *Revisionism: Essays on the History of Marxist Ideas* (New York, 1962). The widely-known histories of Socialism of Carl Landauer, *European Socialism: A History of Ideas and Movements*

(Berkeley and Los Angeles, 1959), in two volumes; and of G. D. H. Cole, *The Second International: 1889–1914* (London, 1956), the third volume of his *A History of Socialist Thought* helps one to put ideas in perspective. Other reliable discussions by respected scholars include Carlton J. H. Hayes, 'The History of German Socialism Reconsidered', *American Historical Review*, XXIII (October, 1917), pp. 62–101; James Joll, *The Second International: 1889–1914* (New York, 1956), and Milorad M. Drachkovitch, *Les socialismes français et allemand et le problème de la guerre: 1870–1914* (Geneva, 1953).

The most valuable work of criticism and analysis dealing with Shaw to appear in the past generation is William Irvine's *The Universe of G.B.S.*, op. cit. I have also derived a number of ideas from E. Strauss, *Bernard Shaw: Art and Socialism* (London: 1942), which is very brief but argues persuasively that Shaw's ambiguous and changing attitude towards Socialism can be seen in his plays. Another short book of considerable merit is Eric Bentley, *Bernard Shaw* (London, 1950). The most important recent contribution to the literature on Shaw's early years is J. Percy Smith, *The Unrepentant Pilgrim: A Study of the Development of Bernard Shaw* (Boston, 1965).

The fundamental tools for the study of Shaw's biography, in addition to his own writings, are the elaborate biographies by Archibald Henderson, *George Bernard Shaw: His Life and Works* (Cincinnati, 1911); *Bernard Shaw: Playboy and Prophet* (New York, London: 1932); and *George Bernard Shaw: Man of the Century*, op. cit. The serious scholar must consult all three, because even though Henderson carried much material from the earlier volumes to the later one, in some cases he omitted material in the more recent study. These works contain a substantial amount of primary material, but they are sometimes cumbersome and difficult to use because of the author's organizational practices. This is particularly true of the last volume, which shows that the remarkable Mr. Henderson—master of many specialties and a scholar in the Renaissance tradition—was being overwhelmed by the burgeoning data on his subject after a half-century of study.

In spite of the volume of material that has appeared on Shaw, a group of Shavian scholars meeting in Chicago in 1959 expressed regret about the relative lack of good studies of Shaw's Socialism and his political ideas. No significant quantity of outstanding work in this field has appeared in the intervening years. See the *Shaw Review*, III (May, 1960), pp. 18–26.

The key work for the study of Morris's art and thought is *The Collected Works of William Morris*, with Introductions by his daughter May Morris, 24 volumes (London: 1910–15). All of Morris's major writings are included, and his daughter's essays contain much biographical material. This collection was supplemented two decades later by two companion volumes: May Morris, *William Morris: Artist Writer Socialist* (Oxford, 1936). The second volume contains much material pertinent to Morris's Socialist activities and some writings not incorporated in *The Collected Works*. Both of these collections were republished in 1966 by Russell & Russell, New York. There is no definitive edition of Morris's numerous letters, but the best collection so far is that edited by Philip Henderson, *The Letters of William Morris to His Family and Friends* (London, New York, 1950). Other important letters and insights can be consulted in J. W. Mackail, *The Life of William Morris*, 2 vols. (London, 1899), long considered the basic biography, and in J. Bruce Glasier, *William Morris and the Early Days of the Socialist Movement* (London, New York, 1921). Glasier was closely associated with Morris in the Socialist League, and he had an extensive correspondence with his subject during his most active years, but it must be treated with some scepticism in those sections where Glasier claims to remember exact conversations and speeches that occurred a quarter century earlier. More revealing letters have been included in R. Page Arnot, *William Morris: the man and the myth* (London, 1964). Several little known lectures have become available in Eugene D. LeMire's 'The Unpublished Lectures of William Morris: A Critical Edition, Including an Introductory Survey and a Calendar and Bibliography of Morris's Public Speeches' (Wayne State University Ph.D. Dissertation, 1962).

The most important single work on Morris's Socialist activities is E. P. Thompson, *William Morris: Romantic to Revolutionary*, op. cit. This volume is the result of intelligent and exhaustive scholarship, but it is marred by the author's intense Marxian bias. All of Morris's experiences in the Socialist movement and many of his artistic efforts are examined through the prism of the class struggle, and the result is a somewhat distorted view of Morris's ideas. Thompson also includes some Morris letters and other pertinent correspondence.

Two significant new books on Morris have appeared since 1966. Philip Henderson, *William Morris: His Life, Work, and Friends* (New York, 1967), presents new material, and the recently-published work of Paul Thompson, *The Work of William Morris* (New York, 1967), is the most valuable contribution to the secondary literature on Morris in a half-century. For the purposes of the general reader, it supersedes such older volumes as Aymer Vallance, *William Morris: His Art, His Writings and His Public Life* (London, 1897); Elisabeth Luther Cary, *William Morris: Poet, Craftsman, Socialist* (New York, London, 1902); John Drinkwater, *William Morris: A Critical Study* (New York, 1912); Arthur Compton-Rickett, *William Morris: A Study in Personality* (New York, 1913); Arthur Clutton-Brock, *William Morris: His Work and Influence* (London, 1914); Holbrook Jackson, *William Morris:*

Craftsman-Socialist, revised edition (London, 1926); and Anna A. von Helmholtz-Phelan, *The Social Philosophy of William Morris* (Durham, N.C., 1927). The work of Lloyd Wendell Eshleman, *A Victorian Rebel: The Life of William Morris* (New York, 1940), served as the most readily available general biography for the past quarter century; it is based on competent research and a sympathetic understanding of Morris. There is, of course, a large body of literary criticism, including the statements of lasting interest by such persons as Alfred Noyes, G. K. Chesterton, W. B. Yeats, and, of course, Bernard Shaw.

II

STEPNIAK

From Terrorism to Liberalism

IT was an ambitious undertaking for an avowed terrorist to enter Victorian England in 1883 with the intention of justifying his policies to the intellectual community of the English-speaking countries. This is what Stepniak set out to do, and to a greater extent than he could have foreseen, he became an agent for shaping British and American opinions of imperial Russia in the last decade and a half of the nineteenth century.

Several persons who knew Stepniak well left descriptions of his striking personal qualities. He was a stout man—occasionally characterized as fat—but he gave the impression of possessing great physical strength. There was an Oriental cast to his face, suggesting Tatar ancestry. He had small sharp eyes that most of his acquaintances found soft and gentle. The 'orthodox Tory' W. Earl Hodgson set down a light-hearted description after hearing the noted exile speak to a small group one evening:

His countenance was devoid of wrinkles, or even of the slightest sign of care. It beamed upon you, placidly, from out of a very remarkable setting. The small brown eyes were somewhat Japanese in shape; the mouth was firm and masterful, but such as broke easily into a smile; the huge square head was crowned by a luxuriant growth of shaggy black hair divided roughly into three sections—one bush of it, as it were, guarding the right ear; another, the left; the third crowning the whole Nihilist edifice. The Russian eagle could have comfortably built its nest in either of the two crevices by which S——'s raven locks were divided.[1]

Stepniak had a captivating manner in small groups, balancing his imposing appearance with gentle speech and self-effacing gestures. Eduard Bernstein, who met him often in the 1890s at the home of Friedrich Engels, found him to be a dreamy, sensitive

[1] W. Earl Hodgson, *A Night with a Nihilist* (Cupar-Fife, 1886), p. 7.

person—a reticent guest who usually spoke only when addressed.[1]
Bernard Shaw testified that he had a charm in private intercourse
because

. . . he betrayed the heart of an affectionate child behind a powerful
and very live intellect.[2]

And James Mavor, the Scottish-born scholar who knew him well
during the 1880s, wrote in later years:

. . . the cast of Stepniak's temperament was that of an artist rather than
that of a political philosopher or that of a revolutionist. Yet I never met
an artist who was so amiable and so gentle in his judgments.[3]

Yet those who knew him had to reconcile what they saw with
his record. More than any other individual living in England in the
1880s, Stepniak personified the Terror, and he became its leading
apologist. He performed this function, however, in an impersonal
way, with a minimum of reference to his specific role in the
revolutionary movement. His acquaintances were generally aware
that he had performed some dramatic and violent deeds, but
apparently none of them knew many of the details. Mavor speculated that Stepniak may have been provoked to assassinate
Adjutant General Mezentsev because his mother had been mis-
treated by the authorities:

Whether or not because he had mingled an act of private vengeance
with a significant revolutionary deed, and on that account felt some
qualms of conscience, I do not know; but this event appeared to cast
a shadow over his mind. He never referred to it.[4]

During a visit to the United States late in 1890, Stepniak denied,
in a newspaper interview, that he had ever killed anyone; he made
a similar denial or evasion on other occasions. Yet the record is
as clear as it can be on such episodes, and Stepniak's writings
provided a justification for assassination. His arguments on behalf
of the Terror in Russia made a significant contribution to Socialist
and anarchist thought as it was expressed in England in the last
decade and a half of the nineteenth century.

---

[1] Eduard Bernstein, *Aus den Jahren meines Exils*, op. cit., pp. 231–2; *My
Years of Exile*, op. cit., p. 214.

[2] Bernard Shaw, 'A Word About Stepniak', *To-Morrow: A Monthly Review*,
No. 2 (February 1896), p. 103.

[3] James Mavor, *My Windows on the Street of the World*, I (London, 1923),
p. 253.   [4] *Ibid.*, I, p. 251.

THE PROLIFIC PROPAGANDIST: 1883-9

Although English-language readers first saw Stepniak's work with the publication of *Underground Russia* in 1883, he had published the general outline of his rationale more than four years earlier, soon after the assassination, in his pamphlet *Smert' za smert'*. The basic argument held that acts of terror against the authorities were fundamentally defensive measures; they were the only recourse available to reformers who suffered under the complete oppression that the Tsarist regime imposed. As long as the bureaucracy tortured and killed men for engaging in legitimate political and propaganda activities, it was necessary to respond with action commensurate with the officially-imposed violence. *Smert' za smert'* was dedicated to the memory of a revolutionary agitator who had committed no offence other than political agitation, but who had been killed by the regime in Odessa. Stepniak (although he was not yet using his pseudonym) wrote his justification almost immediately after the assassination.[1]

The pamphlet referred to the assassination as a collective act of the reformers, and it set forth their grievances and demands. The agitators merely desired to work for reform—primarily economic improvements at this point—without governmental interference. The bureaucracy and police machinery were not the primary opponents of the agitators. 'Our present enemies are the bourgeoisie, who now hide behind your back, even though they hate you,' Stepniak wrote, addressing the governmental agents.

The question of the division of power between you and the bourgeoisie is not our concern at all. Grant or do not grant a constitution; summon electors or do not summon them; nominate them from the landowners, priests, or gendarmes—we are absolutely indifferent on that score. Do not violate our human rights—that is all we want from you.[2]

At the time he wrote *Smert' za smert'*, Stepniak had not progressed far beyond the elementary *narodnik* doctrine of the early 1870s. Like many of his contemporaries of that period, he had only vague political ideas beyond the desire to communicate with the people. Russian liberalism was still in an embryonic stage, and the young Stepniak—only in his middle twenties—had had little

---

[1] S. Kravchinskii, *Smert' za smert'*, (*Ubiistvo Mezentseva*), (Petrograd, 1920). Introduction by V. Petrovskii. Reprinted from the 1878 edition.

[2] Ibid., pp. 19, 20.

opportunity to learn about Western-style representative institutions; he was a product of the generation that had learned avidly from Lavrov, Bakunin, Chernyshevskii, and Pisarev.

Within the next four years, Stepniak became more clearly liberal in his political philosophy. When he wrote the articles that eventually constituted *Underground Russia*,[1] he was living in Italy. This work made many of the same points as *Smert' za smert'*, but its political message was more sophisticated and it was a much more extensive argument. Peter Lavrov contributed a preface rejoicing that it provided readers with 'a faithful and animated picture' of Russian despotism and the struggle against it.

Stepniak began the book with a survey of the evolution of the resistance to autocracy from the relative peacefulness of the nihilists of the sixties through the fruitless *narodnik* period of the early seventies to the period of 'the Terror' in the late seventies. His objective was to prove that the Terror was the logical and necessary result of the brutal policies of the Tsarist bureaucracy. The vastness of the Russian Empire, the relative smallness of most towns, and the overwhelming size of the government's repressive apparatus made it impossible to conduct a revolution of the Western European variety. The ruthless suppression of all opposition kept the people in slavery, and the only effective recourse was direct assaults on those who were guilty of the oppression.

About half the book was devoted to heroes of the struggle who had demonstrated typical bravery and self-sacrifice on behalf of the cause. Stepniak sketched 'Revolutionary Profiles' of several well-known revolutionaries, including Kropotkin, Dmitri Klements, Vera Zasulich, and Sofia Perovskaia. He described the operations of the secret presses of the conspirators and some of the techniques used for prison escapes. He argued that the mass of the Russian people supported the Terrorists, citing as evidence that thousands of people were hiding them, handling their messages, and performing other dangerous assignments without sharing the intimate knowledge of their functions.

In an appendix to the volume, Stepniak inserted a copy of the letter that the Executive Committee of the *Narodnaia Volia* had sent to Alexander III shortly after his father's assassination. This

[1] Stepniak, *Underground Russia: Revolutionary Profiles and Sketches from Life*, op. cit.

petition went beyond *Smert' za smert'* in demanding political concessions, but its tone was moderate and, by the political standards
then existing in Italy and England, the requests were reasonable.
The Tsar was asked not only to grant a general amnesty for
political prisoners, but also to convoke popular assemblies on
political and social questions in various parts of the empire, to
permit free election of deputies to these assemblies, and to
recognize freedom of speech, press, and political activity. In
return, the *Narodnaia Volia* promised an end of the Terror.

Stepniak was obviously convinced that the Terror would and
could end abruptly if such concessions were made.

By yielding to the legitimate requests of the nation, by conceding the
most elementary political rights demanded by the times in which we
live, and by civilisation, everything will enter upon a peaceful and
regular course. The Terrorists will be the first to throw down their
deadly weapons, and take up the most humane, and the most powerful
of all, those of free speech addressed to free men, as they have several
times explicitly declared.[1]

Stepniak's treatment of acts of terror was frank but impersonal.
He referred to the assassination of Mezentsev as one of the
important turning points of the revolutionary movement. With
this action, the revolutionaries threw down the glove to the regime
and engaged in the deadly duel. Subsequent acts of terror, including the killing of Alexander II, were logical sequels to that act.
Underground Russia did not assign individual responsibility for
these acts, treating them rather as the anonymous conduct of men
at war.

The book had a swift impact on the left-wing movement in
Great Britain, just awakening from its mid-century slumbers.
Hyndman saw the work in Italian and proposed a translation. He
was deeply impressed by Stepniak's picture of a newspaper being
printed underground by a dedicated conspirator without regard
for his own safety, health, or pleasure.[2] This was several months
before Hyndman started his own journal *Justice*, the first Socialist
newspaper of this era in Britain.

One of those who read the book with great interest was William
Morris, who at the time was going through the conversion that

---

[1] Stepniak, *Underground Russia*, pp. 280–1.
[2] Henry Mayers Hyndman, *The Record of an Adventurous Life* (New York,
1911), p. 80.

made him a militant Socialist. Morris wrote to one of his daughters that *Underground Russia* was ' . . . a most interesting book, though terrible reading too: it sounds perfectly genuine: I should think such a book ought to open people's eyes a bit here & do good.'[1]

For a reader like Morris, the testimony about the self-sacrificing spirit of the revolutionaries had special appeal; Morris referred to this quality on a number of occasions in his later writings. Stepniak, more effectively than any other writer of the 1880s and 1890s, aroused sympathy for the young men and women who were throwing themselves into the virtually hopeless struggle. Morris and Stepniak soon became friends, and Stepniak contributed one of the first articles to the newspaper *Commonweal* when Morris started it in 1885.[2]

Stepniak soon had a number of English outlets for his prose. In 1884, he contributed articles to *To-day*, the magazine operated by E. Belfort Bax and J. L. Joynes. The topic on this occasion was Russian penal institutions and policies[3] with emphasis on the Peter–Paul fortress prison and on the brutalities inflicted on the victims. At various times in 1884, Stepniak contributed articles to *The Times* on education and censorship and the editorial commentary showed that his work was effective.[4] In December, a *Times* correspondent in Russia wrote:

An extremely sore feeling . . . has lately shown itself here in the highest circles, in which the English Press is accused of having lately taken to basing its opinions about Russia upon the prejudiced writings of disguised and long-expatriated Nihilists.[5]

Stepniak was obviously delighted by such a report, and he had the satisfaction of seeing his book translated into several continental languages, including German, French, and Danish. Such a reception persuaded him to abandon his plans for fighting the Tsarist regime as an underground conspirator and to employ his pen as

[1] William Morris, *The Letters of William Morris to his Family and Friends*, edited by Philip Henderson (London, 1950), p. 172.
[2] Stepniak, 'The Actual Position of Russia', *Commonweal*, I (March 1885), pp. 10–11.
[3] Stepniak, 'Russian Political Prisons', *To-day*, I (June, 1884), pp. 401–15; and II (July 1884), pp. 1–19.
[4] See. e.g., his article 'Student Life in Russian Universities', *The Times*, 18 April 1884, 3: 1–4; and the articles on 'The Russian Press', 2 September 1884, 2: 5–6 and 3: 1–2; and 30 September 1884, 2: 1–4. See also the editorial comment on 2 September 1884, 9: 4–5.
[5] *The Times*, 24 December 1884, 3: 3.

a weapon. A new 'dream' emerged for him, as he wrote several years later, when his journalistic efforts proved so rewarding:

To conquer the world for the Russian revolution; to throw upon the scales the huge weight of the public opinion of civilized nations; to bring to those whose struggle is so hard that unexpected help; to find without a lever to move the minds of the Russians themselves within —this was the dream which glistened before me.

The opportunity was unique.[1]

The book became a 'lever' in unintended places. Translations circulated among groups of conspirators in Europe for many years. In 1893, a Russian-language edition was published in London for distribution in Russia, and more than twenty years later it was still an important reference work for Serbian conspirators, including the circle of Gavrilo Princip—the assassin of Sarajevo.[2]

The articles that Stepniak wrote for *The Times* and other periodicals after 1883 formed the nucleus of a second book, *Russia Under the Tzars*, which appeared in the spring of 1885 in both London and New York. The theme resembled that of *Underground Russia*, but the subject matter was greatly expanded. The volume opened with a brief historical survey of Russia, explaining the rise of despotism. Stepniak looked back to a golden past—a medieval period before tyranny had imposed itself on the people. The typical Russian city was controlled by the *veche* and the village by the *mir*, collective institutions where legislation was achieved by unanimous consent. The princes of the era, Stepniak said, were not despots, but rather they served at the pleasure of the cities. The excellent home rule system embodied the republican features that he endorsed. In this idealized description of early Russia, the reader recognizes Stepniak's aspirations for the future of Russia.

This republican society, Stepniak wrote, had been thwarted by the rise of Muscovy, with its centralized bureaucracy and Orthodox Church. The old institutions were crushed and the new authorities became instruments of slavery and oppression. The story moves rapidly to the emancipation of 1861 and then becomes a catalogue of recent abuses by the authoritarian regime.[3]

[1] Sergius Stepniak, 'What Americans Can Do for Russia', *The North American Review*, Vol. 153, No. 5 (November 1891), p. 600.
[2] Vladimir Dedijer, *The Road to Sarajevo* (New York, 1966), pp. 333, 442.
[3] Stepniak, *Russia Under the Tzars*, rendered into English by William Westall, Authorized edn. (New York, 1885), pp. 1–57.

To the modern reader, Stepniak's anecdotes about the 'Russian Inquisition' are tedious and depressing. Nearly two hundred pages are devoted to testimonials about nocturnal police searches, prison experiences, judicial injustices, censorship, the exile system, and similar matters, and another substantial section describes restrictions on educational institutions and the press. It is not surprising that the editors of the 1958 *Sochineniia* published only a fragment of the book. But what is today dead evidence made a mark in Victorian England, which had heretofore depended primarily on the less unfavourable account of Sir Donald MacKenzie Wallace.[1]

Stepniak was determined not only to arouse the sympathy of the English-speaking nations for the revolutionary cause, but also he repeatedly sought arguments for greater involvement in the struggle by Western sympathizers. He became increasingly adept at managing phrases that were likely to appeal to the Western liberal and patriot:

. . . The Russian despotism must and will be destroyed; for it is not permitted to the stupid obstinacy of one, nor to the infamous egoism of a few, to arrest the progress and light of a nation of a hundred million souls. We can only wish that the mode of execution of the unavoidable may be the least disastrous, least sanguinary and most humane. And there is a force which can strongly contribute to this— it is the public opinion of European countries.

It is strange, but quite true; Russian governmental circles are much more impressed by what is said about them in Europe, than by the wailing of all Russia from the White Sea down to the Euxine . . .[2]

Addressing ourselves now to the English people, we have not the slightest doubt that such an appeal will find echo in many thousands of English hearts. There was never a striving of any country for its liberty which found not the warmest support in England. . . .[3]

The widely-recognized British distrust of Russian foreign policies also provided ammunition for this prolific nihilist. Russia was certain to be more hostile and more dangerous as long as an irresponsible Tsarist regime ruled her destiny, he wrote. 'To have such a State for a neighbour is nearly as unpleasant as to sit by

---

[1] The first edition of Wallace's *Russia* was published in London in 1877. Although it described the gross inefficiencies of the Tsarist regime, it left the impression that great improvements in administration and justice had been made since 1861.

[2] Stepniak, *Russia Under the Tzars*, op. cit., pp. 375–6.

[3] Ibid., p. 379.

an unfettered madman at an evening party. Nobody can answer for what he will do the very next moment.'[1]

This approach, which was only mentioned in passing in *Russia Under the Tzars*, became the theme of another book, published in 1886. Like the earlier works, this volume was assembled largely from occasional articles that Stepniak had contributed to prominent newspapers and magazines. He entitled it *The Russian Storm-Cloud* and undertook to prove that Russia's troublesome expansionism originated in the Tsar's efforts to divert attention from domestic matters.

Why is Russia a conquering country? . . . The fundamental cause of this is perfectly understood in Europe: it is the existence of the Autocracy in Russia . . . Russia alone among European countries is a conquering State in these days.[2]

By the time Stepniak compiled this volume, he had formulated his political philosophy rather precisely, and he had described violence as an abnormal form of political action. By 1886, he was thinking of a social revolution, to be implemented gradually by constitutional means; it was 'a task too complicated and difficult for the resources of an insurrection'.[3] He embraced the concept of a federal system, 'a form of government of which the United States of America furnishes us with an example'.[4]

In these earliest writings, Stepniak had said little about the lot of the peasantry under Tsarist rule. His fourth book, published initially in 1888, concentrated on this and revealed a broader range of interest than any of the first three volumes had demonstrated. It also provided a context within which Stepniak could develop some of his agrarian-based Socialist ideas. This book, *The Russian Peasantry*, was the most successful of his propaganda works, with four editions in eighteen years.[5]

The purpose of this work was to document the worsening of the peasants' condition since the Emancipation of 1861 and to offer insights into the life of the agrarian population. The emphasis called forth an additional justification for the revolutionary activity.

[1] Ibid., p. 380.
[2] Stepniak, *The Russian Storm-Cloud; or Russia in her Relations to Neighbouring Countries* (London, 1886), pp. 47–8.
[3] Ibid., p. 217.　　　　[4] Ibid., p. 89.
[5] Stepniak, *The Russian Peasantry: Their Agrarian Condition, Social Life and Religion* (New York, 1888).

Great are the wrongs, bitter the abuses and sufferings inflicted by this despotism on the whole of educated Russia—arbitrary arrests, detentions, exiles without any trial whatever, the trampling down of all sacred human rights, suppression of freedom of speech and of the Press, violation of the hearth and prevention of the right to work, whereby the lives of thousands of intelligent, well-intentioned, and innocent men and women are either wasted or made miserable. But what are their sufferings compared with those of the dumb millions of our peasantry? What an ocean of sorrow, tears, despair, and degradation is reflected in these dry figures. . . .

Verily, it is here, and not so much in the cruelties inflicted on political offenders, that we must look for the cause of the fierce, implacable hatred of the revolutionists against their Government.

Herein lies the peremptory cause, the permanent stimulant and the highest justification of the Russian revolution and of the Russian conspiracies. . . .[1]

Stepniak tried to demonstrate that the Emancipation had merely compounded the miseries of the peasants by giving them too little land and by increasing their financial burdens. He argued that the basic problems could be solved by equitable land distribution and by ending the exploitive taxes and redemption payments; republican institutions, he believed, would be the prelude to accomplishing these ends. A revitalized *mir*—into which Western style freedoms and principles would be introduced—would put Russia on a corrective Socialist path.

Russia's distinctive religious organizations also made her a candidate for successful democracy and Socialism, Stepniak believed. Nearly half of *The Russian Peasantry* is devoted to popular religious movements among the peasants, with an emphasis on the schismatic, heretical, and secular groups.

Convinced that the Orthodox Church and its priesthood had no important influence on the peasantry, Stepniak believed that great vitality existed in the rebellious sects. He had worked among some of the non-Orthodox peoples during his *narodnik* days, and sensed that some of these groups had revolutionary possibilities. In *The Russian Peasantry*, he had lengthy discussions of such groups as the Raskolniks, Dukhobors, the Stundists, and other non-conformists.

Stepniak had been interested in schemes for the communal control of property and productive resources since his *narodnik*

[1] Stepniak, *The Russian Peasantry*, pp. 69–70.

days, but he had become convinced as early as the 1870s that for Russia, Socialism must wear peasant dress and not a 'German costume'.[1] Thus his Russian experience had endowed him with an immunity to most of the aspects of Marxian Socialism which was becoming more popular among his English associates and fellow Russian exiles during the decade of the 1880s. Stepniak not only had the friendship of Engels but he was well acquainted with G. V. Plekhanov, and he brought these two together. Yet his own Socialism belonged to the lineage of Alexander Herzen, and some of the conclusions near the end of *The Russian Peasantry* seemed to echo that renowned propagandist.

There exist no people on the face of the earth, or to keep within the boundaries of the better known, on the face of Europe, who, as a body, are so well trained for collective labor as our moujiks are.[2]

And later he repeated:

. . . we will say that, supposing socialism is not entirely a dream, of all European nations the Russians, provided they become a free nation, have the best opportunity of realizing it.[3]

The socialism of Stepniak, then, was thoroughly subservient to his liberalizing crusade for Russia. He embraced the doctrine of the class struggle only to the extent that it conformed to events within the jurisdiction of the Tsar. He had no special interest in the proletariat, and he demonstrated no inclination to participate with the Marxists in their exploration of the subtleties of Hegelian philosophy. Furthermore, he had little patience for the perpetual intrigues and intra-party controversies that were so common in the typical Socialist organizations of his time. As his friend Kropotkin wrote at a later time, Stepniak was willing to spend considerable time planning strategy that related directly to revolutionary action, but evidences of conspiracies and bickering within the Socialist movement saddened and disturbed him.[4]

It would not be misleading to compare Stepniak with the Christian Socialists who were his contemporaries in England. Content with many of the liberal solutions and values, prepared to search for social improvement in unorthodox religious experiments,

---

[1] Theodore Dan, *The Origins of Bolshevism* (New York and Evanston, 1964). p. 102.

[2] Stepniak, *The Russian Peasantry*, p. 390.   [3] Ibid., p. 394.

[4] See Kropotkin's introduction to vol. I of Stepniak'-Kravchinskii, *Sobranie Sochinenii* (St. Petersburg, 1907), p. XXVI.

increasingly cautious about the use of violence as a revolutionary technique, Stepniak was settling on the right-wing of the Socialist movement by the end of the 1880s. Or perhaps Bernard Shaw was near the mark when he wrote, shortly after Stepniak's death, that the Russian nihilist was hardly a Socialist at all in Russian terms. His programme was so moderate and his influence on some English liberals so effective that he might with equal justification be classified in that category, despite his personal claims to being a Socialist.[1]

Shaw recalled having seen Stepniak at a protest meeting in Hyde Park in 1884. On that occasion, Socialists and anarchists— Shaw dismissed them as 'toy revolutionists'—had hailed Stepniak as one of their own, to the embarrassment of the Russian propagandist. While he would not reject or disclaim Socialist affiliations, he was interested in a wider audience for his message.

For the first four or five years of his residence in England, Stepniak was reticent about making public addresses on behalf of his cause. Uncertain of his command of the spoken language, he preferred small discussion groups or the printed page. He delivered his first lecture in March of 1886 in the small lecture hall that William Morris maintained for the Socialist League next to his home at Hammersmith, and the *Pall Mall Gazette* carried an account which may have been written by Shaw. Morris took the chair for the meeting, and Stepniak spoke extemporaneously. He then underwent a 'prolonged ordeal' of questioning before the audience, at Shaw's suggestion, adopted a resolution of sympathy for the Russian people. The experience was apparently not pleasant for Stepniak.[2]

Despite his language problems and restricted activities, Stepniak became an enthusiastic student of English and American literature

---

[1] Shaw, 'A Word About Stepniak', op. cit., pp. 99–100.
[2] The clipping from the *Pall Mall Gazette* (29 March 1886) is preserved in the Shaw collection at the British Museum, London. See also Shaw's 'A Word About Stepniak', op. cit., p. 104. In the Socialist League Correspondence preserved at the International Institute of Social History in Amsterdam, there is a letter from Stepniak to the League dated Saturday, 5 June (1886) in which Stepniak declined an invitation to speak because his accent was too poor. He indicated he did not plan to lecture publicly for a year or two. Socialist League Correspondents, ╪ 2859/2. There was also an article published by Stepniak's friend, Robert Spence Watson, shortly after the Russian's death in which he said Stepniak's first speeches had been somewhat unsuccessful but had become progressively better. *Free Russia* (London), VII, 1 February 1896, p. 10.

and improved his grasp of the language by extensive reading. In 1889, he received a visit in his Chiswick home from Harriot Blatch, a correspondent for the *Boston Transcript*, who published a long feature story on their conversation.[1] She found him completely devoted to his self-assigned mission, engaged at his reading and writing for ten or twelve hours a day, and little inclined to travel or relax. As she listened to his comments on the literature of England and America, she learned that Stepniak himself was soon to offer his fifth book—and his first experiment in creative writing in the English language—to the reading public. The publication of this volume later in the year marked the beginning of a new phase of his activities as a revolutionary-in-exile.

LITTERATEUR AND ORGANIZER: 1889–95

Stepniak's novel, *The Career of a Nihilist*, drew on the same body of material and the same set of political considerations as his earlier articles and volumes. He wrote in a preface to the second edition:

Having been witness of and participator in a movement, which struck even its enemies by its spirit of boundless self-sacrifice, I wanted to show in the full light of fiction the inmost heart and soul of these humanitarian enthusiasts, with whom devotion to a cause has attained the fervour of a religion, without being a religion.[2]

For those who had read Stepniak's *Underground Russia*, the title may have been misleading. In that initial work, Stepniak had pointed out that the term *nihilism*—as popularized by Turgenev and employed in Russia—referred to the egocentric rebels of the 1860s, like Bazarov in *Fathers and Sons*. These people were individualistic, negative towards all responsibilities to society and family, oriented towards their personal happiness, non-violent, and preoccupied with 'moral despotism' rather than with social ideas. But when the term *nihilism* had come into vogue in the West, it was erroneously applied to the revolutionaries of the 1870s. These individuals felt a deep sense of obligation to their fellow-men and to the cause of freedom and were prepared for

---

[1] *Boston Transcript*, 18 May 1889, 5: 1–3. A shorter version of the story was reprinted as 'Stepniak on American Authors', *The Critic* (New York), XV (24 January 1891), pp. 48–9.
[2] Stepniak, *The Career of a Nihilist: A Novel*, 2nd ed. (London, n.d.), (1901), p. ix.

ultimate self-sacrifice and terror on behalf of their cause. Stepniak
saw this misapplication of the term as an irony, but he adapted
himself to the error and sought to dispel the pejorative connotation
that expression carried.[1]

The hero of the novel is Andrey Kozhukhov, a dedicated conspirator in his late twenties, affiliated with the Land and Liberty
League. At the beginning of the novel, he is living in Swiss exile
but is summoned to return to Russia to engage in underground
work, which involves primarily illegal propaganda among the
workers and occasional efforts to rescue imprisoned colleagues.
Andrey and his circle of friends emerge as sane, pleasure-loving
young people, ordinary in all respects except their compelling,
selfless dedication to the deadly struggle against the social system
of the Empire. Kozhukhov falls in love with and marries a comrade, Tania Repin, and the sacrifice of their happy marriage to
the cause is a central theme. At the climax, Kozhukhov is driven
by his dedication—intensified by an urge for revenge—to make
an attempt on the life of the Tsar, even though the attempt almost
certainly means his own death. The struggle for Russia's freedom
from bondage becomes submerged in his yearning for a martyr's
role. The 'ego of self-sacrifice' triumphs over his love of life.

The book has a number of skilful characterizations and insights
about the methods and standards of the 'illegal people' of Stepniak's youthful years. It belongs to the romantic tradition. The
central subject is not the Terror, but the torments and pressures
that drive decent, keen-witted persons like Andrey to it. The novel
closes, after his unsuccessful assassination attempt, with a simple
announcement of his arrest, trial, and execution: 'He had perished.
But the work for which he died did not perish. It goes forward
from defeat to defeat towards the final victory, which in this sad
world of ours cannot be obtained save by the sufferings and the
sacrifice of the chosen few.'[2]

After completing this book, Stepniak solicited criticism from
several persons with whom he had established close relationships.
One of his advisers was Edward Pease, the secretary of the Fabian
Society, whose meetings Stepniak occasionally attended,[3] and

[1] Stepniak, *Underground Russia*, pp. 3–13.

[2] Stepniak, *The Career of a Nihilist*, op. cit., p. 320.

[3] A copy of a letter to Pease on the novel has been printed in Charles A. Moser,
'A Nihilist's Career: S. M. Stepniak–Kravchinskij', *The American Slavic and
East European Review*, XX (February 1961), pp. 60–3. The article is not as

another was the American journalist George Kennan, who in 1887 had begun a series of articles in *The Century Magazine* on the Russian exile and prison system. These essays, which continued for more than two years and received wide attention in the United States, complemented Stepniak's own version of internal Russian affairs and lent credence to his reports. Stepniak and Kennan conducted an extensive trans-Atlantic correspondence, in the course of which Stepniak submitted a preliminary draft of the novel and asked for comments. He was worried about his literary style and yet eager to see the book successfully in print; he apparently received a good deal of conflicting advice before committing the book to print.[1]

The novel brought Stepniak additional attention and some new praise, most of it from the British and American Left. Some of his friends apparently believed him to be destined for an impressive literary career—or so some of them said after his death. This proved to be, however, his only notable experiment with English creative writing. According to Mavor, Stepniak was discouraged from further serious efforts as a novelist in English because of a remark by William Ernest Henley, who reacted somewhat unfavourably to *The Career of a Nihilist*.

Following the mixed reaction to his novel, Stepniak devoted much of his energy for the next two years to founding an organization that solicited aid from the intellectuals of the English-speaking countries for the Russian liberation movement. By 1890, the animosity towards the Tsarist regime had increased substantially in England, and Dr. Robert Spence Watson, President of the Liberal Federation of Great Britain and a prominent humanitarian, formed an organization called the Society of the Friends of Russian Freedom. Several members of Parliament lent their names to the cause, and Edward Pease became secretary. Stepniak and other non-Marxian Russian exiles were in close touch with the organization and supplied it with propaganda. The Friends issued a paper known as *Free Russia*, designed to circulate propaganda unfavourable to Tsarist autocracy. Meanwhile, Stepniak and some

---

ambitious as the title implies, dealing primarily with Stepniak's activities in America in 1891.

[1] Two revealing letters from Stepniak to Kennan, dated 20 January and 26 March 1889, are in the George Kennan Papers: Correspondence—Letters received, 1865-1890, Library of Congress Manuscript Collection.

of his fellow exiles formed a Russian Free Press Fund to print Russian-language material for opposition movements both inside Russia and in exile.

From the beginning, Stepniak insisted upon a moderate tone for the propaganda that the Russian Free Press issued. When he described the concept of the organization to Kennan before its inception, Stepniak stressed that there was no plan to advocate insurrection or revolt.

... no appeal or incitement to violence has ever appeared in any decent revolutionary paper abroad. It is considered ignoble to do such things when one is safe in a foreign country.[1]

When the Russian Free Press went into operation in the early 1890s, Stepniak produced tracts calling for co-operation between the Socialists and the liberals who were opposing the imperial regime. By this time, Stepniak had become convinced that acts of violence were not necessary or desirable in the political struggle. The progress of the German Social Democratic Party—in spite of the restrictions of Bismarck's anti-Socialist legislation of the previous decade—suggested that a reform party could advance even under an authoritarian government. Although he had little use for Marxian doctrine, he had warm admiration for the methods of this Marxian party, and in an 1891 essay he proposed it to his fellow Russians as a model of 'political discretion and self-control'.

Profiting by its experience, we propose to take our stand openly in favour of evolutionary socialism, recognising freedom of speech, freedom of the press, and universal franchise as fully sufficient weapons; and, so long as they are guaranteed by inviolable law, the only right weapons to use in the coming social struggle.[2]

Stepniak, then, had adopted a position very similar to that which would be called 'Revisionist' less than a decade later. He reached this position partly by watching events in Germany and while paying frequent visits to the home of Engels. Stepniak and Engels were estranged during the last months of their lives because of a disagreement over a matter of Socialist strategy, but he had obviously reached some of his conclusions in the period when he

[1] George Kennan Papers: Correspondence—Letters received, 1865–1890. Library of Congress Manuscript Collection. Postscript dated 29 March 1889.
[2] From his pamphlet 'Chego nam nuzhno?' translated as 'What is Wanted?' *Nihilism as It Is* (London, n.d., but 1894), p. 35.

was making regular visits to the home of the aged patriarch of German Socialism. And most probably he discussed his ideas often with that other exile who regularly shared the Sunday evenings at the Engels' home—Eduard Bernstein. Parts of Stepniak's 1891 essay might well have come from the pen of the leading German Revisionist a few years afterwards:

We utterly disbelieve in the possibility of reconstructing economic relationships by means of a burst of revolutionary inspiration. That is a huge work which needs great mental efforts on the part of many people, much preparation, much practical experience and correction, and therefore much time.[1]

It is impossible to determine to what extent Stepniak and Bernstein exchanged ideas during the early 1890s, but they obviously shared a good deal. Bernstein's wife read and responded warmly to Stepniak's novel and apparently consulted him about the possibility of a German translation.[2] The warm bond that existed between the two men suggests a large measure of political agreement. Bernstein wrote a tribute to his Russian friend after the latter's death; Stepniak had helped to settle misunderstandings between the German Social Democrats and the revolutionists in Russia, Bernstein said, and he added: 'His was a very open mind. He did what so seldom popular leaders dare—he dared to break with traditions when they proved to be false, or, at least, when he was convinced of their falseness.'[3] When Bernstein wrote this phrase in 1896, he was on the threshold of his own break with the Marxian doctrines.

The year of this proto-Revisionist essay from the pen of Stepniak —1891—was also the year of his lecture tour to the United States. He arranged the trip with the help of George Kennan, and from January until late May he conducted propaganda for his cause in New England, New York, and the Middle West.[4]

[1] Ibid., p. 32.
[2] Bernstein Archives, D 680, International Institute of Social History, Amsterdam. This is a letter from Stepniak to Mrs. Bernstein, thanking her for her interest in *The Career of a Nihilist*.
[3] *Free Russia* (London), VII, 1 February 1896, p. 16.
[4] On Stepniak's visit to the United States, see Charles A. Moser, 'A Nihilist's Career: S. M. Stepniak–Kravchinskij', op. cit., pp. 55–71. The article is not as ambitious as the title implies, dealing primarily with Stepniak's novel *The Career of a Nihilist* and with his visit to America. For Stepniak's account of his American trip, see *Free Russia* (American edition), No. 12 (July 1891), pp. 8–10. A later account by Lillie B. Wyman appeared in *Free Russia* (London), X

Stepniak's reputation had preceded him to America and he made
the usual good impression. An entourage of reporters was awaiting
him when he disembarked in New York City on 30 December
1890, and the newsman representing *The New York Times* wrote:

Anybody, taking a good look at him, would say: 'There's a man over-
flowing with good nature; a warm-hearted sympathetic fellow. He cannot be a Nihilist.' But that is the very sort of man to make a good
Nihilist, according to the definition which Stepniak himself gives, for,
as he puts it, the Nihilist is a man who, touched by the suffering of his
people, feels impelled to espouse their cause and to make a martyr of
himself, if needs be, to right their wrongs. He may do very bad things,
but he does them because he is a very good man.[1]

The *Times* reporter was only the first of Stepniak's American
conquests. A few days later, he spoke to a responsive audience in
the Metropolitan Opera House and a short time later he made his
way to Boston for lectures and private audiences. There, one of his
earliest admirers was William Dean Howells. 'He is a most
interesting and important man'; Howells wrote his father, 'one of
those wonderful clear heads that seem to belong to other races than
ours. He went to the club dinner with me, and talked for an hour
or two about conditions in Russia, with a moderation and lucidity
that enchanted everybody.'[2] Howells heard him lecture effectively
on Tolstoy, showed him some of the local curiosities (such as a
fire-engine house where Stepniak provoked laughter by negotiating
his stout frame down the brass pole) and gave him a letter of
introduction to Samuel Clemens.[3]

The energetic Stepniak contacted several other well-known
Americans, apparently seeking out the surviving abolitionists who
had won reputations for reform a generation earlier. Among his
contacts were T. W. Higginson, William Lloyd Garrison, and
Julia Ward Howe, whom he importuned to sign an appeal expressing sympathy with the Russian revolutionary movement. As he
discussed his project with the American intellectuals, he found it

---

(August–September 1899), pp. 67–8; (1 November 1899), pp. 79–80; and
(1 December 1899), pp. 87–8.

[1] *The New York Times*, 31 December 1890, 8: 3.

[2] William Dean Howells, *Life in Letters of William Dean Howells*, ed. by
Mildred Howells (Garden City, N.Y., 1928), vol II, p. 12.

[3] Henry N. Smith and William M. Gibson, eds., *Mark Twain–Howells Letters:
The Correspondence of Samuel L. Clemens and William D. Howells, 1872–1910*
(Cambridge, Mass., 1960), p. 643.

necessary to compose a petition that specifically did not countenance or support the extreme and violent section of the Russian revolutionary movement, and by so doing he won much support for his cause. Howells, who first responded warmly, declined to give his support to the movement, but Clemens and his wife, then living in Hartford, signed. Eventually such names as John Greenleaf Whittier, James Russell Lowell, and Phillips Brooks appeared on the petition.

Part of Stepniak's objective was also to raise funds for the edition of *Free Russia* that was being published in New York largely through the efforts of George Kennan, and to create an 'American Society of Friends of Russian Freedom', corresponding to the group that existed in London. The group came into existence in Boston in April 1891, but it does not appear to have functioned actively after Stepniak's return to London a few weeks later.

Stepniak was so pleased with America that he considered moving there to continue his work. In a letter written shortly before his departure for England in May, he told Kennan that he hoped to produce more books for his cause, but he was obviously tiring of journalistic activity.[1]

In the last few years before his death, Stepniak shared in the translation of several samples of Russian literature and wrote introductory essays to other translations. Among the translations in which he had a hand were A. N. Ostrovsky's *The Storm* (or *The Thunderstorm*) and V. G. Korolenko's novels *The Blind Musician* and *In Two Moods*. He wrote introductions to English-language editions of Turgenev's *Rudin* and *A House of Gentlefolk*, to a collection of the stories of V. M. Garshin, and to an anthology of Russian humour translated by E. L. Voinich. In 1890 he wrote a story of his own entitled *Domik na Volge*. About two years later, he was at work on another manuscript—not initially conceived as a novel—that finally emerged in novel form. It was published after his death under the title *Shtundist Pavel Rudenko*.

Stepniak had an unfortunate experience with this manuscript. In 1892, the English writer Hesba Stretton, who was sympathetic to the persecuted religious sects in Russia, became interested in the Stundist group that Stepniak had described in *The Russian*

---

[1] George Kennan Papers: Correspondence—Letters received—1891–1904. Library of Congress Manuscript Collection. Letter dated New York, May 19, 1891.

Peasantry. She was the author of a number of books that emphasized fundamentalist Christianity, and the simple, non-ritualistic Stundists seemed to be ready-made for her purposes. She approached Stepniak and proposed that they collaborate on a novel.

According to the account given later by Stepniak's widow, the idea of joint authorship did not appeal to him, but he did consent to write some descriptive and historical matter about the movement for Miss Stretton's use.[1] When he began to compose the promised material he found it easier to use the novel form and to centre the activities around a hero, Pavel Rudenko. He composed initially in Russian and gave a translation to Miss Stretton. When she made the alterations that she considered necessary, the treatment of the religious theme did not meet Stepniak's approval, and he declined to allow his name to appear on the title page. He allowed Miss Stretton to publish the work under her name alone, and she acknowledged the anonymous help of a prominent Russian exile.[2]

All of Stepniak's ventures with novels and translations were extensions of his efforts to acquaint the Western societies with Russian life. Since Stepniak was an eager observer of the London cultural scene and a friend of Shaw, he recognized the theatre as another outlet for his message. He tried to get English dramatic producers interested in Russian plays, and he composed a melodrama of his own in 1894.

Written in the Russian language, the play is entitled *Novoobrashchennyi*, translated into English after Stepniak's death as *The New Convert*. He took the plot of an earlier play and adapted it to his purposes. Stepniak's death occurred before the play was either published or performed, but Shaw took an interest in it, and his wife had it published in Geneva in 1897. It was produced in the Avenue Theatre in London on 14 June 1898.[3]

The New Convert is a crude melodrama about a young woman dedicated to the revolutionary cause but pursued by a villain—

[1] This episode is described in Stepniak's *Sochineniia* (1958), II, pp. 571–3.
[2] The English version is Hesba Stretton and ********, *The Highway of Sorrow* (New York, 1894). The Russian version is S. Stepniak, *Shtundist Pavel Rudenko* (Geneva, 1900; several later editions).
[3] B. Piskun, in the introduction to Stepniak, *Sochinennia* (1958), II, pp. 582–5. According to *Free Russia* (London), vol IX (July–October 1898), p. 51, Kropotkin spoke briefly at the end of the play.

a representative of the Tsar's military and police. Early in the play, the heroine, Katia, rejects the villain as a prospective husband, and near the end he nearly succeeds in arresting her as an illegal person. The girl's wealthy, upper-class father, who initially tried to arrange the marriage, finally kills the discredited pursuer and dedicates himself to the revolutionary cause.[1]

This is the kind of sentimental theatre that Bernard Shaw lambasted unmercifully in his *Saturday Review* articles in the middle 1890s, and he undoubtedly had some reservations about this play. He seems to have submerged them, however, in the interests of Stepniak's widow, whom he tried to help after the fatal accident.[2]

In Shaw's testimonial to Stepniak written a few weeks after the accident, he acknowledged his own debt to the peripatetic Russian. Apparently the two men had discussed a wide range of subjects, including books, theatre, and music, and Stepniak offered much information on Bulgarian manners and customs when Shaw—still struggling for recognition as a playwright—was writing *Arms and the Man*. 'He studiously encouraged me to think well of my own work,' Shaw wrote, expressing an unusually warm regard for the deceased friend.[3]

For all his experiments in translating, play writing, and criticism, Stepniak remained most comfortable in the field of political propaganda. He continued to produce articles on current Russian affairs, and in the last year of his life he helped to draft a proposed constitution for the Russian Empire.[4] Once again, his proposals were modest and reasonable by Western standards, a reflection of his own personal gentleness and the spirit of compromise that had grown during the years of his English residence.

Yet he did not abandon the old techniques of vilification against the hated regime. His final work, *King Stork and King Log*, was largely a compilation and revision of some of his last articles, describing still more episodes of persecution under Alexander III and Nicholas II. The reign of Nicholas II was still young at the

---

[1] The English translation is Sergei Stepniak, *The New Convert: A Drama in Four Acts*, translated from the Russian by Thomas B. Eyges (Boston, 1917).

[2] For Shaw's letters in which he proposed a means of assisting Fannie Stepniak, see Bernard Shaw, *Collected Letters: 1874–1897*, edited by Dan H. Laurence (New York, 1965), pp. 587, 588.

[3] Shaw, 'A Word About Stepniak', op. cit., p. 106.

[4] 'Proekt' 'Russkoi Konstitutsii (Sostavlennyi v' Rossii) 1895g.', in *Sobranie Sochinenii*, VI (St. Petersburg, 1908), pp. 65–95.

time the volumes appeared, so only the final pages are concerned with his regime. There is more discussion of the administrative system, of the governing of such minority groups as the Finns, Jews, and Poles, and of the continuing revolutionary movement.[1]

Many of the arguments are essentially redundant; one finds him discussing the meaning of nihilism again and explaining the special qualities of Russian socialism. He was eager to establish that the Russian people—though different in some respects from their Western neighbours—were capable of governing themselves in the Western fashion. He concluded that the Russians were better prepared for self-government than some of the other West European peoples had been when they won representative institutions.

Thus the buoyant, energetic Stepniak finished his career with a work of considerable size on the theme that had preoccupied him during all his adult years. He was on his way to a meeting at which further organizational and propaganda plans were to have been made when he was struck by a train. When his funeral was held on 29 December 1895, an international collection of prominent revolutionaries assembled to pay tribute to him.

STEADFAST NARODNIK

For one who had such wide-ranging interests, Stepniak demonstrated relatively little intellectual growth between his first and last books. Although *King Stork and King Log* shows more sophistication than some of his earlier works, it is not on a significantly higher intellectual level. Stepniak remained an old-fashioned liberal revolutionary, more moderate than he had been in his twenties, but still hardly concerned with any problems or objectives beyond the immediate political ones. He was more like his mid-century predecessors in his thinking than he was like his Socialist and anarchist acquaintances in England. His was the simple message and the eloquent rhetoric of the romantics when he wrote in the *North American Review*:

But what is this dream of mine?
This dream is to see one day a new crusade started in the West against the great sinner of the East, the Russian Tzardom; to see an

[1] S. Stepniak, *King Stork and King Log: A Study of Modern Russia* (London, 1896), 2 vols.

army spring into existence—not a host, but a well-selected army like that of Gideon—composed of the best men of all free nations, with unlimited means at their command, making common cause with the Russian patriots, fighting side by side with them, each with their appropriate weapons, until that nightmare of modern times, the Russian autocracy, is conquered, and compelled to accept the supremacy of the triumphant democracy.[1]

The 'dream' includes an afterthought—'the land of the future co-operative civilization' which will replace the old 'competitive, pugnacious, man-a-wolf-to-man civilization'—but Stepniak does not dwell on or develop this theme. For him, it would have been infinitely rewarding to see modest progress towards representative institutions and individual freedoms in his homeland. He was not interested in a fundamentally new moral order for all mankind, as many of his companions in London were.

In all significant respects, Stepniak's work is less complex than that of those contemporaries who are studied here. His writing is not burdened with the intricate analysis that became a common feature of the revolutionary prose of his time. He did not trouble himself with meditations about a new ethical basis for the future society; he contented himself with the affirmation that most men —and specifically the Russian peasants—were basically good, and that was enough:

First of all, we take for granted the absolute independence of pure ethics from any religious doctrines. Human ethics, the moral principles which regulate the relations between man and man, have a much broader basis than the doctrines of Christianity, or any religion whatsoever. They spring from the human heart, from man's social nature, and are manifested wherever men are thrown peacefully together. When tribes first broke up into families, their founders learned, from the very nature of this new institution, the first lessons of morality, and at once grasped the necessity of putting the common good before their private benefit. They learned to suppress their narrow and selfish interests for the sake of wider and far-reaching ones; the needs of the family ranked before those of the individual.[2]

The moral instinct had expanded as human contacts had increased, and the ideal of human brotherhood emerged. The instinct of sympathy for fellow men is innate; only its application has been widened.

---

[1] 'What Americans Can Do for Russia', op. cit., pp. 596–7.
[2] Stepniak, *The Russian Peasantry*, pp. 211–12.

The social conditions under which our peasantry lived for centuries have been favorable to the spontaneous development among them of such 'pan-human' morals. They are Christ-like as a matter of course.[1]

In one of the scenes at the climax of *The Career of a Nihilist*, the hero Andrey engages in a searching exchange with his father-in-law, Repin, which suggests Stepniak's attitude towards the more formal thinkers. Andrey asks:

'. . . Has not a great philosopher said, "The higher your estimation of the majority of men, the smaller your chances of mistake?" '

Repin observed, that as far as his knowledge of great philosophers went, none of them had said this, and one of them had said the very reverse.

'Then they ought to have said it,' Andrey answered. 'If they have not, I would not give a brass farthing for the lot.'[2]

Because Stepniak did not concern himself with some of the more challenging questions that had arisen in the left-wing movement in the 1880s and 1890s, after his death his writings did not remain in vogue for long. Although his wife collected funds and managed to get most of them translated into Russian during the next few years, they commanded little attention in the West in the twentieth century. Many of his anecdotes and arguments slipped out of date quickly, as propaganda often does, and the point of view that he represented did not prevail in Russia. Had the intellectual level of the works been higher, perhaps they would have fared better, but this would not have suited Stepniak's immediate ends.

Writing in 1913, Thomas Masaryk commented on the Russian revolutionaries generally and reached this conclusion:

. . . the Russian, who continues to believe uncritically in myth, still expects the revolution to work miracles. What Russians need, in a word, is a Kant to apply criticism to their revolutionary doctrines. For lack of such a Kant, they have never got beyond Stepniak's Old Testament theory of a life for a life.[3]

Stepniak's friend Kropotkin fared better at the hands of posterity because his range of interest was broader and his ethical speculations were more engaging.

---

[1] Stepniak, *The Russian Peasantry*, p. 217.

[2] Stepniak, *The Career of a Nihilist*, p. 297.

[3] Thomas Garrigue Masaryk, *The Spirit of Russia: Studies in History, Literature, and Philosophy*, translated from the German by Eden and Cedar Paul (London, 1955), II, p. 542. The German original was published in Jena in 1913.

III

KROPOTKIN

The *Philosophe* of Anarchism

PRINCE KROPOTKIN was much like his friend Stepniak in temperament and manner: those who knew him could not regard him as a desperate revolutionary. He was balding, short, and stocky, and he peered at the world through tiny eye-glasses that gave him more the appearance of the quaint continental professor than of Europe's leading theoretical anarchist. Bernard Shaw wrote of him as 'amiable to the point of saintliness, and with his full red beard and lovable expression (he) might have been a shepherd from the Delectable Mountains'.[1]

There was a quality of serenity and personal warmth that many of his acquaintances mentioned when they wrote of him. As he changed from a man of middle years to one of old age in England between 1886 and 1917, increasing numbers of middle-class Englishmen were added to the ranks of those who respected his integrity. He was admired generally, however, for his personal qualities and for his scientific work rather than for the social ideas that were most dear to him.

When Kropotkin arrived in England in 1886, his Communist-anarchist ideas were little known, although he had published a number of articles in English. He had written several scientific reviews for *Nature* and had contributed to *Encyclopedia Britannica* and *The Nineteenth Century*, but most of these articles had dealt with subjects other than anarchism. His articles in *The Nineteenth Century* resembled the works of Stepniak during the same period, bearing such titles as 'Russian Prisons' (January 1883), 'The Fortress Prison of St. Petersburg' (June 1883), 'Outcast Russia' (December 1883), 'The Exile in Siberia' (March 1884), 'Finland: A Rising Nationality' (May 1885), and 'The Coming War' (May 1885) which dealt with Central Asian tensions. While such articles

---

[1] Quoted in Woodcock and Avakumović, p. 225.

identified Kropotkin as a revolutionary, they provided little explanation of his distinctive political theories.

Most of Kropotkin's writing on anarchism was initially in
French, and during the period of his incarceration in 1883–6, his
friend Élisée Reclus had assembled several of the articles from
Le Révolté and published them in a booklet entitled *Paroles d'un
révolté*.[1] From this work came most of the earliest samples of his
anarchist arguments to be put into English. Hyndman, whom
Kropotkin had met and urged to begin a revolutionary newspaper
during his 1881–2 sojourn in London, reprinted the section entitled
'An Appeal to the Young' in 1884.[2] This was issued as a pamphlet
in the following year, and other parts of the *Paroles* followed in
quick succession in 1886. Some of the selections were published by
the press of *The Anarchist*, a small newspaper under the editorship
of Henry Seymour. In the autumn of that year Kropotkin had
helped to form the Freedom Group and to establish the tiny
propaganda newspaper *Freedom*. This periodical, edited by Mrs.
Charlotte Wilson, became an important forum for Kropotkin's
ideas, but it had only a small circulation.

It was clear at an early date that Stepniak and Kropotkin had
different approaches to the reform movement. Kropotkin did not
share his friend's interest in winning political rights from the Tsar.
He acknowledged that there are some rights worth fighting for,
'which are so dear to the people that the people will rise if an
attempt is made to violate them'.

But there are others, such as universal suffrage, the liberty of the
press, and so on, towards which the people to-day remain cold and
indifferent, because the people feel that these rights, which serve so
well to defend the governing bourgeoisie against the invasions of power
and the aristocracy, are simply an instrument in the hands of the
dominating classes to maintain their dominion over the people. These
rights are not even real political rights, since they protect nothing for
the mass of the people; and if they are still decorated with the pompous
title of rights, it is only because our political language is simply a
jargon elaborated by the governing classes for their own use and in
their own interest.[3]

[1] Peter Kropotkin, *Paroles d'un révolté*, edited by Elisée Reclus (Paris, 1885).
[2] *Justice*, vol I, 23, 30 August, 6, 13, 20, 27 September, 4, 11 October 1884.
The instalments are on p. 3 of each issue.
[3] Quoted from *Paroles d'un révolté*, in William H. Hurlbert, 'State Christianity
and the French Elections', *The Nineteenth Century*, XVIII (November, 1885),
p. 750.

Thus Kropotkin rejected the political values that were fundamental to Stepniak and proceeded from a different set of assumptions, even though the two men had come from the same background.

Kropotkin's first book published in England followed the Stepniak pattern. In 1887, he combined his articles on the Russian prison system with some new ones on his experiences in French cells and issued them as a volume entitled *In Russian and French Prisons*. But he continued to devote a major part of his energy to writing in French for *Le Révolté*,[1] and this work proved to have greater significance than his English efforts, since it was these articles that were combined into his first major exposition of anarchism—*La conquête du pain*.

THE CONQUEST OF BREAD

La conquête du pain appeared as a book in 1892. There was no English edition until 1906, but a number of chapters appeared in *Freedom* and elsewhere in the 1890s, so that its propositions were readily available to London readers who were interested.

The writing that Kropotkin had done before his arrival in England might be regarded as a rough draft for this work. Even though *La conquête du pain* was, like *Paroles*, a combination of journalistic articles, it had the benefit of Kropotkin's editing of his more mature thinking. During his years in the French prisons, Kropotkin had done much reading and some experimental gardening that had helped to shape his theories about future revolutionary efforts. He had been especially moved by the ideas of Professor Karl Kessler, a zoologist of St. Petersburg University, about the co-operative instinct in nature. He had, in short, added to the raw material from which his ultimate anarchist theory was fashioned. The articles that went into *La conquête du pain* were the first systematic expression of that theory.

When he wrote these pieces, Kropotkin obviously envisioned a new French revolution and he seems to have assumed that the new social order would begin there. He had studied the great Revolution of the 1790s and also the episode of the Commune, and on

[1] After August 1887, the paper was renamed *La Révolte*. Articles in *Le Révolté* and *La Révolte* were usually unsigned, but it is clear that most of the theoretical and scholarly material came from Kropotkin's pen. Editorial notes occasionally give guidance, and a substantial amount of this material was later republished under his name.

this record he made his important calculations and projections. His rhetoric is often emotional and provocative, and there is much repetition; *The Conquest of Bread* is not one of his carefully prepared books, but it is a fundamental document of anarchism.

The basic assumptions were elementary. The great revolution could be expected soon, and to be successful it would have to accomplish a total transformation of society very quickly. Revolutionary leaders of the past had spent too much time fulminating over the forms of office and the types of authority they would establish; they had given too little thought to the immediate elimination of human suffering. What was needed were not merely new institutions and regulations, but a complete abolition of government and a new spirit that would swiftly convince the lower classes that the old order was dead.

The great metamorphosis of the masses depended on a new principle of distribution, according to this line of argument. The populace must be convinced by tangible evidence—primarily consisting of an equitable distribution of food—that the day of liberation was at hand. It was the want of basic foodstuffs that had caused previous revolutionary efforts to founder. If this could be overcome, the idlers would become fighters and workers for the common cause and would be equal to any reactionary challenge.

The solution that Kropotkin proposes, after many diversions and generalizations, is common storehouses of food and other essential supplies in the cities where the revolutionary movement has begun:

Thus the really practical course of action, in our view, would be that the people should take immediate possession of all the food of the insurgent districts, keeping strict account of it all, that none might be wasted, and that by the aid of these accumulated resources every one might be able to tide over the crisis. During that time an agreement would have to be made with the factory workers, the necessary raw material given them and the means of subsistence assured to them while they worked to supply the needs of the agricultural population.[1]

Kropotkin consistently avoided more specific suggestions than this. He was convinced that there could be enough foodstuffs for all insurgents during a revolutionary situation if it were well handled, and it was almost axiomatic that the people had the talent and the will to make an equitable distribution, once they became

[1] P. Kropotkin, *The Conquest of Bread* (London, 1906), p. 74.

convinced that the day of liberation had come. He categorically rejected the argument that a government bureau must to manage the division. One looks in vain through the work for a substitute or for more precise information about the procedures to be used. Kropotkin had unlimited faith in the people, expecting all the significant problems to evaporate with the political institutions that have been devised to deal with them.

Once the initial hurdle is passed and the revolutionary movement has survived the first trying weeks, its creative collectivity will rapidly provide an abundance for all. In his mind's eye, Kropotkin visualized Paris as he wrote, and he conceived a new commune that would be strong enough to prevent a recurrence of 1871 because it could not be starved. Such a commune could quickly begin to solve its own supply problems:

'What about land?' It will not be wanting, for it is round the great towns, and round Paris especially, that the parks and pleasure grounds of the landed gentry are to be found. These thousands of acres only await the skilled labour of the husbandman to surround Paris with fields infinitely more fertile and productive than the steppes of southern Russia, where the soil is dried up by the sun. Nor will labour be lacking. To what should the two million citizens of Paris turn their attention when they would be no longer catering for the luxurious fads and amusements of Russian princes, Roumanian grandees, and wives of Berlin financiers?[1]

Each great city would be thus made self-sufficient, and its own factories and shops could supply local needs. Kropotkin enjoyed the luxury of living and developing his theories before the age of the aeroplane and sophisticated weapons of bombardment, and in the 1880s he was not able to imagine types of warfare more deadly than those employed in his own day and in the previous century. His buoyant optimism carried him easily over brutal and bloody aspects of the revolution to the rich life beyond:

. . . Imagine a society, comprising a few million inhabitants, engaged in agriculture and a great variety of industries—Paris, for example, with the Department of Seine-et-Oise. Suppose that in this society all children learn to work with their hands as well as with their brains. Admit that all adults, save women, engaged in the education of their children, bind themselves to work 5 *hours a day* from the age of twenty or twenty-two to forty-five or fifty, and that they follow occupations

[1] Ibid., pp. 100–1.

they have chosen in any one branch of human work considered *necessary*. Such a society could in return guarantee well-being to all its members; that is to say, a more substantial well-being than that enjoyed to-day by the middle classes. And, moreover, each worker belonging to this society would have at his disposal at least 5 hours a day which he could devote to science, art, and individual needs which do not come under the category of *necessities*, but will probably do so later on, when man's productivity will have augmented, and those objects will no longer appear luxurious and inaccessible.[1]

The use of labour for projects that serve only the idle rich, the division of labour in factories which forces thousands to do tedious boring work, the placing of artificial restrictions on production to elevate prices—all these practices would be eliminated in Kropotkin's ideal community. He confidently believed that land and other resources were available in abundance in every corner of the world, and he expected science and technology to provide many new vistas.

Having read extensively in agricultural journals and having observed new machinery, new fertilizers, and experimental green-houses in use, Kropotkin gave free rein to his imagination. More completely than most of his contemporaries, Kropotkin foresaw an era when the productivity of land would multiply several times under intensive cultivation. He patiently assembled elaborate statistics and worked out production estimates to demonstrate the possibilities of some types of agriculture. Fortified with figures on hot-house experimentation on Jersey and Guernsey and in the suburbs of London, on practices employed on the American plains, on the raising of cattle, on shipping costs, on labour-time invested in various food-products, he concluded that the earth's potential had been badly underestimated. Only poor systems of cultivation and distribution caused shortages.

The seizure of 'bread' during the revolutionary epoch, then, constituted only the first step in the reordering of man's procedures for obtaining food. Kropotkin even anticipated that men would come to see the wisdom of communal kitchens, where the needs of a whole community could be prepared on a single fire. This was a provisional and qualified suggestion however; he would leave open the option of individual kitchens and restaurants.

---

[1] P. Kropotkin, *The Conquest of Bread*, pp. 132–3. The italics are Kropotkin's.

In many other areas of human life, similar drastic reorientations would begin immediately. His proposals on housing are suggestive. It would be within the ability of the revolutionaries to distribute available housing fairly by expropriating completely the buildings that received too little use. 'Groups of volunteers' would probably arise in every district and street to make housing surveys, prepare lists of those that were overcrowded and those that could accommodate the poorly housed. Within a few days, the self-appointed groups would have complete statistics and would make the new distribution of quarters. Again the patience of the underprivileged and aroused populace was assumed. Even if there were not enough buildings to solve all the housing needs immediately, new quarters will be quickly provided.

When the masons, and carpenters, and all who are concerned in house building, know that their daily bread is secured to them, they will ask nothing better than to work at their old trades a few hours a day. They will adapt the fine houses which absorbed the time of a whole staff of servants, and in a few months homes will have sprung up, infinitely healthier and more conveniently arranged than those of to-day. And to those who are not yet comfortably housed the anarchist Commune will be able to say: 'Patience, comrades! Palaces fairer and finer than any the capitalists built for themselves will spring from the ground of our enfranchised city. They will belong to those who have most need of them. The anarchist Commune does not build with an eye to revenues. These monuments erected to its citizens, products of the collective spirit, will serve as models to all humanity; they will be yours.'[1]

Kropotkin regarded a building—like any of the other creations of society—as the product of collective skills and of material gathered from many places and produced by many hands. Hence it is the possession of the community, not the property of him whom the state regards as its owner. He does not indicate how different claims will be adjudicated or how disputes over possession will be settled when expropriation has put all the dwellings under the Commune; he rested on his expectation that good will would prevail. Again he reminded his readers that no central authority could handle the transformation or make the arrangements. Only spontaneous groups, exercising their native communal instincts, will be capable of meeting the challenge.

[1] Ibid., p. 112.

Even in the more esoteric fields, the new era will provide unprecedented opportunities and abundance. The arts and the professions of writing and publishing would flourish as never before. The artists, by spending parts of their days in the fields or factories, will achieve magnificent results, drawing inspiration from *'ideals held in common'*.[1] A writer who prepared a manuscript will no longer seek someone with capital to publish his works; he will be obliged only to 'look for collaborators among those who know the printing trade, and who approve the idea of his new work. Together they will publish the new book or journal.'[2]

Thus the argument advances, always stopping short of specific description, always leaving technical and practical questions in the minds of the readers. Wages are to be abolished completely and the division of labour will be drastically reduced. International trade will be greatly diminished as region after region becomes self-sufficient in most goods. Toll bridges will become free, museums and libraries will be open to all without charge, and free water will be available in each home. Even the drudgery of the housewife will soon disappear under the impact of technology; Kropotkin anticipated the development of such devices as the automatic washing machine, dishwasher, vacuum cleaner, and other labour-saving household equipment.

Only a lack of collective imagination could provoke a failure, Kropotkin said at several points; ' . . . cowardice of the spirit is the rock on which all revolutions have stranded until now'.[3] The final passage of the book summarizes and captures the mood of the later sections:

Inspired by a new daring—thanks to the sentiment of solidarity —all will march together to the conquest of the high joys of knowledge and artistic creation.

A society thus inspired will fear neither dissensions within nor enemies without. To the coalitions of the past it will oppose a new harmony, the initiative of each and all, the daring which springs from the awakening of a people's genius.

Before such an irresistible force 'conspiring kings' will be powerless. Nothing will remain for them but to bow before it, and to harness themselves to the chariot of humanity, rolling towards new horizons opened up by the Social Revolution.[4]

[1] P. Kropotkin, *The Conquest of Bread*, p. 151. The italics are Kropotkin's.
[2] Ibid., p. 144.   [3] Ibid., p. 291.   [4] Ibid., pp. 295–6.

FIELDS, FACTORIES AND WORKSHOPS

Kropotkin's next book, *Fields, Factories and Workshops* may be regarded as a supplement to *The Conquest of Bread*. The essays that went into this volume were written during the same period—the late 1880s and early 1890s. One notable difference is that they were written primarily for English readers and examples were drawn from the English situation; some of the essays appeared first in *The Nineteenth Century*. At the time Kropotkin issued *Fields, Factories and Workshops* in book form in 1898, he may not have anticipated that *The Conquest of Bread*, then available only in French, would be issued in an English edition a few years later.

One of the initial objectives of the essays and the book was to convince Englishmen that their unique leadership in the industrial field was in jeopardy and that their neglect of agriculture in favour of manufacture and trade was an error. Kropotkin deplored the fact that British farm production had declined during the last third of the century, a trend that ran counter to the balanced economic self-sufficiency that he desired for each region. With the same kinds of statistics and some of the same examples that had served him in the earlier work, Kropotkin argued that Great Britain could more than double her food production. He omitted from this work, however, the revolutionary justification for such a development.

The British reliance on her industrial leadership could only be of short duration, according to Kropotkin's reasoning, because manufacturing skills and facilities were developing in all parts of the world. He accurately anticipated that Britain would be embarrassed by her competitors, but he less accurately anticipated that the solution to this would be more reliance on local and domestic industries.

Kropotkin looked at the data that showed ever-larger industrial firms crowding the small producer and handicraft operator out of business, and he refused to accept the conclusion that the evidence suggested.

Altogether, it may be taken as one of the fundamental facts of the economical life of Europe that the defeat of a number of small trades, artisan work, and domestic industries came through their being incapable of organising the *sale* of their produce—not from the *pro-duction* itself.[1]

In his view, the ultimate trend in industry and agriculture would have to be away from great centralized enterprises and towards small, locally-oriented productive units. On this score he found fault with the Marxian Socialists and asserted that Marx himself, had he lived into the 1890s, probably would have abandoned his theories about the concentration of capitalistic enterprises.[2]

Only under special conditions or in certain situations could large and specialized industries exist—ship-building operations and iron foundries were examples. Kropotkin recorded, with obvious delight, a number of instances in which handicraft work of high quality continued to flourish. He was not advocating destruction of mass-production machinery where labour-saving functions could be performed, but artistic design and special types of work would remain in the realm of the craftsman. At several points, Kropotkin's arguments run parallel to those of William Morris.

Complementary to this theme was the idea that 'brain work' and 'manual work' would be integrated, with virtually all adults sharing the opportunities and the obligations of each kind of work. The great inventions of the nineteenth century had usually not come from the men of science and from the laboratories, he argued, but from the humble workers who knew how to use their hands and 'had breathed the atmosphere of the workshop and the build-ing-yard'. Division of labour generally was deplored in anarchist thought, and Kropotkin especially disliked it when mental work had no relationship with physical production. The new creativity that he sought depended on their interaction.

For Kropotkin, the growing population of the world did not constitute a problem; it offered an opportunity. Although some men of his generation were noticing population increases with concern, Kropotkin characteristically welcomed it and took pains to refute the Malthusian hypothesis. He predicted the land could be made so productive that 1,000 people living on 1,000 acres could produce 'luxurious vegetable and animal food, as well as

---

[1] P. Kropotkin, *Fields, Factories and Workshops or Industry Combined with Agriculture and Brain Work with Manual Work*, Illustrated and Unabridged, Second Impression. (New York, London, 1901), pp. 169–70.

[2] Ibid., p. 163 n.

the flax, wool, silk and hides necessary for their clothing' simply by using known methods.[1]

We know that a crowded population is a necessary condition for permitting man to increase the productive powers of his labour.[2]

Not only was Malthus's theory wrong from a technical point of view, but it was also repugnant for the social use that had been made of it:

. . . Malthus's theory, by shaping into a pseudo-scientific form the secret desires of the wealth-possessing classes, became the foundation of a whole system of practical philosophy, which permeates the minds of both the educated and uneducated, and reacts (as practical philosophy always does) upon the theoretical philosophy of our century.[3]

The idea that the thinking of European men had gone astray, that they had been tricked by wilful exploiters was an important aspect of Kropotkin's thought. Like the later Bolsheviks, who explained many of their failures in terms of erroneous or treacherous use of ideology, Kropotkin regarded the formulation and publicizing of the correct ideology as a most important assignment. This was one of the main reasons for his devotion to the task of creating an anarchist literature during the 1880s and 1890s. He felt the need for a definitive argument—a fresh ideology—that would remedy the damage done by Hobbes in political philosophy, Malthus in economics, and the Darwinians in science. He felt he had the weapons to fashion the correct and 'scientific' social philosophy for the new era.

MUTUAL AID

Kropotkin's third significant literary contribution to the body of revolutionary doctrine was a series of articles that eventually became well known under the title of *Mutual Aid*. The point of departure for this series was the Darwinian philosophy of Thomas H. Huxley. In February 1888, the English naturalist had published an essay entitled 'The Struggle for Existence in Human Society', which was primarily an argument for an enlarged programme of technical training in Great Britain as a service to citizens in the industrial society. Kropotkin objected not only to this kind of specialization—he took up this question in *Fields*,

[1] Ibid., p. 70.   [2] Ibid., p. 71.   [3] Ibid., pp. 84-5.

Factories and Workshops—but also he took exception to the fundamental assumptions the famous Darwinist made at the beginning of his article.

One of Huxley's offensive points was that primitive men—like animals—tend to multiply until food resources are insufficient to sustain the whole population, leading to a vicious struggle in which the strong will prevail. This was simply a restatement of the ideas of Malthus and Darwin, specifying the absence of any moral code in the natural state. The history of civilization, however, is a record of man's efforts to escape this Hobbesian condition, according to Huxley. Hence the desirability of governmental action to try to mitigate the struggles between men and to prepare them for social roles.

Kropotkin disliked not only the conclusions but also the premise, and he had been pondering similar questions for about half a decade when the Huxley article appeared. Returning to the articles by the Russian biologist Kessler that he had read during the period of his incarceration at Clairvaux, and adding to it a variety of information that he had assembled from scholarly works, Kropotkin took issue with Huxley. He willingly consented to write a rebuttal when offered a chance to do so by James Knowles, editor of *The Nineteenth Century*.

The answer to Huxley emerged as eight essays and appeared over a period of more than six years—from the summer of 1890 to the summer of 1896. In 1902, the essays were combined and published as a book. The work was re-issued in 1914, soon after the beginning of the war. Kropotkin hoped at that time that his arguments on communal instincts would help to counteract impressions arising from the barbarities of the war.

Mutual Aid became more than a response to the Darwinists. An elementary philosophy of history is sketched here, and the theories enunciated in *The Conquest of Bread* and *Fields, Factories and Workshops* receive further development.[1] The arguments of the Darwinians are given relatively little attention, most of it in the earliest essays. *Mutual Aid* argues that the Darwinians have ignored some basic facts about the struggle for life and have over-

[1] For a helpful edition of the work, see Peter Kropotkin, *Mutual Aid: A Factor of Evolution*, Foreword by Ashley Montagu (Boston, 1955). This contains not only the informative foreword but also Huxley's essay to which Kropotkin was replying and the author's Preface to the 1914 edition.

emphasized the occasional competition between members of the same species. Those creatures most likely to survive and prosper are not usually those who have triumphed in adversity, but those who have experienced little natural adversity, and this is often a matter of chance, according to Kropotkin. The elimination of birds' eggs by rats, unfavourable weather, and other natural factors have more influence on survival and development of birds than does any struggle for existence within the species. The horses of Siberia, often starved and stunted by the terrible winters, do not grow more fit by virtue of their struggles for existence. It is the horses of more favourable climates that thrive and contribute finer attributes to their progeny, partly because they and their ancestors have escaped the struggles enforced by Siberian winters. Nature's indiscriminate slaughter of individuals in a species more often determines the survivors than do some special qualities of the individuals.

A more important reservation of Kropotkin related to the question of ethics. Huxley drew a sharp line between 'nature' and society, finding in nature (and in primitive man) bitter competition for survival, and in society the establishment of methods to diminish the competition. Kropotkin rejected this distinction summarily. The most common characteristic of birds, animals, or men, he believed, was co-operation of individuals within a species, and in the highest orders of creatures the greatest amount of mutual aid existed:

> The first thing which strikes us as soon as we begin studying the struggle for existence under both its aspects—direct and metaphorical—is the abundance of facts of mutual aid, not only for rearing progeny, as recognized by most evolutionists, but also for the safety of the individual, and for providing it with the necessary food. With many large divisions of the animal kingdom mutual aid is the rule. Mutual aid is met with even amidst the lowest animals, and we must be prepared to learn some day, from the students of microscopical pond-life, facts of unconscious mutual support, even from the life of micro-organisms.[1]

Kropotkin then described a large selection of rodents, mammals, insects, and sea-creatures that associate for self-protection and assistance to their neighbours, and he drew from zoological literature some remarkable examples of intuitive co-operation. His own

[1] Ibid., pp. 9-10.

experiences in Asiatic Russia, he testified, provided evidence contrary to the Darwinian thesis.

As he moved on to his consideration of man in the primitive state, Kropotkin revived the theme of the noble savage. The gentle anarchist reviewed an extensive body of writing by anthropological and archaeological scholars to find support for his argument that the typical savage condition involved collective co-operation. Kropotkin proposed that even those practices of savages that troubled Europeans most—infanticide, parricide, blood-revenge, and cannibalism—were founded on the principle of serving the needs of the community as a whole. The clan arrangement had worked well until it was disturbed by the establishment of separate family groups, a preliminary to the accumulation of wealth and property by hereditary units within the clan.[1]

As man passed from the stage of the savage to that of the barbarian—when he accomplished the Neolithic revolution—his preference for collective activity continued, according to Kropotkin's thesis. The natural approach to agriculture was communal, and the great migrations were accomplished collectively. The remarkable achievements of the phase of man's development—the conquering of the wilderness, the developing of domestic industries, and the development of fundamental codes of justice—were among the fruits of this activity. If we think of barbarians in terms of war and slaughter, this is the fault of the historians and chroniclers. The record-keepers have a 'pronounced predeliction for the dramatic aspects of history'. In our own time, there are many reports of crimes and offences in society, but relatively few of the more frequent and more typical acts of mutual support. So it was with the barbarians, and the epic poems, the annals and the historical remnants inform us of the exceptions, not of the typical circumstances. He argued that contemporary evidence of peoples who are in a transitional stage, just emerging from barbarism, demonstrates the peacefulness of barbarian men.

Kropotkin risked tedious repetition in his argument that man was essentially peaceful, and he even contended that it was the natural peacefulness of man that made possible the rise of the warriors' caste.[2] Because most barbarian men preferred their non-combatant pursuits to warfare, they allowed specialists to under-

[1] Peter Kropotkin, *Mutual Aid: A Factor of Evolution*, p. 113.
[2] Ibid., p. 137.

take the duties of fighting, and this made possible a group of men
devoted to militarism, leading to the 'States period' of history.

. . . the deeper we penetrate into the history of early institutions, the
less we find grounds for the military theory of origin of authority. Even
that power which later on became such a source of oppression seems,
on the contrary, to have found its origin in the peaceful inclinations
of the masses.[1]

With the rise of militarism, the village communes which were
the standard form of social organization fell victim to the military
rule of the feudal era, with Europe dominated by thousands of
petty rulers who could command armed strength. As a result,
Europe lapsed into a dark era. In *Mutual Aid*, Kropotkin does
not deal with the development of Greek and Roman cultures
chronologically. Only later in his essays does one find any substantial comment on the role of the classic civilizations. As the
villages fell under the yoke of the local despots, they maintained
their habits of mutual aid, and this eventually created the framework for liberation.

In many parts of Europe, medieval towns evolved into institutions which were able to free themselves from the despots and
defend themselves from the ravages and exploitation of feudalism.
Beginning in about the tenth and eleventh centuries—Kropotkin
is not precise with his time references—the medieval city began
to emerge with remarkable uniformity throughout Europe. Here,
Kropotkin elaborated a thesis that had been briefly foreshadowed
in the early sections of *The Conquest of Bread*. The flowering of
the medieval city between about the twelfth and fifteenth centuries
was one of the outstanding manifestations of mutual aid. He
became ecstatic as he discussed the benefits and accomplishments
of those communities; he regarded them as the ideal social form.
During the era when free cities operated without the restrictions
of centralized authority or military rule, they conceived the 'truce
of God' to limit warfare, developed the craft guilds, erected
magnificent cathedrals, cultivated philosophy, improved navigation, and made many other advances that have benefited subsequent generations. According to Kropotkin's reading of medieval
studies, the city labourer was well respected and well compensated
and his personal liberties were honoured. He was not subjected

[1] Ibid., p. 159.

to long hours and unpleasant conditions of labour, as his descendants have been. 'To guarantee liberty, self-administration, and peace was the chief aim of the mediaeval city . . .'[1] The 'fundamental principle' in each city was to assure adequate food and lodging to all. The reader gets the impression that hunger and privation were unknown in the typical city when the federalism of mutual aid existed. Each section and profession within the city exercised its sovereignty wisely and in the public interest.

Yet many of the cities shared unfortunate flaws, and all of them became victims of external pressures that ruined their idyllic conditions. They were frequently at war with the feudal lords who remained in control of the countryside, and they had to maintain armies for defence. All too often, as they liberated the peasantry and their land from the despots, the cities failed to extend the principles of liberty and mutual aid to the countryside. Exploitation of the rural populations continued, creating a gulf of misunderstanding between the urban areas and the rural hinterlands. Compounding the error, the cities neglected agriculture and overemphasized commerce and industry. Such practices had become common by the sixteenth century, which Kropotkin saw as the twilight of the golden age. Commercialism led the cities into distant trading enterprises, which involved colonial ventures and new military commitments. Mercenary armies were a necessary corollary. Once again, the co-operative instinct proved inadequate to withstand militarism.

In addition, another evil idea existed to undermine the foundations of the medieval city:

. . . Self-reliance and federalism, the sovereignty of each group, and the construction of the political body from the simple to the composite, were the leading ideas of the eleventh century. But since that time the conceptions had entirely changed. The students of Roman law and the prelates of the Church, closely bound together since the time of Innocent the Third, had succeeded in paralyzing the idea—the antique Greek idea—which presided at the foundation of the cities. For two or three hundred years they taught from the pulpit, the University chair, and the judges' bench, that salvation must be sought for in a strongly-centralized State, placed under a semi-divine authority; that *one* man can and must be the saviour of society, and that in the name of public salvation he can commit any violence: burn men and women at the

---

[1] Peter Kropotkin, *Mutual Aid: A Factor of Evolution*, p. 181.

stake, make them perish under indescribable tortures, plunge whole provinces into the most abject misery. Nor did they fail to give object lessons to this effect on a grand scale, and with an unheard-of cruelty, wherever the king's sword and the Church's fire, or both at once, could reach. By these teachings and examples, continually repeated and enforced upon public attention, the very minds of the citizens had been shaped into a new mould. They began to find no authority too extensive, no killing by degrees too cruel, once it was 'for public safety'. And, with this new direction in mind and this new belief in one man's power, the old federalist principle faded away, and the very creative genius of the masses died out. The Roman idea was victorious, and in such circumstances the centralized State had in the cities a ready prey.[1]

Such cities as Paris, Madrid, and Moscow, strategically located and endowed with cunning and unscrupulous lords, became the centres of the revived authoritarian tendencies, and the free cities could not adapt the principles of mutual aid widely enough—either internally among their own populations or externally by defensive federations—to prevent the rise of the monarchies. Their failure to resist successfully permitted the rise of narrow-minded religious and commercial individualism. The determination to seek one's own happiness at the expense of others became common, and the arts and sciences, so vigorous in the medieval period, declined. For Kropotkin, the period from the fifteenth to the eighteenth century was one of decay and lethargy in science and technology.

In spite of this, the mutual aid instinct had survived. At times it is difficult to reconcile this assertion with some of the earlier categorical remarks about the decline of the co-operative idea; Kropotkin's emphatic statements do sometimes seem to be contradictory. But he remained convinced that mutual co-operation prevailed primarily among the poorer classes, among the labourers and in the countryside, in the slums of the modern cities and in the trade union movement. Such institutions as the *artels* of contemporary Russia and collectively-oriented villages of France and Switzerland have survived the ravages of the authoritarian regimes, and the impulse to form co-operatives becomes manifest whenever centralized authorities allow. Kropotkin found a number of examples in France and England in the nineteenth century to support his thesis.

Kropotkin's effort to support his philosophy with scholarly

[1] Ibid., pp. 220–1.

evidence is not quite as successful as he believed it to be. There are many internal indications of his extensive reading and his patience; his command of several languages and his propensity for research directed him to monographs in a broad range of fields, and *Mutual Aid* is generously footnoted. Yet, like *Das Kapital*, it is essentially a polemic and the documentation is obviously selective. The sub-title informed the reader that Kropotkin was considering only one of the factors of evolution, and he was not reticent about the fact he was under-emphasizing some other factors that had been stressed too heavily by the Darwinians.

At times, the evidence that Kropotkin elicits does not seem adequate to sustain the burden of his argument; his characteristically romantic and optimistic sentiments often carry him beyond the facts, and grandiose generalizations follow upon the heels of mundane, narrow data. He was inclined to regard man's experience as basically uniform, acknowledging few important variations. When men passed from the feudal era to the age of the medieval villages and thence to the medieval cities, for example, the experience was basically the same across the continent and in England. One gets no appreciation of the differences between England, France, and eastern Europe, or the various rates of development of the centralized monarchies.

But the fact that Kropotkin ignored some of the historical evidence in fashioning his argument is not as significant as his criticism of scholars of the past, who had selected for their emphasis 'the ways and means by which theocracy, military power, autocracy, and, later on, the richer classes' rule have been promoted, established and maintained'.[1] He hoped that future historians would find more occasion to document man's co-operative achievements, rather than concentrating on examples of competition and struggle.

As he worked on his articles of the 1886–96 period, Kropotkin obviously thought of providing an example of the kind of history he had in mind, and his attention returned occasionally to the era of the French Revolution. He wrote short pieces and spoke about it from time to time, and like so many of his colleagues, he spent many hours in the Reading Room of the British Museum. From these studies and reflections he eventually produced his large history of the French Revolution, in which he intended to demonstrate

[1] Peter Kropotkin, *Mutual Aid: A Factor of Evolution*, p. 295.

the desirable historical technique. However, in the mid-1890s the end of this project was still more than a decade away.

Another need that Kropotkin recognized as he fashioned the basic documents of Communist Anarchism was in the field of ethical philosophy. The movement would have to be provided with a new morality, he believed, since the old values and standards of Europe were inadequate. As early as 1890, he had sketched his ideas on this subject in *La Révolte*, and the *Freedom* press issued the articles as a thirty-six page pamphlet entitled *Anarchist Morality*.[1] Intermittently for the next two decades Kropotkin worked on this project, but he was not able to give it sustained attention until near the end of his life, when he had returned to post-revolutionary Russia and found himself in a kind of involuntary seclusion. His *Ethics*, like his history of the French Revolution, although a logical continuation of the first three major books, belongs to a later phase of his career.

THE ECLIPSE OF ANARCHISM

Perhaps Kropotkin would have written a better *Ethics* had he set himself to work at it in the late 1890s, because he was more vigorous then than he was twenty years later, and all of his fundamental concepts on the subject had already been formed. But events combined to turn his attention in other directions. Beginning in about 1895, he gave increased attention to Russian affairs, on which he had done relatively little writing for nearly a decade. Although he was sympathetic to Stepniak and others who were active in the *Free Russia* movement, he did not contribute to their early propaganda efforts. Shortly before Stepniak's death, Kropotkin revealed new interest in the reform movement of his homeland, and for the next twenty years he wrote and commented often on its problems.

Kropotkin was deeply saddened by the death of Stepniak, as he indicated in letters to the Danish critic Georg Brandes, but it cannot be ascertained whether the death was a reason for his return to the ranks of the active anti-Tsarist propagandists. There were other factors that drew him in that direction in the final years

[1] The articles appeared irregularly in *La Révolte* from March through August 1890. *Anarchist Morality* is Freedom Pamphlet No. 15 and is undated, but it was issued in either 1891 or 1892 in London.

of the century. A trip to America in 1897, for example, brought
him invitations to speak on Russian subjects and eventually he
was commissioned to write his memoirs for the *Atlantic Monthly*.
A second trip brought similar opportunities and obligations a few
years later. In a sense, a renewal of interest in Russia was forced
upon him by an enlarged audience.

Beyond this, Kropotkin was experiencing disappointment over
the fact that the great revolution had been delayed, and he sensed
that the Socialist movement was taking a wrong turn. When he
had arrived in England in 1886, he ardently believed that the great
change was imminent, and *The Conquest of Bread* was written in
this spirit. It became customary for Kropotkin to speak at the
annual gathering in commemoration of the members of the Paris
Commune in March, and he usually conveyed the impression that
the great day could occur soon. When the usual gathering occurred
at South Place Institute on 17 March 1887, for example, he spoke
of Western civilization as being 'on the eve of one of those great
uprisings which periodically visit Europe'.[1] But it became increasingly difficult to sustain such an expectation as the years passed.

In 1886, the anarchists seemed to be the peers of the Fabians
and the Marxists in Britain, but a decade later they had obviously
fallen far behind their left-wing rivals. The Fabians and Social
Democrats were building favourable political records, while the
very name of 'anarchist' was a term of fear and derision. The word
Kropotkin used to express his libertarian ideal was increasingly
associated in the popular language with the bloody deeds of
fanatics. As Bertrand Russell expressed it in later years, 'Anarchism
attracts to itself much that lies on the borderland of insanity and
common crime,'[2] and the spectacular bombings and assassinations
that became increasingly frequent in the 1890s were often attributed to the influence of the theoretical anarchists. While Kropotkin regretted the acts of violence, he refused to join those who
expressed public outrage on such occasions. He contended that
the authentic anarchists hated violence with a much greater passion
than governmental authorities who condoned officially-approved
killings and punishment, but he frequently argued that members
of the privileged classes had no right to pass judgement on one
who had committed a desperate act against society. Only those

---

[1] *Freedom*, I (April 1887), pp. 25–6.
[2] Bertrand Russell, *Proposed Roads to Freedom* (New York, 1919), p. 53.

who shared the hopelessness of men driven to desperate means could properly judge an assassin, he argued, and he would not allow himself to pass judgement, unless the wanton destruction of innocent lives had seemed evident. The fact that he was loath to condemn the 'darker side' of anarchism—to use another of Russell's terms—apparently convinced a few Englishmen and Americans that Kropotkin shared personal responsibility for the crimes. Even some of the outstanding leaders of the Socialist movement were prone to lump the bloody deeds and the noble, humanitarian ideals together—with emphasis on the former—when they spoke or wrote of anarchism. William Morris was among those who could not learn to think of 'anarchism' without revulsion, in spite of his respect for Kropotkin and his sympathy for the objectives of Anarchist-Communism. So it was for many well-intentioned citizens of the European world.

Even those who recognized the distinction between the half-crazed bomb-thrower and the high-minded work of a Kropotkin were usually inclined to dismiss the latter as a dream. Kropotkin disliked the term 'Utopian' at least as much as the Marxists did; perhaps he disliked it more because it was probably more often applied to him and his theories. Even a friend like Stepniak had little faith in the ideal. In a speech to the Fabian Society on 21 October 1892, he had been called upon to express his views about the resemblances between nihilism and anarchism. He acknowledged that the 'psychology' of the two movements had much in common but he believed that anarchism was an impractical idea. Yet its principles were admirable, and it was an idea without which the world would be poorer.[1]

The observation that the anarchists were unrealistic seemed to be emphasized by the achievements of the Fabians in Great Britain and the Marxists on the continent in the 1890s. The 'permeation' tactics of the British Fabian Socialists and the electoral successes of the Social Democrats, especially in Germany, demonstrated that some successes could be achieved by competing within the existing political and economic framework.

To a purist like Kropotkin, such gains were not worth the price; they contaminated the revolutionary movement with statist, authoritarian ideas—at least in Western and Central Europe. Looking back in retrospect after the turn of the century, Kropotkin

[1] The speech is summarized in *Freedom*, VII (January–February 1893), p. 7.

saw the period between 1884 and 1890 as the high point of revolutionary activism in England. True revolutionary Socialism had been represented by several groups and there was much evidence in the strikes and riots of the working classes that the potential for change existed. But after 1890 many Socialist groups had become apathetic and had turned aside from the proper course. The English movement had fallen under the spell of German Social Democracy, according to Kropotkin's recapitulation. Many of its leaders had begun to crave for political office and this in turn had sowed distrust among the workers.[1] The revolutionary opportunity had been allowed to slip away.

German Socialism was equated in the mind of Kropotkin with the authoritarian practices of the Prussian dynasty and Bismarck, and his antipathy for it grew as its success in the German electoral system became more obvious. He disliked the dogmatism of its leading figures, and he foresaw that doctrinaire Marxists in power could be as tyrannical as any capitalists. Yet he did not believe such a regime could survive: 'Should an authoritarian Socialist society ever succeed in establishing itself, it could not last; general discontent would soon force it to break up, or to reorganize itself on the principles of liberty.'[2]

Kropotkin was never as harsh with the British or French Socialists for their political activities as he was with the Germans, largely because of his special animosity for the latter. This attitude coloured Kropotkin's thinking to the end of his life and emerged in several of his later writings.

While Kropotkin could find almost nothing to approve in the German reform movements, he accorded a good deal of latitude and praise to the Russians who were striving for the kind of institutions that the Germans were using. This led to an interesting ambivalence in his writings in the late 1890s. Without abandoning his anarchist position, he entertained the idea that desirable evolutionary changes might occur in Russia to replace the existing autocracy. In his article published in the summer of 1895—the essay that indicated the renewal of his interest in Russian affairs —he expressed interest in proposals for a national assembly in

---

[1] See his articles 'The Coming Revival of Socialism', in *Freedom*, XVIII (February 1904), 1, and (March 1904), 1–2; and '1886–1907: Glimpses into the Labour Movement in this Country', *Freedom*, XXI (October 1907), pp. 1–2. The former article was later issued as a Freedom Pamphlet.

[2] Kropotkin, *The Conquest of Bread*, p. 188.

Russia. Kropotkin was sceptical about this, but he was clearly not opposed to a suggestion for regional popular assemblies to deal with social and economic problems. The village *mir* and the *zemstvo* did not seem to be inconsistent with his anarchist ideal, and it was only a short step from such institutions as these to regional assemblies. The article seems to bear the stamp of Stepniak's influence, since it deals with many of the topics that had been treated in his articles and books, and since the suggestions about the regional assemblies had been advanced earlier by him.[1]

Despite the differences between their political philosophies, they shared enough common ground on Russian matters for Kropotkin to take the arguments, as well as the mantle, of Stepniak when the latter was killed.

By 1898, Kropotkin had moved a long way towards the liberal position on Russian affairs. He spoke approvingly of a scheme to establish several parliaments for the Empire: ' . . . I am firmly persuaded that the only possible solution for Russia would be to frankly acknowledge the Federalist principle, and to adopt a system of several autonomous Parliaments, as we see it in Canada, instead of trying to imitate the centralized system of Great Britain, France, and Germany.'[2]

Kropotkin wrote these lines not long after his first voyage to America, which included a long trip to Canada and a study of Canadian institutions. He had frequently spoken of the need for territorial and functional decentralization of administrative responsibilities, and his first trip to America in 1897 suggested to him that the political structures of the United States and Canada might not be as far from his ideal as they at first appeared to be. In short, Kropotkin had hardly finished his basic anarchist documents when he began to see—in the writings of Stepniak, in his American travels, and in the Russian political situation—that conventional government on a limited, regional scale might not do violence to his fundamental anarchist principles.

In the meantime, some of Kropotkin's acquaintances and friends in England were struggling with their own political ideas and programmes. William Morris and the Socialist League went

---

[1] P. Kropotkin, 'The Present Condition of Russia', *The Nineteenth Century*, vol 38 (September 1895), pp. 519-35.

[2] P. Kropotkin, 'On the Present Condition of Russia', *The Outlook*, Vol. 58 (8 January 1898), p. 117.

through an anarchist phase, in spite of Morris's antipathy for the term, and in the last few years before his death in 1896, Morris was uncertain about the direction the social reform movement should take. The Fabian Society also flirted briefly with the anarchist theory before its leaders defined their position in the Fabian Essays of 1889, and Shaw revealed a considerable amount of sympathy for Kropotkin's ideas in *The Impossibilities of Anarchism*. The network of personal and political relationships among the London social reformers of the 1880s and 1890s considerably enriched the ideas of all of them.

IV

WILLIAM MORRIS

Pilgrim of Hope

SINCE the death of William Morris in 1896, there has been an intermittent debate about where this versatile artist really stood on social matters. There is no agreement on the question of whether he retreated from Socialism in his final years or whether he remained as dedicated as he had been earlier. The record is ambiguous, with the result that, as Eugene D. LeMire has said in his study of Morris, each commentator has been 'claiming Morris's ideas as the image of his own'.[1]

No group has been more persistent than the Marxists in trying to prove that the great poet and craftsman was one of their apostles. They can produce some impressive support for their case. Bernard Shaw, in his famous 'William Morris as I Knew Him', asserted that 'He was on the side of Karl Marx *contra mundum*'. Shaw had offered conflicting testimonials earlier, and in the course of this essay he qualified the assertion considerably, but this line provided the kind of ammunition that Marxian scholars thrive on. Shaw wrote this statement in the 1930s when he, like many other intellectuals, was more inclined to favour the Marxian position than at other periods of his life.

Another influential critic who in the 1930s assessed Morris as a thorough Marxist was Granville Hicks. He argued that the Marxism of Morris was a healthy antidote to Fabianism in the British Socialist tradition, and he contended that Morris got his cue from Marx about the ultimate goal of the Socialist process. He came to the conclusion that 'his essays show how consistently he was guided by Marxism'.[2]

The most elaborate and insistent attempts to prove that Morris was a 'scientific socialist' have come from two British scholars.

[1] LeMire, op. cit., p. 55.
[2] Granville Hicks, *Figures of Transition: A Study of British Literature at the End of the Nineteenth Century* (New York, 1939), p. 86.

R. Page Arnot contends that Morris's reputation has been subjected to several myth-making efforts in England to minimize his
revolutionary ideas, and he insists with considerable vehemence
that Morris was deeply influenced by Marxian thought.[1] And E. P.
Thompson, in the most thorough study of Morris's Socialism yet
to appear, also asserts that his biographers wilfully distorted his
work by ignoring or denying such a relationship.[2] If the influence
was unacknowledged for many years, as Arnot and Thompson
argue, the pendulum has now swung in the opposite direction and
the debt has been greatly over-emphasized.

The relationship between Morris and some of the non-Marxian
revolutionaries, however, deserves more analysis than it has had.
From the time that Morris became active in the Socialist movement in the early 1880s until his death about fifteen years later,
he had extensive contacts with the leading revolutionaries in
London. In the early years of his Socialist activity, he was an
occasional visitor to the Engels home. More often his own home
and meeting-hall at Hammersmith was a gathering place, and his
activities brought him into close contact with the whole range of
the Socialist and anarchist movement. The written record certainly
does not prove that he was primarily a Marxist; it rather suggests
that he was receptive to the ideas of Stepniak, Kropotkin, and
Shaw, in spite of occasional differences and misunderstandings,
and that his revolutionary philosophy was not fixed or rigid. In
1883 and 1884, while he was allied with Hyndman in the Social
Democratic Federation, he accumulated some Marxian ideas and
arguments. At the end of 1884 he broke with Hyndman and
established the Socialist League, and during the next five years
his theories became less Marxian than anarchist in spirit. After
1890, he gradually withdrew from active Socialist propaganda,
but he left the impression that he had become more moderate.
Like the pilgrims in his romances, Morris wandered from one
camp to another, searching for the answer—or perhaps the magic
—that would satisfy his quest.[3]

[1] R. Page Arnot, op. cit., pp. 9–14.

[2] E. P. Thompson, op. cit.; see especially Appendix IV, pp. 886–9. Even the
excellent new volume by Paul Thompson, *The Work of William Morris*, has
incorporated this point of view; see pp. 229–34.

[3] For an excellent article discussing the differences between Marx's ideas and
those of Morris, see Bernard Wall, 'William Morris and Karl Marx', *The Dublin
Review*, Vol. 202 (January 1938), pp. 39–47.

THE SEARCH FOR A PROGRAMME: THE MIDDLE 1880s

When Morris joined the Democratic Federation in January of 1883, he had no affirmative political theory; he was driven by discontent with the state of art and the condition of politics in Britain. He testified a few years later that he had learned from the writings of John Stuart Mill, contrary to Mill's intention, 'that Socialism was necessary', but he had no clear idea of the technical side of Socialism.[1] It is not surprising that Morris was not well read in the literature of Socialism at that time; even if he had been disposed to study politics and economics, he would have found relatively little recent Socialist information. Marx's works were hardly known in England and *Das Kapital* was not published in English until several years later. Morris, like several of his associates, read it first in the French edition. When he became a Socialist he was 'blankly ignorant' of economics:

... I had never so much as opened Adam Smith, or heard of Ricardo, or of Karl Marx. . . . Well, having joined a Socialist body (for the Federation soon became definitely Socialist), I put some conscience into trying to learn the economical side of Socialism, and even tackled Marx, though I must confess that, whereas I thoroughly enjoyed the historical part of 'Capital', I suffered agonies of confusion of the brain over reading the pure economics of that great work.[2]

Morris came to rely on others for instruction on the technical side of Socialism. Ernest Belfort Bax, Andreas Scheu, and Hyndman all had a better grasp of economics than he, and Morris relied heavily upon them. He also visited the Engels home occasionally during this period of his apprenticeship, and during his first year in the movement he read the efforts of a young dissident named George Bernard Shaw, whose incomplete novel *An Unsocial Socialist* was published in *To-Day* in 1883. Since Shaw was learning his own Socialism at this time, Morris probably learned little of a technical nature from him at this stage, but the friendship did provide new ideas for his consideration.

Morris was in this receptive, inquisitive frame of mind when he read Stepniak's *Underground Russia*, only about four months after joining the Federation. When Morris wrote to his daughter that

[1] William Morris, 'How I Became a Socialist' (1894), *Collected Works*, op. cit., Vol. 23, p. 278.   [2] Ibid., pp. 277–8.

' . . . such a book ought to open people's eyes a bit here & do
good . . .'[1] he was appraising the book in his own case as well as
evaluating it for the reading public. Edward Burne-Jones,
Morris's lifetime friend who probably knew him as well as anyone
outside his immediate family, attached considerable importance
to his interest in the persecution of the Russian intellectuals, as
described in Stepniak's first book. It was 'one of the inciting
causes of his Socialism'.[2] On a number of occasions in his lectures
of the 1880s, Morris made reference to the Russian oppression
and identified himself with the cause of the revolutionaries there.

Several new doors were opened to Morris, then, in the first two
years of his Socialist activity, and Marx was not the predominant
influence. The influence of his English mentors—especially Carlyle
and Ruskin—remained stronger than that of Marx throughout his
last years. It was the hopes and animosities—rather than the technical formulae—of the Socialists that converted and held him.
When he tried to explain his new commitment to a friend in a
letter in July of 1883, he wrote:

Also of course, I do not believe in the world being saved by any
system—I only assert the necessity of attacking systems grown corrupt,
and no longer leading anywhither: that to my mind is the case with the
present system of capital and labour: as all my lectures assert, I have
personally been gradually driven to the conclusion that art has been
handcuffed by it, and will die out of civilization if the system lasts. That
of itself does to me carry with it the condemnation of the whole system,
and I admit has been the thing which has drawn my attention to the
subject in general. . . .[3]

Morris dedicated himself to the task of removing the conditions
that created the abominable situation. 'Now it seems to me that,
feeling this, I am bound to act for the destruction of the system
which seems to me mere oppression and obstruction,' he wrote in
the same letter; 'such a system can only be destroyed, it seems to
me, by the united discontent of numbers . . .'[4] The propaganda
that he wrote for *Justice* and the hundreds of lectures that he
delivered for the Cause in the next few years were efforts to
stimulate this 'discontent'. He was an English equivalent of the
narodniki, which perhaps helps to explain his interest in the

[1] William Morris, *Letters*, op. cit., p. 172.   [2] Ibid., p. lv.
[3] May Morris, op. cit., II, p. 83.   [4] Ibid., p. 84.

Russian struggle during the period of his own conversion to the revolutionary movement.

During 1883 and 1884, his major Socialist lectures dealt primarily with the state of art. Their titles alone suggest the extent to which his attention was focused on his favourite theme: 'Art and the People' (1883?), 'Art, Wealth, and Riches' (1883), 'Art Under Plutocracy' (1883), 'Art and Socialism' (1884), and 'Art and Labour' (1884).[1] The lecture entitled 'Art, Wealth, and Riches' delivered at Manchester on 6 March 1883, was presented only two months after he had joined the Democratic Federation. Morris had gone into the lion's den, approaching an audience that was hostile towards Socialism and making an attack on the existing competitive economic system. This system has not created wealth, he argued, but riches on the one hand and poverty on the other, and it has destroyed wealth—the fruits of artistic work. He specified that he wanted a Utopia in which all men have equal opportunities in education, in which riches are no longer worshipped and regarded as the only means to advancement, in which the division of labour is restricted, and in which work of artist-craftsmen will be admired, preserved, and honoured. This early Socialist lecture—and this also applies to nearly all of the lectures of this period—does not advocate a bitter class struggle. On the contrary, it suggests 'useful work in forestalling destructive revolution' by 'trying to fill up the gap that separates class from class'.[2]

The doctrine of the class struggle was one of the Marxian ideas that was only gradually and partially assimilated by Morris. He was not intellectually ready for the notion that the proletariat was the class with the special destiny, but he saw much evidence of growing friction between the capitalist property-owners and the poor. The Marxian doctrine of the inevitability of the change appealed to him, however, and the theory of the certain class struggle seemed to follow later. In the second of his major Socialist lectures, delivered at Oxford in November 1883, he asserted:

. . . I am 'one of the people called Socialists'; therefore I am certain that evolution in the economical conditions of life will go on, whatever

[1] The first lecture is reproduced in May Morris, op. cit., II, pp. 382–406; the date of initial delivery is uncertain. The next three were published by Morris during his lifetime and are available in *The Collected Works*, Vol. 23, pp. 143–214. The fifth is reproduced in full in LeMire's dissertation, op. cit., pp. 188–218. See also LeMire's calendar of lectures for these years, pp. 446–58.

[2] William Morris, *Collected Works*, Vol. 23, p. 153.

shadowy barriers may be drawn across its path by men whose apparent
self-interest binds them, consciously or unconsciously, to the present,
and who are therefore hopeless for the future. I hold that the condition
of competition between man and man is bestial only, and that of
association human; . . .[1]

Would it not be worth while, he asked this academic audience,
to combat the idea that society can only be changed by violence?
He offered his programme as an example of 'reconstructive
Socialism' that hoped to avoid chaos. He may have been thinking
of Stepniak's first book—which he had read in the spring of the
same year—when he warned:

. . . yet I well know that the middle class may do much to give a peaceable
or a violent character to the education of discontent which must precede
it (i.e. the new sense of social justice). Hinder it, and who knows what
violence you may be driven into, even to the renunciation of the morality
of which we middle-class men are so proud; advance it, strive single-
heartedly that truth may prevail, and what need you fear? At any rate
not your own violence, not your own tyranny?[2]

The class struggle, then, was an undesirable development that
might be modified and reduced—or so he thought during his first
year as a Socialist. During these early months, he was inclined to
look upon the struggle in much the same way as the Russian
revolutionaries of Stepniak's stripe regarded the Russian situation.
In 'Art and Socialism', a lecture delivered initially at Leicester on
23 January 1884, he said,

Or will you say that here in this quiet, constitutionally governed
country of England there is no opportunity for action offered to us?
If we were in gagged Germany, in gagged Austria, in Russia where a
word or two might land us in Siberia or the prison of the fortress of
Peter and Paul; why then, indeed—— Ah! my friends, it is but a poor
tribute to offer on the tombs of the martyrs of liberty, this refusal to
take the torch from their dying hands! Is it not of Goethe it is told,
that on hearing one say he was going to America to begin life again, he
replied: 'Here is America, or nowhere'? So for my part I say: 'Here is
Russia, or nowhere.' To say the governing classes in England are not
afraid of freedom of speech, therefore let us abstain from speaking
freely, is a strange paradox to me. Let us on the contrary press in
through the breach which valiant men have made for us: if we hang

[1] William Morris, 'Art Under Plutocracy', *Collected Works*, Vol. 23, p. 172.
[2] Ibid., p. 190.

back we make their labours, their sufferings, their deaths, of no account. Believe me, we shall be shown that it is all or nothing: or will any one here tell me that a Russian moujik is in a worse case than a sweating tailor's wage-slave? Do not let us deceive ourselves, the class of victims exists here as in Russia. There are fewer of them? Maybe; then are they of themselves more helpless, and so have more need of our help.[1]

Morris sympathized with and identified himself with the heroic opponents of autocratic tyranny before he accepted the concept of the proletariat locked in deadly struggle with the bourgeoisie, because the romantic origins of his rebellion were more fundamental than the abstract formulas of his newly-found comrades. This address once again was an appeal to the middle class and an effort to enlarge the 'discontent' of the general public; it was not a summons to engage in class conflict but a challenge to individual men of integrity to come to the aid of the oppressed.

In other lectures that survive from the year 1884, one can trace the growth of the Marxian approach to the class struggle. In 'Art and Labour', delivered initially at Leeds on 1 April, he relied heavily on the Marxian idea, but he still finished with an appeal to his middle-class colleagues to change sides in the contest. To fail to do so, he asserted, was to 'brand yourself as an oppressor and a thief'.[2] His language became more provocative as his Socialist education expanded.

The lecture entitled 'Useful Work *versus* Useless Toil', probably written very early in 1884, reveals further additions from Scientific Socialism. The class struggle is described at length and the concept of surplus value is incorporated in some detail.[3] By the late summer, Morris was trying patiently to convey an elementary concept of the Marxian message to the proletariat; his 'Misery and the Way Out', delivered on several occasions during the autumn and winter, is the best example of his platform technique in this context.[4] Near the end of the year, he wrote and first delivered 'How We Live and How We Might Live', which contained the basic economic arguments that had already served his

[1] William Morris, 'Art and Socialism', ibid., pp. 212–13.
[2] Reproduced in LeMire, op. cit., pp. 188–218.
[3] William Morris, 'Useful Work *versus* Useless Toil', *Collected Works*, Vol. 23, pp. 98–120. According to LeMire's Calendar for 1884, this lecture was delivered at least ten times during the year (LeMire, op. cit., pp. 448–58). It was probably modified and refined during the course of the year.
[4] This lecture is partially reproduced in May Morris, op. cit., pp. 150–64.

propaganda purposes, as well as a brief exposition of the theme
that imperialism and international war were the common result
of capitalist competition.[1] By this time, Morris had incorporated
the most obvious and most characteristic Marxian debating points
into his orations. He was to use them intermittently for the
remainder of his life.

Such an accumulation of arguments, however, did not preclude
the development of his revolutionary speculations in other directions. The romantic side of Morris that had responded to the
oppressed Russians continued to be nourished by his readings of
history and literature and his speculations about art. The Lord
Mayor's Show of 1884 provoked him to reflect on the story of
Wat Tyler and John Ball, as told by Froissart, and to find contemporary significance in their martyrdom.[2] He continued to
lecture on the fine arts and the crafts, incorporating his idealized
pictures of the workmen of the past—especially of the Middle Ages
—and his admiration for their achievements. Thus some of
Morris's lectures of his early Socialist years constituted still another
'embodiment of dreams', and they contain much more of the
spirit of Ruskin and of Rossetti than of Marx and Engels.[3]

As Morris's education in Socialism progressed in the mid-
1880s, he became convinced that customary political and parliamentary activity would not help the 'Cause', and he became
alarmed because the Hyndman faction was prepared to engage in
campaigns for elective office and for gradual changes in the
economic order. Such 'palliatives'—as Morris called these efforts
to implement piecemeal reforms—would only deceive the poor
and delay the complete transformation of society. Hyndman's
approach was to seek gains on this front while at the same time
threatening violent revolution, and this also offended Morris. Such
'theatrical boasts and warnings about immediate violent revolution' tended to frighten or disgust those who might otherwise join
the movement, according to Morris. In addition to all this,
Hyndman was too authoritarian for Morris's taste; his dictatorial

[1] William Morris, Collected Works, Vol. 23, pp. 3–26. The Table of Contents
gives the date of 1885 to this lecture, and it was most frequently delivered in that
year. LeMire's Calendar, however, shows that it was first delivered late in 1884.
[2] May Morris, op. cit., II, pp. 143–7.
[3] The major lectures on art in 1884 were entitled 'Textile Fabrics' and
'Architecture and History'. They are included in the Collected Works, Vol. 22,
pp. 270–317.

manner, his militance, and his programme of reform through
conventional political means all seemed to suggest a kind of 'Bismarckian State Socialism, or as near it as we can get in England'.
Morris wrote to a friend at the time of the schism:

I cannot stand all this, it is not what I mean by Socialism either in aim
or in means: I want a real revolution, a real change in Society: Society
a great organic mass of well-regulated forces used for the bringing
about a happy life for all. And means for attaining it are simple enough,
education in Socialism and organization for the time when the crisis
shall force action upon us: nothing else will do us any good at present:
the revolution cannot be a mechanical one, though the last act of it may
be civil war, or it will end in reaction after all.[1]

It is one of the ironies of Morris's Socialist experience that he broke
with the Social Democratic Federation at the time when his lectures
and other writings were most completely coloured by Marxian
thought. At the end of 1884, when Morris and some of his friends
—including Ernest Belfort Bax, Edward Aveling, and Eleanor
Marx-Aveling—left the Federation to found their own Socialist
League, they were eager to claim themselves the legitimate heirs
of Marxism. The Manifesto of the Socialist League, written in its
original form by William Morris soon after the break with Hyndman's Social Democrats, is a kind of summary of Morris's position
at the time. It incorporates several of the Marxian arguments, but
the basic tone was moderate. Morris found it necessary to make the
break because Hyndman's faction was too authoritarian, too wildly
militant, and too opportunistic—in short, too Marxist. Morris
had adopted some of the propaganda arguments of the Marxists
without their hatreds and their flexible political techniques.[2]

When the Socialist League initiated its own newspaper, *The
Commonweal*, early in 1885 with Morris as editor and main
financial supporter, it claimed to represent the legitimate Marxist
tradition. Engels himself lent support to this claim by contributing
his well-known article comparing England of 1885 with that of
1845. It may have been his personal dislike for Hyndman—rather

---

[1] William Morris, Letters, op. cit., p. 228.
[2] The details of the split have been described in a number of places. See, for
example, G. D. H. Cole, *Socialist Thought: Marxism and Anarchism, 1850–1890*,
Vol. II. of *A History of Socialist Thought* (London, 1957), pp. 398–402; E. P.
Thompson, op. cit., pp. 384–421, and Chushichi Tsuzuki, *H. M. Hyndman and
British Socialism* (London, 1961), pp. 62–7.

than his faith in the Socialist League's correctness—that led to this act. In an often-quoted letter to Bernstein, Engels referred to Aveling, Bax and Morris as 'the only honest men among the intellectuals—but men as unpractical (two poets and one philosopher) as you could possibly find'.[1] Engels was never to become very enthusiastic about the English Socialist movement during the remaining decade of his life.

Undoubtedly the continuing close contact with Bax and Aveling after 1884 helped Morris to carry on his tutelage in Marxism. Both men were better informed on the subtleties and ambiguities of that school of thought, and Morris was willing to yield to others on technical questions. But in the middle years of the decade he was also giving a sympathetic ear to the anarchists within and without the Socialist League, and for a few years carried on his work in alliance with them.

It was Bax who was most responsible for the Marxism in Morris's published lectures and articles in the last half of the decade. Morris had a much warmer respect for Bax than he ever held for Hyndman or Aveling, and even after Bax left the Socialist League to return to the Social Democratic Federation in 1888, the two men remained on cordial terms.

Bax was Morris's guide to contemporary German thought and culture. Bax had studied music in Stuttgart and had practised journalism in Berlin shortly before he met Morris in the Federation in 1883. He knew the German language well—as Morris did not—and he had studied German philosophical writing extensively. He knew *Das Kapital* well and had written a commentary on it that had won the praise of Marx himself about two years before his death. He was one of the few Englishmen to visit the Engels home regularly. It is understandable that Morris—unsure of himself on the intricacies of Marxism—should rely heavily on Bax on economic questions, even though the latter was nearly a generation younger. Charmed by his mannerisms, delighted at times by his 'naive side in the ordinary matters of every-day life', Morris nevertheless respected his intellect and they worked well together.[2]

Bax was one of the most frequent contributors to *The Common-*

[1] Friedrich Engels, as translated in 'Marx and Engels on the British Working-Class Movement—II: 1879–1895', *The Labour Monthly: A Magazine of International Labour* (London), October 1933, p. 649. The letter was dated 29 December 1884.

[2] May Morris, op. cit., II, p. 174.

weal and its leading authority on Socialist theory. When he and
Morris collaborated on a series of articles entitled 'Socialism from
the Root Up' in 1886 and 1887, Morris still relied heavily on
Bax for the economic sections of the articles, confessing his own
ignorance even though he had been studying Marxism for more
than three years. There is a revealing entry in his Socialist Diary
for 15 February 1887:

> Tuesday to Bax at Croydon where we did our first article on Marx:
> or rather he did it: I don't think I should ever make an economist even
> of the most elementary kind: but I am glad of the opportunity this
> gives one of hammering the some [*sic*] of Marx into myself.[1]

The two men met each week for a time to continue the composition
and Morris's diary reveals his continuing uncertainty. It was 'a
very difficult job', he wrote on 22 February; 'I hope it may be
worth the trouble.'[2] Later, the work seemed to progress more
easily, but Morris never claimed to have a very profound understanding of the ideology.

Bax was Morris's teacher in yet another branch of theory. Like
several of his reformist compatriots in the 1880s, Bax was interested
in the moral implications of the Socialist movement. If respect for
religion, property, and traditional governmental authority were to
be challenged, would not new ethical principles have to be defined
for the new social order? Several important agitators asked this
question and tried to provide an affirmative suggestion in the
1880s. Bax was one of the pioneers in this field of Socialist ethical
philosophy, and he did not find much guidance in the writings of
Marx and Engels. He did, however, try to enunciate a collectivist
morality. The highest expression of the new ethic would be willingness to sacrifice all—even life—for the cause. Such martyrdom
would be more noble than that of the Christian victims, because
the Socialists had no expectation of everlasting reward in another
realm. The Socialist martyrs were not motivated by 'rarefied self-
seeking' but only by the hope of eventual social happiness and the
solidarity of mankind.

Bax published his ideas on 'The New Ethic' in the *Neue Zeit* of
Stuttgart in January of 1888, and the same articles appeared in the
following month in *The Commonweal*. He not only rejected the
'theologico-metaphysical' basis for ethics on which the Christian

[1] British Museum Additional MS 45335, p. 17.   [2] Ibid., p. 21.

tradition relied, but he also dismissed the empirical-utilitarian tradition that had been developed in English thought, which he believed to be 'the speculative formulation of the principle obtaining under the competitive capitalistic system . . .'[1] Both of these ethical systems were individualistic, rooted in personal self-interest and not directed towards the well-being of a class or society.

These ideas appear to have taken final form at the same time that Bax and Morris were writing their series on 'Socialism from the Root Up'. And they were woven into the final part of those articles. Bax was primarily responsible for this formulation, but it complemented Morris's own thoughts about the values and significance of the movement. In the final paragraphs of the series they wrote:

As regards the future form of the moral consciousness, we may safely predict that it will be in a sense a return on a higher level to the ethics of the older society, with the difference that the limitation of scope to the kinship society in its narrower sense, which was one of the elements of the dissolution of ancient society, will disappear, and the identification of individual with social interests will be so complete that any divorce between the two will be inconceivable to the average man.

We may say in conclusion that this new ethic is no longer a mere theoretic speculation, but that many thousands of lives are already under its inspiration. Its first great popular manifestation was given in the heroic devotion of the working-classes of Paris in the Commune of 1871 to the idea of true and universal freedom, which was carried on by the no less complete devotion of the little band of Russian revolutionists who made so little account of their individual lives in their engrossing passion for the general life of humanity.[2]

While Bax believed that the new economic era would be accompanied by the development of the new ethical standard, he did not believe the one to be founded upon the other. Thus he did not subscribe to the Marxian idea that the material relations of production were the basis for moral systems. In his reminiscences, Bax recounted a discussion with Engels in which he challenged the co-founder of Marxism to use the materialist conception of history to account for the appearance and rise of the Gnostic sects during

---

[1] The *Commonweal*, IV, 11 February 1888, p. 42. The essay is reprinted in Ernest Belfort Bax, *The Ethics of Socialism: Being Further Essays in Socialist Criticism, &c.* (London, 1893), pp. 1–30.
[2] *The Commonweal*, IV, 19 May 1888, p. 155.

the second century of the Roman Empire. Engels, according to
Bax, could not do so, and this apparently encouraged Bax in his
deviation from Marxism on ethical questions.[1] The conduct of
heroic martyrs could be as responsible for social evolution as the
economic circumstances of society, and they were the authors of
the new morality, independently of their class relationships.

In brief, Bax accepted the same ethical principle as Stepniak
on the question of revolutionary conduct; he, like Morris, was
obviously impressed by the example of the Russian agitators. In
a country like Russia, he wrote, where all other means of public
protest and expression are denied, acts of terror are both expedient
and just. As long as free discussion exists, however, 'there can be
no excuse for the use of terrorist methods, which are in this case
at once a crime and a blunder . . .'[2] The moral obligation to
support the existing legal establishment is suspended if its institutions are the habitats of criminals. It is not economic or material
conditions, but political policy, that can justify a violent struggle
against the authorities.

The philosophical speculations of Bax are important not only
because they complemented those of Morris during the years of
their closest collaboration—1885 to 1888—but also because they
reveal the limitations of Marxian influence on one of the leading
English disciples of Marx and Engels. On the question of ethics,
Bax's reflections carried him along some of the same paths that
Kropotkin was to follow in his *Anarchist Morality* (1890). Even
though he returned to the Social Democrats in 1888 because the
Socialist League was becoming too anarchistic, he declined to
embrace the standard Marxian doctrine on moral matters.

In the same manner, Morris declined to incorporate Marxism
into his social goals and his aesthetic theory, and his conclusions
had more in common with Communist Anarchism than with
Scientific Socialism. Despite the phraseology of Social Democracy
that occurred so often in Morris's later lectures, his social and
moral values—as reflected in his statements about the future of
society—were more like those of Kropotkin than of Marx and
Engels. His antipathy for the word 'anarchism' has tended to
obscure his fundamental acceptance of one special variety of it.

[1] Ernest Belfort Bax, *Reminiscences and Reflexions of a Mid and Late Victorian*
(London, 1918), pp. 46–8.
[2] Bax, 'Legality' in *The Ethics of Socialism*, p. 74.

THE ANARCHIST PHASE: THE LATE 1880S

In the League, Morris found himself in a middle position between two tendencies that he disliked in the Socialist movement, but as an advocate of unity and tolerance, he tried to keep the proponents of both factions together within the League. On the one hand there were those who advocated conventional politics, including in some cases attempts to influence parliamentary elections and decisions. Such a policy, to Morris, meant 'palliation' and compromise with the existing system. On the other hand, the opponents of such political activity—broadly described as anarchists—often sought little more than turbulence and disorder, advocating riotous action and threatening to erect barricades. Morris had broken with Hyndman because he seemed to represent both of these undesirable tendencies, and in the League, he tried to discourage both tendencies, adhering to his original programme of 'education' for the poor, but he devoted much of his energy to maintaining a tenuous alliance between them from 1885 until 1888. As his efforts failed, he identified himself with the anarchists.

There is no evidence that Morris had any substantive acquaintance with Communist Anarchism in 1885 when the Socialist League was being formed. The literature of this movement was as little known in England as the writings of Marx and Engels. Yet Morris's opposition to 'palliatives' and to conventional political action, his concept that all of society's values would have to be altered, and his suspicion of authoritarian Socialism as represented by Hyndman put him near the anarchist position even before the Socialist League was created.

Once the Socialist League was operating, there were several comrades on hand to cultivate this inclination. Frank Kitz, the militant product of East-end poverty, and Joseph Lane, who had been identified with a variety of London social protest movements during the 1870s, became energetic participants in the League's work, and they brought to it an attitude of 'destructivism'. When disagreements developed within the League over the question of parliamentary action, Morris tried to remain neutral and to prevent another division, but he was strongly against parliamentary action. As the quarrel became more intense during the second and third years of the League, Morris became increasingly identified with the anarchists on issues of strategy. This situation continued until the

middle of 1888, when several prominent leaders of the League
—including the Avelings and Bax—withdrew from the League.

Morris found himself in sympathy with men like Lane and Kitz
because of what they opposed rather than what they believed. Too
many of the East-enders were hot-headed, Morris felt, more eager
for a confrontation with the authorities than was necessary. In
his emphasis on education and propaganda, and in his willingness
to work patiently until the masses were prepared by hope and
discontent, he resembled Kropotkin and the Communist-Anar-
chists more than he did his own confederates within the League.

Morris and Kropotkin first met each other shortly after the
Russian *émigré* had been released from the Clairvaux prison.
Kropotkin had only been in England a few days when, on 18 March
1886, both men attended a rally in commemoration of the Paris
Commune and exchanged greetings. A few days later, they met
again at a meeting of the Social Democratic Federation and had
a long discussion.[1] Thereafter they were in close contact, and
when Kropotkin and Mrs. Wilson began issuing *Freedom* in
October, they were given the use of *The Commonweal* press facilities. Kropotkin spoke on occasion at the Kelmscott meeting house
and attended some of the Sunday suppers at the Morris home. It
is doubtful that Morris made any systematic study of Kropotkin's
anarchist writings, but he did have ample access to Kropotkin's
ideas and arguments during the last years of his participation in
League affairs.[2]

The early years of Morris's friendship with Kropotkin coincided
with the period of conflict within the League, and the propaganda
work of the famous Russian proved to be a help to Morris on
occasion as he tried to keep peace and to maintain an anti-parliamentary position for the League. In March of 1887, Morris paid
a visit to the League's branch at Glasgow shortly after Kropotkin
had been there, and he wrote with obvious approval that Kropotkin's appearance had 'turned them a little in the Anarchist direction, which gives them an agreable [*sic*] air of toleration, and they
are at present quite innocent of any parliamentary designs'.[3]

The anarchism of the Socialist League and of Morris himself

[1] William Morris, *Letters*, p. 251.
[2] For an uneven but interesting effort to demonstrate the influence of Kropotkin on Morris, see Gustav Fritzsche, *William Morris' Sozialismus und anarchistischer Kommunismus* (Leipzig, 1927), pp. 91–119.
[3] British Museum Add. MS 45335, p. 43.

did not escape the attention of Engels, who frequently commented on the English movement in his letters to German comrades on the continent. On several occasions in 1886, the patriarch of the Marxist movement remarked that Morris and Bax were both victims of anarchist thought. 'And these muddle-headed people want to lead the English working class,' Engels wrote to F. A. Sorge on 29 April 1886. 'Fortunately, the working class does not want anything to do with them.' Two weeks later, Engels described this affinity for anarchism as a 'children's ailment' of the young British Socialist movement, employing the phrase that Lenin was to put to good use more than thirty years later.[1] Engels recognized clearly that Morris had removed himself substantially from the Marxian camp.

The poet's inclination for a variety of anarchism was strengthened by confrontations with the police and the courts. The so-called Dod Street affair of October 1885, and the Trafalgar Square demonstration of February 1886, opened a period of recurring trouble with the authorities that caused some Socialists to believe that the rights of free speech and public assembly were in jeopardy. Morris was among those who engaged in demonstrations and attended police court hearings—risking personal abuse and arrest —to support the right of the Socialist League and other left-wing organizations to continue their propaganda. Even though he wanted to avoid premature violence in the class struggle, he recognized that freedom of expression was essential to the pro-gramme of education that he regarded as the main work of the League. The possibility of physical confrontation and prison seemed very real to Morris in 1886. Government appeared to be an implacable enemy, and the oppression to which Stepniak and his comrades in Russia had been subjected seemed to be not a remote possibility in the emotion-charged situation that existed during these months. Speaking to the Fabian Society in June of 1886, shortly after the beginning of the Haymarket affair in Chicago, Morris tried to demonstrate the futility of a policy of conventional political activity:

Will you think the example of America too trite? Anyhow, consider it! A country with universal suffrage, no king, no House of Lords, no

---

[1] Two of the letters containing Engel's disparaging references to Morris and Bax are translated in *The Labour Monthly*, Vol. 15 (November, 1933), pp. 710–11.

privilege as you fondly think; only a little standing army, chiefly used for the murder of red-skins; a democracy after your model; and with all that, a society corrupt to the core, and at this moment engaged in suppressing freedom with just the same reckless brutality and blind ignorance as the Czar of all the Russias uses.[1]

This willingness to look at events in England and America in the context of the Russian experience and the willingness to risk physical abuse for free speech carried Morris into other demonstrations, including the famous 'Bloody Sunday' affair in Trafalgar Square on 13 November 1887. This experience fortified his antipathy to government authority in general, but also convinced him of the inadequacies of mob action against well-organized police. It had needed only a few officers to disperse the crowd and to prevent the planned rally in the square. Morris's immediate reaction was one of militance, but after his immediate anger had passed, he was even less willing to embrace either the compromising policies of the parliamentarians or the invitations to violence of the League's anarchist faction, and he was less able to hold them together.

After the parliamentary faction left the Socialist League in 1888, its drift towards militant anarchism was more pronounced and Morris found himself once more in controversies because of his effort to hold the League on its course of education and 'agitation for discontent'. In his polemics against the Socialist League anarchists, he often took issue with anarchists generally, not excluding—in his hastily written journalistic pieces—the Communist Anarchists. Occasionally he seems to have confused them with the Individual Anarchists of the Benjamin Tucker variety, understood to propose absolute individual freedom and an absence of social responsibility. But in his most carefully written pieces, one often finds statements on the future political regime that have a remarkable resemblance to those of Kropotkin. In a letter to the Reverend George Bainton written on 10 April 1888—one of four letters to the minister in which Morris took special pains to make his arguments carefully—he wrote:

But to return to our 'government' of the future, which would be rather an administration of *things* than a government of *persons*. Without dogmatizing on the matter I will venture to give you my own views

[1] William Morris, 'Whigs, Democrats, and Socialists', *Collected Works*, XXIII, pp. 30–1.

on the subject, as I know that they are those held by many Socialists. Nations, as political entities, would cease to exist; civilization would mean the federalization of a variety of communities great and small, at one end of which would be the township and the local guild, in which administration would be carried on perhaps in direct assemblies 'in more majorum', and at the other some central body whose function would be almost entirely the guardianship of the *principles* of society, and would when necessary enforce their practice; e.g. it would not allow slavery in any form to be practised in any community. But even this shadow of centralization would disappear at last when men gained the habit of looking reasonably at these matters. It would in fact be chiefly needed as a safeguard against the heredity of bad habits, and the atavism which would give us bad specimens now and again. Between these two poles there would be various federations which would grow together or dissolve as convenience of place, climate, language, &c. dictated, and would dissolve peaceably when occasion prompted. Of course public intercourse between the members of the federation would have to be carried on by means of delegation, but the delegates would not pretend to represent any one or anything but the business with which they are delegated; e.g. we are a shoemaking community chiefly, you cotton spinners, are we making too many shoes? Shall we turn some of us to gardening for a month or two, or shall we go on?—and so forth.[1]

Of course the Marxists, too, talked of the eventual withering away of the state, but for them such an eventual transformation was of secondary importance; it was overshadowed by the impending struggle and short-range political tactics. Morris, like Kropotkin, liked to leap beyond the problems of the transition to the description of the coming social order. Although he often spoke of the class struggle, he gave it less emphasis in his writings than Marxists usually do. And without engaging in the kind of speculations about morality that Bax and Kropotkin undertook, he embraced a concept of ethics that resembled theirs. In an article of 1889, he wrote:

Surely we all of us feel that there is a rascal or two in each of our skins besides the other or two who want to lead manly and honourable lives, and do we not want something to appeal to on behalf of those better selves of ours? and that something is made up of the aspirations of our better selves, and is the *social conscience* without which there can be no true society, and which even a false society is forced to imitate, and so have a sham social conscience—what we sometimes call hypocrisy.

[1] William Morris, *Letters*, op. cit., p. 287.

Now I don't want to be misunderstood. I am not pleading for any form of arbitrary or unreasonable authority, but for a *public conscience* as a rule of action: and by all means let us have the least possible exercise of authority. I suspect that many of our Communist-Anarchist friends do really mean that, when they pronounce against all authority. And with equality of condition assured for all men, and our ethics based on reason, I cannot think that we need fear the growth of a new authority taking the place of the one which we should have destroyed, and which we must remember is based on the assumption that equality is impossible and that slavery is an essential condition of human society. By the time it is assumed that all men's needs must be satisfied according [to] the measure of the common wealth, what may be called the political side of the question would take care of itself.[1]

Morris was often willing to concede that the Socialist movement might eventually reach a period when participation in political and governmental activities of the existing order would be necessary and helpful, but he felt this period to be a long time away. In this, he differed with the *Freedom* group and some of the other anarchists, but he regularly affirmed that an anti-parliamentary, anti-political movement should be kept alive, and he wanted to be identified with it. In spite of his frequently expressed desire for Socialist unity and toleration, he did not want to be in the same organization with men who devoted their time and energy to conventional politics.

As G. D. H. Cole has pointed out, Morris differed from Kropotkin in his expectations about the speed with which the existing regime could be removed.[2] He was more patient than Kropotkin and, at least in the 1880s, more willing to accept a gradual transition. He also placed greater stress on the importance of handicrafts and had a less favourable view of the advantages of modern machines. Kropotkin was a scientist and a proponent of modern technology; Morris was an artist, suspicious of all machines that did not have unmistakable and inoffensive labour-saving functions. But these were differences in emphasis; from the standpoint of political and economic theory they were of little consequence. In an important sense, Morris's literary efforts in these years were an artistic counterpart of Kropotkin's scholarly arguments on behalf of anarchism.

[1] May Morris, op. cit., II, p. 316.
[2] G. D. H. Cole, *Socialist Thought: Marxism and Anarchism, 1850–1890* (London, 1957), p. 419.

Burdened as he was by the propaganda duties, the administrative chores, and the controversies of the movement, Morris did not achieve nearly as much in the field of poetry in the middle 1880s as he had done in the previous periods of comparable length. His least productive period was 1883, 1884, and 1885 when, coincidentally, he was acquiring the Marxian façade of his Socialism. His most significant Socialist poems and prose pieces emerged during his anarchist period, and as the frustrations of these years accumulated, he was increasingly driven back into his dream world. His literary output reflects both the hopes and frustrations of his years on the League.

Morris scholars and literary critics do not attach much importance to most of the Socialist poems that he wrote for *Justice* and *The Commonweal*. Most of them are simple chants, marching songs or other ephemeral pieces offered to the working class as part of the education in discontent. Morris himself chose to reproduce only a few of them in his final years when he printed selections of his verse from that period. One of the first verses of this *genre*, 'The Day Is Coming', has been one of the most durable of its kind; it typifies the summons and the promise that runs all through Morris's propaganda. It begins with an invitation to dreaming:

> Come hither, lads, and harken, for a tale there is to tell
> Of the wonderful days a-coming, when all shall be better
>   than well.

> And the tale shall be told of a country, a land in the
>   midst of the sea
> And folk shall call it England in the days that are going
>   to be.

After about twenty such couplets comes the moderate finale, a call for dedication:

> Come then, since all things call us, the living and the dead,
> And o'er the weltering tangle a glimmering light is shed,

> Come, then, let us cast off fooling, and put by ease and rest,
> For the Cause alone is worthy till the good days bring the best,

> Come, join in the only battle wherein no man can fail,
> Where whoso fadeth and dieth, yet his deed shall still prevail.

Ah! come, cast off all fooling, for this, at least, we know:
That the Dawn and the Day is coming, and forth the Banners go.

Several of Morris's poems of this decade, like many of his lectures, invoked the vision of a happier England, free of the troubles and oppressions of the nineteenth century, often set in either the past or the future. *The Pilgrims of Hope*, the poem series that he wrote for *The Commonweal* in 1885 and 1886, opens with images of lovely countryside and the happy lovers; 'The Message of the March Wind' suggests a state of English life that has been and—when the evils of the day have been removed—will be again. The nostalgia, the dreaming, and even the yearning for the struggle that emerge in the poems of this group epitomize Morris's thoughts about the revolution during the middle 1880s. Some of the scenes are set in the Paris of the period of the Commune, but the struggle is seen as international. The heroes are imaginary English equivalents of Stepniak's Russian *nihilists*.

A Dream of John Ball, written soon afterwards, constitutes another blending of the world of Morris's imagination with the facts of his own day, but here the poet has retreated a bit further into dreams. He transports himself to medieval Kent, hears the stirring speech of John Ball, and engages in conversation with the soon-to-be-martyred rebel. John Ball retains something of the spirit of Morris's earlier epic heroes and he shares the devotion to social justice of the modern revolutionaries. When he delivers his rallying message from the foot of the cross, his theme is the essential unity of mankind. 'Forsooth, brothers,' Morris has him say, 'fellowship is heaven, and lack of fellowship is hell: fellowship is life, and lack of fellowship is death: and the deeds that ye do upon the earth, it is for fellowship's sake that ye do them, and the life that is in it, that shall live on and on for ever, and each one of you part of it, while many a man's life upon the earth from the earth shall wane.'[1] It is true that he is summoning a class to throw off its oppressors, but he is looking beyond the struggle towards the ultimate goal. He is affirming that voluntary community of men is more fundamental than the institutions and authorities of contemporary society, and more elementary than the strife that temporarily troubles mankind.

This yearning for fellowship—for social co-operation and

[1] William Morris, 'A Dream of John Ball' in *Collected Works*, Vol. 16, p. 230.

tranquillity based on man's communal instincts—coloured all of
Morris's writings in the last seven or eight years of his life. It is
especially evident in *News from Nowhere*, written during his last
months in the Socialist League and published serially in *The
Commonweal* in 1890, just before he resigned from the League in
November. It is the work of a man who has become tired of the
day-to-day strife of the Cause and who seeks to live, at least
vicariously, in the future created by his fancy.

News from Nowhere is the best known of Morris's late prose
romances, and more than any of the other works of this period,
it is a transitional piece. It is a combination of the polemics of his
essays and of the fantasy that became the predominating characteristics in his later creative writing. Morris was prodded into
this kind of utopian speculation partly at least by reading Edward
Bellamy's *Looking Backward*.[1] In a review of this work for *The
Commonweal*, Morris decried Bellamy's projection of a centralized
authority, large and tightly-organized communities, based on a
machine economy. His reaction to this picture was that of a
philosophical anarchist:

. . . it is necessary to point out that there are some Socialists who do
not think that the problem of the organisation of life and necessary
labour can be dealt with by a huge national centralisation, working by
a kind of magic for which no one feels himself responsible; that on the
contrary it will be necessary for the unit of administration to be small
enough for every citizen to feel himself responsible for its details, and
be interested in them; that individual men cannot shuffle off the business
of life on to the shoulders of an abstraction called the State, but must
deal with it in conscious association with each other. That variety of
life is as much an aim of true Communism as equality of condition,
and that nothing but a union of these two will bring about real freedom.
That modern nationalities are mere artificial devices for the commercial
war that seek to put an end to, and will disappear with it. And, finally,
that art, using that word in its widest and due signification, is not a mere
adjunct of life which free and happy men can do without, but the
necessary expression and indispensable instrument of human happiness.[2]

[1] Several of Morris's essays and articles of the 1880's include speculations on
the future society. Of special interest is his series entitled 'The Society of the
Future', in *The Commonweal*, V, 30 March 1889, pp. 98–9; 6 April 1889, pp. 108–
109; and 13 April 1889, pp. 114–15. This was reprinted in May Morris, op. cit.,
Vol. II, pp. 453–68.
[2] *The Commonweal*, V, 22 June 1889, pp. 194–5.

Kropotkin must have concurred with this reaction to Bellamy, if he read it, and it is highly probable that he had a hand in the conception of *News from Nowhere*, which Morris wrote at least in part as an alternative to Bellamy's utopian projection. In the first paragraph, Morris offered a clue about the event that sparked his imagination. There had been a lively discussion 'up at the League' one evening about 'what would happen on the Morrow of the Revolution, finally shading off into a vigorous statement by various friends of their views on the future of the fully-developed new society'. Among the participants had been four persons with 'strong but divergent Anarchist opinions'.[1]

While one cannot ascertain whether Kropotkin was present on this occasion, his ideas were obviously well known and Morris could not have been unaware of Kropotkin's own speculations about the future. Not only was Kropotkin working on the articles that were collectively entitled *The Conquest of Bread* during this same period, but he was also producing with regularity other essays that carried predictions about the sequels to the existing society. Within the previous two or three years, he had published in the *Nineteenth Century* pieces entitled 'The Coming Anarchy', 'The Coming Reign of Plenty', and 'The Industrial Village of the Future'.[2] All such statements not only summarized and advanced Kropotkin's ideas about the rejuvenation of the social system, but they invited anticipation and discussion of coming events. Even if Kropotkin were not on hand on the evening when Morris was launched on his most famous utopian statement, his ruminations certainly had a bearing on the occasion. Kropotkin, in any event, thoroughly approved of the final product. When he wrote a tribute to Morris after his death in 1896, Kropotkin called *News from Nowhere* '. . . perhaps the most thoroughly and deeply Anarchistic conception of future society that has ever been written'.[3] It was largely a blending of Morris's aesthetic opinions and preferences with Kropotkin's economic and social ideas.

The tale begins with the narrator of *News from Nowhere* returning home from the meeting of the League and falling asleep. He dreams that he finds himself in London about two centuries after

---

[1] William Morris, *Collected Works*, Vol. 16, p. 3.

[2] 'The Coming Anarchy', *Nineteenth Century*, Vol. 22 (August 1887), pp. 149–164; 'The Coming Reign of Plenty', *Nineteenth Century*, Vol. 23 (June 1888), pp. 817–37; and 'The Industrial Village of the Future', *Nineteenth Century*, Vol. 24 (October 1888), pp. 513–30.   [3] *Freedom*, X, November 1896, p. 109.

the Victorian era, and his basic discovery is that men have become
instinctively co-operative and happy, because the exploitive pressure of capitalism and the divisive influence of property are gone.
An Arcadian existence has replaced the grimy, slum-ridden,
unhappy civilization of the nineteenth century.

As the visitor is guided through London and up the Thames to
Oxfordshire, he sees repeated examples of people undertaking
labour voluntarily and happily helping others. In many samples of
dress and design, the visitor is reminded of the fourteenth century.
Industrial concentration has been abolished and the ugliness of
nineteenth-century manufacturing cities has disappeared. Those
mills that still exist are small, tastefully designed, and, of course,
operated by volunteers. According to Morris's vision, the handicrafts had been revived and nearly all able-bodied persons engaged
in one or more of them. Machinery is used primarily for those
tasks that are unpleasant to do by hand; Morris was clearly more
interested in returning to the rustic forms of life than was Kropotkin, but their basic objective of getting all men into some kind of
productive, utilitarian activity was the same.

Salaries and money are of course entirely gone; most of the population seemingly has no indication that such devices ever existed.
All goods are produced for the joy of working, and freely given to
whoever chances to desire them. Morris repeatedly depicts the
new Englishmen as being devoted to the artistic possibilities of
their work.

For a short time in the post-revolutionary era, the visitor to
emancipated England is told, there had been concern about the
possibility that well-being and material abundance would make
people dull and lethargic, but they had learned to engage in

. . . the production of what used to be called art, but which has no
name amongst us now, because it has become a necessary part of the
labour of every man who produces.

. . . The art or work-pleasure, as one ought to call it, of which I am
now speaking, sprung up almost spontaneously, it seems, from a kind
of instinct amongst people, no longer driven desperately to painful and
terrible overwork, to do the best they could with the work in hand—
to make it excellent of its kind; and when that had gone on for a little,
a craving for beauty seemed to awaken in men's minds. . . .[1]

[1] William Morris, *Collected Works*, Vol. 16, p. 134.

The details of the economic system are essentially in harmony with the arrangements that Kropotkin proposed in *The Conquest of Bread* and *Fields, Factories, and Workshops*, except that Morris has forecast a minimum of industrialization. The guide reports to his visitor that ' . . . we have long ago dropped the pretention to be the market place of the world. . . .' The 'world market'—that archaic device for providing useless items to the wealthy classes— has been abolished, and the exchange function has been radically transformed. The shop-keepers are now children instructed to give products to those who desire them, and the 'commercial morality' which made the nineteenth century so greedy and unhappy is extinct.

What of government? The picture could hardly be more compatible with the ideas of Kropotkin. There is no government and there are no politics. The Houses of Parliament are preserved, but they are used for storing fertilizer and are commonly known as the 'Dung Market'. There are no laws, courts, or police; they vanished when there was no longer property or special privilege to protect. There is no criminal class, since there is no idle, rich class to breed enemies of society. When crimes occur, the conscience of the offender proves much more effective than courts or prison.

There are 'units of management', or wards, or parishes for handling problems of administration. We do not get very specific information about how they function, but they respond to local needs, presumably, in much the same way that Kropotkin's voluntary committees would have done. There is no central authority.

Formal schooling has disappeared. On the whole, children educate themselves in the fields and shops, and formal training comes only when motivation for it exists. It is leisurely, practical, and voluntary. As for higher institutions, the same principle operates. Morris took delight in chiding his *alma mater*, Oxford, which the visitor is told:

. . . has reverted to some of its best traditions; so you may imagine how far it is from its nineteenth-century position. It is real learning, knowledge cultivated for its own sake—the Art of Knowledge, in short— which is followed there, not the Commercial learning of the past. Though perhaps you do not know that in the nineteenth century Oxford and its less interesting sister Cambridge became definitely commercial. They (and especially Oxford) were the breeding places of a peculiar class of parasites, who called themselves cultivated people; . . .[1]

[1] Ibid., p. 70.

So much for the economic and institutional forms. Morris decorated his fantasy with descriptions of the pastoral loveliness of the countryside, the architectural delights that dot the landscape, smiling healthy people who live much longer than their oppressed ancestors did, and simple, honest relationships that have replaced the false amenities and bitter enmities of the nineteenth century. Legal marriages have been abolished, and a variety of free love, described in the circumspect Victorian manner, is suggested. There are no longer 'such lunatic affairs as divorce courts', and marital relationships are subject to change without formal arrangements. The equality of the sexes is taken for granted and domestic work has become a joy since women are no longer slaves to it. Not all situations are perfect; domestic strife occasionally occurs, and now and then a crime of passion is reported. But in such cases the difficulties are nearly always settled calmly, without retribution or penalty, to the satisfaction of all. One does not buy or sell hospitality, since any home is open to anyone who finds his presence acceptable both to himself and to the present occupants. Kropotkin could have hardly found any work that more completely incorporated the spirit of his anarchistic writings.

There is a non-utopian feature of *News from Nowhere* that also blends with Kropotkin's work. Two chapters in the middle of Morris's book describe how the revolution had come about. The visitor to the new Britain gets a graphic description of the great turmoil which accompanied the overthrow of commercialism—including the battles in Trafalgar Square that Morris reconstructed partly from memory. Here Morris is suggesting a formula for revolution which incorporates past experience. The visitor learns of a general strike which paralysed the economy of London, affecting especially the wealthy and middle classes. The poor—operating spontaneously and with remarkable instinctive co-operation—caused the old regime to surrender. A Committee of Public Safety organized food supplies and other provisions, operated the bakeries, and assured the essential items to everyone in need. It is not unlikely that Morris had read some of the Kropotkin chapters that later went into *The Conquest of Bread* shortly before he wrote these passages; in any event, the resemblance between these passages and those of Kropotkin's work at the same time is so strong that it is easier to believe that the two men shared ideas than it is to assume a coincidence.

News from Nowhere was the last significant piece of creative writing that Morris gave to the Socialist cause. As he finished the final chapters of this work and contributed them to *The Common-weal*, he was near breaking-point with those who had won control of the League and the newspaper. He was still speaking rather frequently for the cause at this time, and he still carried some of the Marxian baggage in the lectures of this period, but there is little that can be identified as Marxian in his creative works. During this time, Morris was turning more and more of his attention back to the crafts and to Gothic-style romances that contained only a minimum of social commentary. In 1890, he founded the Kelmscott Press and helped to revive the art of fine printing that had virtually disappeared in Europe. The production of the renowned Kelmscott books occupied most of his last five years. Thus he gradually substituted non-political writing and the advancement of a newly-found art for most of his political activities.

The special touch of the poet seems to be necessary to deal adequately with most of Morris's last literary efforts. The scholars who are mainly interested in Morris's socialism have usually found little material of interest in the later works besides *A Dream of John Ball*, *Pilgrims of Hope*, and *News from Nowhere*. Those long, rambling tales with which he amused himself with increasing frequency during the final decade of his life are certainly more understandable as the work of an intellectual anarchist than as products of the class struggle.

Those who insist upon the essential Marxism of Morris's work have tried to find elements of scientific socialism in the late romances, but with little success. The *House of the Wolfings*, written in the period between *A Dream of John Ball* and *News from Nowhere*, seems to invite some of this kind of critical interpretation; E. P. Thompson and R. Page Arnot have both tried, rather superficially, to prove the existence of Marxian influence in this work. But Morris himself suggests that, to the extent that this work did have a social message, it was a simple one: 'It is meant to illustrate the melting of the individual into the society of the tribes: I mean apart from the artistic side of things that is its moral—if it has one.'[1]

If it has a moral message—and that conditional expression reveals Morris's own indifference on the point—it is deeply buried

[1] William Morris, *Letters*, p. 302.

in the imagery and the archaic prose in which the tale is offered. The Gothic tribes of *The House of the Wolfings* are struggling almost instinctively for a continuity of their way of life, against the crowded and dreary Roman cities of the south about which they have only the most vague notions. One senses that in those cities, some men who are idle can dictate the terms of work to those who call themselves free, but the joy of fellowship is absent, and this is the crucial omission.

The operation of a communal instinct is described or implied in a number of places in the late prose romances, and the political forms that exist, where they are not enshrouded in magic or fantasy, are simple. These works are essentially a-political, and for this reason they yield little to those who would enlist Morris's reputation in their own causes. But the fact that there is such a great volume of this kind of prose, dating from the last seven or eight years of his life, testifies to his abandonment of most political activity. By comparison with his meagre output of new Socialist material, consider the long list of romances that appeared after 1889—*The Roots of the Mountains, The Story of the Glittering Plain, The Wood Beyond the World, Child Christopher, The Well at the World's End, The Water of the Wondrous Isles,* and *The Sundering Flood.* Only a fragment of his energies went into Socialism after his resignation from the League.

Morris's departure from the League in November 1890 was the occasion for a rather long letter to *The Commonweal* which has often been quoted—and not infrequently misquoted or awkwardly abridged—by biographers and scholars. He said in part:

It is now some seven years since Socialism came to life again in this country. To some the time will seem long, so many hopes and disappointments as have been crowded into them. Yet in the history of a serious movement seven years is a short time enough; and few movements surely have made so much progress during this short time in one way or another as Socialism has done.

For what was it which we set out to accomplish? To change the system of society on which the tremendous fabric of civilisation is founded, and which has been built up by centuries of conflict with older and dying systems, and crowned by the victory of modern civilisation over the material surroundings of life.

Could seven years make any visible impression on such a tremendous undertaking as this?

Consider, too, the quality of those who began and carried on this business of reversing the basis of modern society! Who were the statesmen who took up the momentous questions laid before England of the nineteenth century by the English Socialists? Who were the great divines who preached this new gospel of happiness from their pulpits? . . .

Those who set out 'to make the revolution'—that is, as aforesaid, to put society on a new basis, contradictory to the existing one—were a few working-men, less successful even in the wretched life of labour than their fellows, a sprinkling of the intellectual proletariat, whose keen pushing of Socialism must have seemed pretty certain to extinguish their limited chances of prosperity; one or two outsiders in the game political; a few refugees from the bureaucratic tyranny of foreign Governments; and here and there an impractical, half-cracked artist or author.

Yet such as they were, they were enough to do something. Through them, though not by them, the seven years of the new movement toward freedom have, contrary to all that might have been expected, impressed the idea of Socialism deeply on the epoch. . . .[1]

This valedictory message does not attribute the relative success of the Socialist movement to a scientific ideology or to the influence of Social Democracy. It is in spite of the errors of those who proposed 'palliation' and those who advocated premature revolt that Socialism has made its progress. Morris reiterated his old argument that the only reasonable programme was continued propaganda and education, to convince people that Socialism was good for them and was possible. He did not feel the necessity for planning the details of the revolution; like Kropotkin, he felt that when the hour of action had arrived, the Socialists would know 'what action is necessary for putting their principles into practice'.[2]

THE FINAL YEARS: 1891–1896

The Morris that emerges from his later articles and essays is a subdued man, troubled by ill-health, chastened by the controversies that he had passed through, and eager to re-establish friendships that had been damaged by the quarrels of the previous years. The Hammersmith Socialist Society, which constituted itself from the old Hammersmith Branch of the Socialist League,

---

[1] William Morris, 'Where are We Now?' *The Commonweal* (15 November 1890), p. 361.   [2] Ibid., pp. 361–2.

became the agency through which Morris conducted his limited Socialist work in the 1890s, and it was clearly less militant than the League had been. Morris collaborated with Bax in republishing some of their earlier essays, and he wrote articles for Hyndman's *Justice* once again. He gave the Fabians cause to believe that he was coming around to their point of view, and he even participated in election campaigning in a modest way. He left, in short, an ambiguous record in those last years. At times he seemed to be standing by his old principles, but at other times he indicated that he believed that the undesirable period of working within existing bourgeois institutions might be at hand. He seems to have been eager to find areas of agreement—rather than points of disagreement—in his relations with his fellow left-wingers. A few scholars have suggested that Morris became more moderate because he was increasingly regarded as a guide and mentor of British Socialism after 1890. His foremost biographer, Mackail, wrote that 'in these latter years his whole personality ripened and softened'.[1] It was the Morris of this period, invariably dressed in 'shabby blue'— Bernard Shaw called him the worst-dressed person he ever knew —with ragged beard and unkempt hair, resembling most of all a Viking patriarch, that his survivors and friends remembered with affection.

The poet-craftsman had one period of rather intense activity on behalf of Socialism in late 1892 and early 1893, but it was of short duration. It was during this time that Morris, moved by the spirit of reconciliation that characterized his last years, participated in the efforts to achieve a measure of unity among his own Hammersmith Socialists, the Fabians, and the Social Democratic Federation. This was the period when the various branches of British Socialism and trade unionism were seeking a ground for common action; the establishment of the Independent Labour Party was one result of this invigorated climate of opinion. Morris, who had been an advocate of mutual tolerance among the factions even when they were most afflicted with dissension, was one of the active proponents of a plan to draft a joint manifesto. He, Shaw, and Hyndman, representing their respective organizations, met on several occasions and tried to find a basis for co-operation. Morris seems to have drafted the working document and to have expended considerable energy and patience, adjusting it to the objections

[1] Mackail, Vol. 2, p. 267.

and idiosyncrasies of Shaw and Hyndman, who quarrelled incessantly. In the final Joint Manifesto, issued in the name of the
three organizations in May 1893, Morris yielded more than either
of his two contentious colleagues, and the final compromises made
the document so general that it served little purpose. As Shaw
wrote forty years later: 'Morris's draft, horribly eviscerated and
patched, was subsequently sold for a penny as the Joint Manifesto
of the Socialists of Great Britain. It was the only document any
of the three of us had ever signed and published that was honestly
not worth a farthing.'[1]

One of his last major Socialist lectures, entitled 'Communism',
which he delivered in February 1893 at Kelmscott House and
which he later published, testified to his continuing worries about
the future of the movement and his second thoughts about his
own assumptions in the latter years. Although he and his colleagues
in the Hammersmith Socialist Society did identify themselves
with some of the Socialist political activities of the early 1890s,
he felt constrained to pronounce his well-worn reservations once
again. He looked on the efforts to form a labour-oriented political
party with misgivings. Speaking specifically of both the Fabians
and the Social Democrats, he expressed the fear that gradual gains
on the political front and partial implementation of Socialism
might cause the working classes to be distracted from the ultimate
goals. He warned that immediate material advantages and the
'machinery' of Socialism should not be mistaken for the final
objective—the creation of a 'new Society of Equals'. The immediate political gains could serve the ends of Socialism only if they
proved to be part of the education of the masses for Communism.

Most of the essay is simply a restatement of his earlier discussion
about the danger of palliatives, the evils of waste and idleness, and
the results of inequality. But there is a tone of uncertainty and
indecision in this essay that does not appear in the earlier major
Socialist essays. Morris was not sure, as he wrote this piece, that
the working classes were ready for the kind of lessons that must
be learned to make progress towards Communism possible. He
wondered whether the poor were so hopelessly oppressed by the

---

[1] Shaw, 'William Morris as I Knew Him', in May Morris, op. cit., p. xxxvi.
For a more detailed Shavian account, see his letter of 1895 to Walter Crane on
the same subject, printed in Henderson, *George Bernard Shaw: Man of the
Century*, pp. 247–50. It is also discussed in Mackail, Vol. II, pp. 289–91.

intellectual slavery that was a counterpart of their material slavery that there was no possibility for an early transformation. He clearly lacked the enthusiasm that characterized his earlier published lectures.[1]

On 10 March 1893 he delivered another of his lectures on 'Communism' to a meeting sponsored by the *Freedom* Fund Publication Committee at Grafton Hall.[2] There were a few remarks in the speech that defended a limited concept of property and that indicated that he was reconciled to the need for some kind of authority to assure that all men would perform their fair shares of the necessary labour in the new society. It is not surprising that anarchists in the audience—some of whom were disappointed in Morris's conduct anyway—took offence at this suggestion and prodded him with questions.

According to a report of the meeting in *Freedom*, one listener asked Morris specifically what line of conduct he recommended, and he replied, 'Upon my word I don't know. I came here to see if I could learn myself what to do. People must go their own road.'[3] Perhaps the account in *Freedom* was intentionally unfavourable to Morris, but this remark is consistent with the uncertainty that troubled him in his last years.

Elsewhere in one of his speeches of early 1893, possibly in the same lecture that he delivered to the *Freedom* group, he revealed the extent to which he adopted a policy of non-violence as part of his Socialist philosophy. He said:

I confess I am no great lover of political tactics; the sordid squabble of an election is unpleasant enough for a straight forward man to deal in: yet I cannot fail to see that it is necessary somehow to get hold of the machine which has at its back the executive power of the country, however that may be done, and that the organization and labour which will be necessary to effect that by means of the ballot-box will, to say

[1] William Morris, 'Communism', in *The Collected Works*, XXIII, pp. 264–76.
[2] There are two Morris lectures entitled 'Communism'. The one delivered at Kelmscott House in February 1893 was a more polished work and was later published not only by Morris but also by the Fabian Society as Fabian Tract No. 113, in 1903. The other remained unpublished for many years and was provisionally entitled 'Communism, i.e. Property'. The original manuscript is British Museum Additional Manuscript 45–333/13; parts have been printed in May Morris, op. cit., II, pp. 345–52. LeMire, op. cit., p. 526, lists the first lecture as the one that was delivered to the *Freedom* group, but it may have been the other one—'Communism, i.e. Property'—in view of the response to it.
[3] *Freedom*, VII (May 1893), p. 27.

the least of it, be little indeed compared with what would be necessary
to effect it by open revolt; besides that the change effected by peaceable
means would be done more completely and with less chance, indeed
with no chance of counter-revolution. On the other hand I feel sure
that some action is even now demanded by the growth of Socialism,
and will be more and more imperatively demanded as time goes on. In
short I do not believe in the possible success of revolt until the Socialist
party has grown so powerful in numbers that it can gain its end by
peaceful means, and that therefore what is called violence will never
be needed; unless indeed the reactionists were to refuse the decision
of the ballot-box and try the matter by arms; which after all I am pretty
sure they could not attempt by the time things had gone so far as that.
As to the attempt of a small minority to terrify a vast majority into
accepting something which they do not understand, by spasmodic acts
of violence, mostly involving the death or mutilation of non-combatants,
I can call that nothing else than sheer madness. And here I will say once
for all, what I have often wanted to say of late, to wit that the idea of
taking any human life for any reason whatsoever is horrible and abhor-
rent to me.[1]

Increasingly weak, beset by doubts about the best strategy, and
deeply engrossed in his Press and his romances, Morris played
little part in the Socialist activities in 1894, 1895, and 1896. He
did appear often enough on the platform or in print to maintain
his reputation as one of the leaders of the movement, but it was
often ceremonial occasions that brought him into public, and he
added nothing of substance to the Socialist message. He appeared
at the inauguration of the Oxford Socialist Union late in 1895,
and one of his last speeches was an address at Waterloo Station
on the day of Stepniak's funeral. There is a touch of irony in the
fact that this farewell message, Morris's last open-air address to
a gathering of revolutionists, should have been occasioned by the
death of one of the men who helped to introduce him to revolutionary movement. Within a year, the survivors of Morris placed
his body in the churchyard at Kelmscott.

It serves little purpose to insist that Morris belonged more to
one branch of Socialism, or Communism, or anarchism, than to
another. He obviously borrowed fragments of his working
Socialism from several sources, and different points of view
predominated in his thinking at different times. The leading

[1] Brit. Mus. Add. MS 45-333/13, pp. 13–14. It is reproduced with minor
alterations in May Morris, op. cit., II, pp. 350–1.

biographers of Kropotkin have observed that Morris's thinking on anarchism was muddled, and they have offered a provocative suggestion; if Kropotkin's theory of mutual aid had been fully elaborated before Morris's death, perhaps Morris's objections to anarchism would have been answered. It is evident that the spirit of Morris's Socialism is at least as similar to that of *Mutual Aid* as to any other of the Socialist documents. Morris's Socialism might best be described as catholic, borrowing from the Middle Ages and from Russian nihilism, as well as from Mill and from Marx. And in this respect, Morris's most famous successor and disciple was Bernard Shaw.

V

SHAW

Socialist Maverick

THE most eclectic member of the London Socialist community in the last fifteen years of the nineteenth century was George Bernard Shaw. Before he became a successful dramatist, and even before he made a reputation as a critic of art and music, Shaw sampled the several varieties of Socialism then available in that remarkable city, and eventually he became disenchanted in some measure with each of them. He flirted with anarchism and Marxism during his earliest period as a Socialist before he finally became the outstanding propagandist of the Fabian Society. But this organization only partially satisfied him, and in the final analysis, after many years of devoting much time and energy to it, he turned his back on most of its enterprises and became one of its most caustic critics. Yet he never completely abandoned any of the Socialist attitudes that he had momentarily embraced as a young man, and it can expand one's understanding of the Prefaces and of the Plays if one recognizes that his early allegiances affected the attitudes he expressed in his fully-developed art.

That Shaw began his Socialist career by discovering Henry George and Karl Marx is well known, because he often referred to the influence of these two men. Having heard George speak and having responded to a challenge to read *Das Kapital*, like Morris, in French, Shaw became a convert to the movement in 1883, but unlike Morris, he was not content to follow the guidance of others on technical matters. Naturally contentious and instinctively sceptical, he quickly went beyond George and he whimsically challenged some of the basic ideas of Marx when most of the newly-aligned British Socialists were just learning to repeat his slogans. In March of 1884, he submitted his well-known brief letter entitled 'Who is the Thief?' to Hyndman's newly-established newspaper *Justice*, raising a question about the Marxian theory of value. Shaw made it clear then and later that he was joking—he signed the letter 'G.B.S. Larking'—but the inquiry pointed to a soft spot in Marxian doctrine, and it raised a difficulty that the advocates of scientific socialism could not answer. Shaw had expected a rebuttal from informed colleagues, but nothing substantial came.[1]

His early heresy notwithstanding, for some time Shaw remained an admirer and advocate of Marxian ideas. One of the little known labours to which he devoted himself in 1884 was the editing of Laurence Gronlund's book *The Co-operative Commonwealth*, the Marxian-oriented study that became one of the first volumes on Socialism to be widely read in English. It was initially published in 1884, and Shaw apparently recognized some propaganda value in it. He had no high regard for Gronlund as a writer; he reviewed another of Gronlund's books rather negatively in 1888.[2] But he obviously approved of Gronlund's effort to subject German socialist thinking—i.e. primarily Marxian thinking—to a digesting and refining process that would make it acceptable to Anglo-Saxon readers. Shaw's objective was to take this process one step further, tightening the language, altering the word order in places, and generally tidying up Gronlund's presentation.[3] Shaw's was one of several re-issues of the book to appear in the 1880s and 1890s, and it demonstrates his devotion to Marxian ideas in his early Socialist period. Shaw was rather brutal in his alterations in places, particularly when the more romantic passages were involved, and he aroused Gronlund's wrath. It was a preview of Shaw's subsequent attitude towards Socialism generally. He would support the movement to the end of his life, but he could not avoid pointing out its weaknesses.

Shaw's drift away from Marxian economics was caused largely

[1] This and the other important Shaw articles on Marxism from the 1880s are republished in R. W. Ellis, ed., *Bernard Shaw and Karl Marx: a Symposium, 1884–1889* (New York, 1930). See also Shaw's long letter to Matthew Edward McNulty dated 15 April, 1884, on the same subject, in Shaw, *Collected Letters*, op. cit., pp. 81–7.

[2] There is a Shaw review, published in the *Pall Mall Gazette* of 5 September 1888, in the Shaw Papers, British Museum Add. MS 50692.

[3] Laurence Gronlund, *The Co-operative Commonwealth*, edited by G. B. Shaw. (3rd edn, London, 1892.) See the comments of Edward Aveling on an earlier printing of this edition in *The Commonweal*, I (September 1885), p. 88 supplement. See also the references in Shaw, *Collected Letters*, op. cit., pp. 101–2; 112, and the bibliographical data in Henderson, *George Bernard Shaw: Man of the Century*, op. cit., p. 232.

by his journalistic encounter with Philip Wicksteed, the Unitarian minister and scholar who was also versed in the economics of Stanley Jevons. Their exchange of articles in *To-Day* in 1884 and 1885 convinced Shaw that he had been bettered; it was one of the few arguments of his long life that he admitted losing. Shaw studied Jevons for some time, and by 1887, armed with a theory of value that was more utilitarian than Marxian, he turned his journalistic talents against Marx and the Social Democrats. In August of that year, he published three articles in *The National Reformer*, reviewing the English-language edition of *Das Kapital* and effectively demonstrating some of its weaknesses.

In the course of his conversion, Shaw did not lose his admiration for Marx as a critic of bourgeois society, but he did lose the respect of the devoted Marxists like Hyndman and his followers. The fate of socialism did not depend on the truth or error of Marx's theory of value, Shaw argued repeatedly, and Marx had done a substantial service to the cause of social reform by his moral indignation. Shaw would not accept the Marxian line about the class struggle or about the special virtues and mission of the proletarian class, and after the 1880s he usually was as harshly critical of Marxolotry as he was of Marxophobia. 'Marx's "Capital" is not a treatise on Socialism,' Shaw wrote in 1901, expressing the view that he had adopted several years before and he was to reiterate often:

... it is a jeremiad against the bourgeoisie, supported by such a mass of evidence and such a relentless Jewish genius for denunciation as had never been brought to bear before. It was supposed to be written for the working classes; but the working man respects the bourgeoisie, and wants to be a bourgeois; Marx never got hold of him for a moment. It was the revolting sons of the bourgeoisie itself—Lassalle, Marx, Liebknecht, Morris, Hyndman, Bax, all, like myself, bourgeois crossed with squirearchy—that painted the flag red. . . . I threw Hyndman over, and got to work with Sidney Webb and the rest to place Socialism on a respectable bourgeois footing; hence Fabianism . . .[1]

Shaw did indeed throw Hyndman aside in the process of modifying his own Marxism, and he put his own genius for denunciation to good use; he seemed to relish the prospect of a

---

[1] Published first in May 1901 in *The Candid Friend*, in response to questions from Frank Harris. This statement was reissued in several forms by Shaw on later occasions. See Bernard Shaw, *Selected Non-Dramatic Writings of Bernard Shaw* edited by Dan H. Laurence (Boston, 1965), pp. 448–9.

quarrel with the Social Democrats who were worshippers of Marx. Unlike Morris, Shaw was most happy in the middle of controversy, and he developed a deft polemical style which paid his opponents sarcastic half-compliments while pointing out the fallacy of their arguments. He became the *bête noire* of the orthodox Marxists.

His conversion to gradualism and democratic reform in the Fabian Society was, of course, the complement of his repudiation of Marxism, but this was not completed until he had also briefly tested the waters of anarchism and found them unsatisfactory. When Shaw joined the Fabian Society late in the summer of 1884, its programme was still undefined. During the infancy of the movement, Mrs. Charlotte Wilson, later to be the close associate of Kropotkin and co-editor of *Freedom*, was one of its active members, 'and a sort of influenza of Anarchism soon spread through the society'.[1] For a year or two, Shaw affirmed, the Fabian Society was 'just as Anarchistic as the Socialist League and just as insurrectionary as the Federation'. Shaw's only reason for joining the Society rather than the other organizations was the feeling that the former would be more likely to attract men who shared his bias and intellectual habits.[2]

In 1884, Shaw wrote for Mrs. Wilson an article entitled 'What's in a Name? (How an Anarchist might put it)', suggesting a means by which the advocates of anarchism might make the name of their movement respectable, in the same way that the early Christians and Quakers had turned their early pejorative labels to good account. There is no objection to the autocracy of Tsarist Russia that cannot also be made against any form of popular government, Shaw wrote, and the only valid protest against such autocracy is that of the anarchist, who refuses to call any man his master. Slavery, he continued, is the complement of authority, and will disappear with it.[3] Whether this short statement reflected Shaw's point of view at the time he wrote it is a debatable question; he seems to have been reticent about the publication of it the following year, and he was embarrassed by its reissue in 1889, after he and the Fabian Society had adopted a moderate, anti-

[1] Bernard Shaw, *The Fabian Society: What it has Done & How it has Done It*, Fabian Tract No. 41 (London, 1892), p. 3.

[2] Ibid., p. 4.

[3] *The Anarchist* (London), March 1885.

anarchist position.[1] At the very least, the statement shows that
Shaw had considered carefully the arguments of individual
anarchism and had constructed a serious statement—which was
not his usual method—on behalf of that ideology.

It is significant that Shaw did not address himself to Communist Anarchism, but only to the individualist variety that was
then being advocated in the embryonic left-wing circles of London.
Kropotkin's *Freedom* group did not come into existence until
more than a year later, and the literature of Communist Anarchism
was nearly non-existent. Shaw, again like Morris, meant individualist anarchism when he used the term in the period before the
Freedom press made the communal variety better known.

The Fabian Society did not take its definitive turn away from
anarchism and towards its characteristic policy of gradual democratic reform until 1886, and then it did so in the heat of controversy with Social Democrats and the Socialist League. The
former, following Hyndman's example, was still preaching violent
revolution, but it had suffered the embarrassment of the 'Tory
Gold' scandal of 1885—having taken money secretly from the
Conservatives to oppose two Liberal candidates for parliament.
As we have seen, the League had categorically denounced all
conventional political activity. The Fabians who shared executive
responsibilities with Shaw in these formative years—Sidney Webb,
Annie Besant, Graham Wallas, Hubert Bland, and Sydney
Olivier—did not share either of those inclinations. They—and
particularly Webb—brought to Fabianism the moderation and the
respectability of the Benthamite Utilitarian tradition, which in the
previous fifty years had been substantially modified in the person
and work of Mill. At an early stage in their Fabian partnership
Shaw urged Webb to read *Das Kapital*; Webb did so and was
unimpressed. He was already 'saturated' with Mill, as Shaw wrote
later, '. . . a ready-made Socialist, and had nothing to learn from
Marx theoretically or from me'.[2]

[1] For Shaw's letter to Henry Seymour relating to its publication in *The
Anarchist*, see Dan H. Laurence, Bernard Shaw, *Collected Letters*, op. cit., pp.
109–10. Consult also the informative article by Geoffrey Ostergaard, 'G.B.S.—
Anarchist', *The New Statesman and Nation*, Vol. 46 (21 November 1953), p. 628.
[2] In Margaret Cole, ed., *The Webbs and Their Work* (London, 1949), p. 6.
The evolution of the Fabian Society in its earliest period and its debts to earlier
English thinkers has been well summarized in Pease, op. cit., pp. 13–85; Mac-
Briar, op. cit., pp. 1–28; Margaret Cole, *The Story of Fabian Socialism*, op. cit.,
pp. 3–25; and Anne Fremantle, op. cit., pp. 24–80.

This is a key to Shaw's relationship with his fellow Fabians. He, alone among the leaders, had studied Marx thoroughly and had experienced an emotional conversion. He, more than any of his colleagues, knew the humiliations of poverty and of unemployment, and he did more to seek out the available alternatives to contemporary society. His training, such as it was, was less traditionally English and left him more open to the varieties of Socialism. On the tactical and political side, the Fabian Society took the road of its moderates, and on this level Shaw followed the leadership of others. Yet he became the leading polemicist and the chief humorist of the movement, and in this respect he put his mark upon it. Blessed with much free time, skilled in the art of drafting statements of consensus, and motivated by a love of argument, he became its most talkative spokesman. As the Fabian Society undertook its famous policy of persuasion and 'permeation', his talents were a remarkable asset.

In this capacity, he was one of the leading participants in the debates that divided the English Socialist movement in 1886–7. Many of the militants in the Social Democratic Federation and in the Socialist League were ready to denounce some kinds of moderate action and policy as service to capitalism. In February 1886, Shaw joined other members of the Society in proposing that Socialists organize a political party, and with this decision they initiated a debate of several months' standing with the Socialist League. A year later, the Fabian Parliamentary League was formed for the specific purpose of using existing machinery and available political techniques to advance the cause of Socialism. This development set the pattern of compromise and gradual reform that guided Fabianism for many years.[1]

The Fabian Essays of 1889, to which Shaw contributed two essays and his editorial talents, became the definitive statement of the Fabian belief that common sense attitudes and gradual improvements, achieved by democratic political means, could overcome the ills of society. Graham Wallas, one of the essayists, probably represented the Fabian consensus of the late 1880s when he wrote

The growing recognition, due in part to Darwin, of causation in the development of individuals and societies; the struggles and disappointments of half a century of agitation; the steady introduction of Socialistic

[1] Shaw, *The Fabian Society*, op. cit., pp. 12–14.

institutions by men who reject Socialist ideas, all incline us to give up any expectation of a final and perfect reform. We are more apt to regard the slow and often unconscious progress of the Time spirit as the only adequate cause of social progress, and to attempt rather to discover and proclaim what the future *must* be, than to form an organization of men determined to make the future what it should be.[1]

And Annie Besant, the only woman among the essayists, added:

It is therefore necessary to bear in mind that I am only trying to work out the changes practicable among men and women as we know them; always seeking to lay down, not what is ideally best, but what is possible.[2]

Although Shaw shared these antipathies to hasty, violent actions and to the utopian expectations that he saw in the rival Socialist groups, he could not be quite so placid about the pace at which change was occurring, and in the long run it was impatience with democratic methods that dominated his thinking.

'The Transition to Social Democracy', the most important Shavian essay of 1888, constitutes a summation of his arguments of the middle years of the decade. This article, which later became one of the *Fabian Essays*, was composed while Shaw was visiting at Kelmscott Manor,[3] and it bears some imprints of Morris's influence. The early, historical passages are enough like Morris's historical lectures of the same period to be identified as his if it were not for the characteristic Shavian barbs. The middle paragraphs, however, are anti-Morrisian, since they constitute an argument demonstrating how the State can be used to achieve reform. He discussed the variety of municipal socialism with which the Fabians were beginning to experiment. It was a slow, 'humdrum programme' that he advocated, and at the end there was a revealing passage testifying to his own frustration with the method of reform that he had embraced:

Let me, in conclusion, disavow all admiration for this inevitable, but sordid, slow, reluctant, cowardly path to justice. I venture to claim your respect for those enthusiasts who still refuse to believe that millions of their fellow creatures must be left to sweat and suffer in hopeless toil and degradation, whilst parliaments and vestries grudgingly muddle and

---

[1] Bernard Shaw, ed., *Fabian Essays*, Jubilee edition (London, 1948), p. 165.
[2] Ibid., p. 185.
[3] Archibald Henderson, *George Bernard Shaw: Man of the Century*, p. 177.

grope towards paltry instalments of betterment. The right is so clear,
the wrong so intolerable, the gospel so convincing, that it seems to them
that it *must* be possible to enlist the whole body of workers—soldiers,
policemen, and all—under the banner of brotherhood and equality; and
at one great stroke to set Justice on her rightful throne. Unfortunately,
such an army of light is no more to be gathered from the human product
of nineteenth-century civilization than grapes are to be gathered from
thistles. But if we feel glad of that impossibility; if we feel relieved that
the change is to be slow enough to avert personal risk to ourselves; if
we feel anything less than acute disappointment and bitter humiliation
at the discovery that there is yet between us and the promised land a
wilderness in which many must perish miserably of want and despair:
then I submit to you that our institutions have corrupted us to the most
dastardly degree of selfishness. The Socialists need not be ashamed of
beginning as they did by proposing militant organization of the working
classes and general insurrection. The proposal proved impracticable;
and it has now been abandoned—not without some outspoken regrets—
by English Socialists. But is still remains as the only finally possible
alternative to the Social Democratic program which I have sketched
today.[1]

That he wrote this half-warning, half-threat on to the end of his
essay on 'The Transition to Social Democracy' suggests his
personal impatience and perhaps uncertainty about the method
that might eventually be used. He could argue vehemently against
his fellow Socialists on occasion, but he would usually take their
part against the bourgeois establishment. His own education in
Socialism became more elaborate during the encounters of the
middle 1880s.

In 1888 he also composed *The Impossibilities of Anarchism*. The
original essay was revised slightly and delivered as a lecture to the
Fabian Society in 1891, and published as a Fabian Tract in 1893.
Although the final title suggests a categorical rejection of anarchism, Shaw demonstrated a somewhat fuller understanding and a
considerable amount of sympathy for the ideals of Kropotkin.
Most writers who have commented on this essay have failed to
distinguish between his dismissal of the individualist anarchism of
Benjamin Tucker, the American agitator, and his uncommon
deference for the Russian exile with whom he occasionally shared
a platform.

Shaw employed against Tucker some of the same arguments

[1] Shaw, *Fabian Essays*, pp. 235-6.

and condescending language that he used against the Marxists, but he took pains to show respect for the ideas of the Communist Anarchists. He said

. . . we shall not have any great reason to stand on the dignity of our humanity until a just distribution of the loaves and fishes becomes perfectly spontaneous, and the great effort and expense of a legal distribution, however just, is saved. For my own part, I seek the establishment of a state of society in which I shall not be bothered with a ridiculous pocketful of coppers, nor have to waste my time in perplexing arithmetical exchanges of them with booking clerks, bus conductors, shopmen, and other superfluous persons before I can get what I need.[1]

In his elaboration of his attitude on Communist Anarchism, Shaw specifies that his reservations are not on the objectives of the movement and not even on the same level as his criticisms of Individualist Anarchism. Rather, he is just not convinced that mankind is morally ready for the experiment that Kropotkin is proposing. Shaw was too Hobbesian in his view of man to believe that an instinctive public morality could operate to influence individuals to do their share of the necessary toil. Existing public opinion seemed to him to deplore manual labour and to applaud the class that finds it possible to live in idleness from the fruits of other men's toil, and he found no reason to believe that this would change quickly. Kropotkin, in short, is too optimistic about the willingness of men to work for the new society:

I submit, then, to our Communist Anarchist friends that Communism requires either external compulsion to labor, or else a social morality which the evils of existing society shew that we have failed as yet to attain. I do not deny the possibility of the final attainment of that degree of moralization; but I contend that the path to it lies through a transition system which, instead of offering fresh opportunities to men of getting their living idly, will destroy those opportunities altogether, and wean us from the habit of regarding such an anomaly as possible, much less honorable.[2]

In short, Communism cannot be entirely anarchistic; men must be compelled, at least in the foreseeable future, to do their share of the essential labour. But this does not mean political despotism or tyranny must be imposed, because an alternative exists in the

---

[1] Shaw, 'The Impossibilities of Anarchism', reprinted in *The Collected Works*, Vol. XXX, p. 81.   [2] Ibid., p. 86.

form of Democracy. Shaw would repudiate this political concept also in a few years, but at the moment he placed his hopes there, and he believed himself to be basically close to Kropotkin:

Indeed, in the mouths of the really able Anarchists, Anarchism means simply the utmost attainable thoroughness of Democracy. Kropotkin, for example, speaks of free development from the simple to the composite by 'the free union of free groups'; and his illustrations are 'the societies for study, for commerce, for pleasure and recreation' which have sprung up to meet the varied requirements of the individual of our age. But in every one of these societies there is government by a council elected annually by a majority of voters; so that Kropotkin is not at all afraid of the democratic machinery and the majority power.[1]

There is no *carte blanche* for Kropotkin's school, of course, but Shaw did make an impressive effort to demonstrate the respectability and the desirability of the ends of Communist Anarchism. He even gave a qualified endorsement to Bakunin's 'comprehensive aspiration to destroy all States and Established Churches, with their religious, political, judicial, financial, criminal, academic, economic and social laws and institutions', in view of the existing conditions. But it was on practical grounds that he finally demurred on Kropotkin's position.

... Kropotkin, as I have shewn, is really an advocate of free Democracy; and I venture to suggest that he describes himself as an Anarchist rather from the point of view of the Russian recoiling from a despotism compared to which Democracy seems to be no government at all, than from the point of view of the American or Englishman who is free enough already to begin grumbling over Democracy as 'the tyranny of the majority' and 'the coming slavery'. I suggest this with the more confidence because William Morris's views are largely identical with those of Kropotkin: yet Morris, after patient and intimate observation of Anarchism as a working propaganda in England, has definitely dissociated himself from it, and has shewn, by his sketch of the communist folk-mote in his *News from Nowhere*, how sanely alive he is to the impossibility of any development of the voluntary element in social action sufficient to enable individuals or minorities to take public action without first obtaining the consent of the majority.[2]

The latter part of this statement is ambiguous but titillating. Shaw's final remark, suggesting that *News from Nowhere* is an

[1] Shaw, 'The Impossibilities of Anarchism', reprinted in *The Collected Works*, Vol. XXX, p. 96.   [2] Ibid., p. 102.

argument against anarchism, is obviously against the evidence. *News from Nowhere*, contrary to the implications of Shaw's statement, does not assume that the 'consent of the majority' must be obtained in any formal manner for 'individuals or minorities' to take public action. In *News from Nowhere*, of course, the communal sense was so strong and life so simple that co-operation was instinctive, and the problem of conflict between society and individuals or minorities was virtually non-existent. Shaw may have read something into Morris's utopian scene that was not there, or—more likely—he may have confused *News from Nowhere* with *The House of the Wolfings*, about which his remark would be much more logical. In all probability, the latter romance had been written when he composed the initial draft of his essay on anarchism, and *News from Nowhere* did not appear until more than a year later. Perhaps, in his later revising or editing of the essay, he inserted reference to the later Morris work in error. This conjecture seems to be supported by the reference to the 'folk-mote', the social form that Morris had given to his Wolfings.

In any case, Shaw was willing to align himself and Fabianism with Kropotkin to a limited extent, and the moderation that Kropotkin expressed in some of his essays beginning in the late 1880s may have been a factor. It is not possible to ascertain how much of Kropotkin's work Shaw knew in the early 1890s; it would be easy to argue from the evidence that his familiarity with the literature of Communist Anarchism was rather superficial. On the other hand, there was his continuous combat against the rivals of Fabianism and he may have known more of Kropotkin's work than he referred to in his writings.[1]

Shaw's admiration for Kropotkin remained high to the end of his life. He 'was the most simple and unassuming of all the people I had ever met', Shaw told Stephen Winsten.[2] Ranking him above Darwin as a scientist, he also paid him a compliment that, for Shaw, approached the ultimate:

[1] As one example, there is a contentious letter in the September 1890 issue of *Freedom*, which seems clearly to be the work of Shaw. It is signed only 'A Fabian' and it deals with the subject of strikes. The rhetoric, the distinctive compound sentences, and the illustrations all reveal the Shavian touch. He was taking issue with the anarchist tendency to oppose all forms of collective administration, defending the democratic technique of government, and probing for weak spots in the anarchist argument.

[2] S. Winsten, *Days with Bernard Shaw* (London, n.d.), p. 85.

I knew Kropotkin and I regard him next to William Morris as the saint of the century. . . .[1]

SHAW AND MORRIS: 1884–96

During the years when Shaw was defining his own position within the Socialist movement, he was in continual communication with Morris. The two men engaged in a substantial Socialist dialogue over the years, in addition to developing a rewarding interchange of ideas on art during the last months of Morris's life.[2] Shaw's later intellectual development and the evolution of his political attitudes can in part be explained by the influence of Morris.

When Shaw and Morris first met in 1884, the young Irishman knew something of the reputation of the famous artist-craftsman, but little of his work. Morris, on the other hand, knew almost as much about Shaw as his meagre success with the publishing world would allow. Morris had been reading Shaw's *An Unsocial Socialist* in the periodical *To-Day*, apparently with some pleasure. The two men apparently liked each other almost immediately, and in short order Morris was taking steps to put Shaw on the platform in his lecture hall at Kelmscott House.[3]

Judging from Shaw's many complimentary statements about Morris in the last half of his life, it is easy to assume—as some commentators have done—that the two men had a consistently warm and placid friendship, becoming especially close in the final years of Morris's life. The best-known account of the relationship is Shaw's 'Morris as I Knew Him', contributed as a preface to May Morris's commentary on her father's work nearly forty years after his death.[4] In this essay, the now famous dramatist

[1] S. Winsten, *Days With Bernard Shaw*, p. 83.

[2] The most extensive study of this relationship is an unpublished doctoral dissertation by E. E. Stokes Jr., 'William Morris and Bernard Shaw: A Socialist-Artistic Relationship' (Austin: University of Texas, 1951). Stokes has summarized his findings in articles such as 'Shaw and William Morris', *The Shaw Bulletin*, No. 4 (Summer 1953), pp. 16–19, and 'Morris and Bernard Shaw', *The Journal of the William Morris Society*, Vol. I (Winter 1961), pp. 13–18. Stokes relied almost entirely on the readily available published works of the two men and made an impressive case for Shaw's great debt to Morris.

[3] Brit. Mus. Add. MS 50541 (provisional category) contains three postcards from Morris to Shaw, sent in the summer of 1884, about arrangements for speaking engagements for Shaw at Hammersmith.

[4] In May Morris, op. cit., Vol. II, pp. ix–xl.

paid a high tribute to Morris's art and character. Shaw's testimony that they shared basic aesthetic ideas as well as distaste for contemporary society, his statement that Morris's 'painfully written lectures survive as the best books in the Bible of Socialism',[1] and his anecdotes suggest a high degree of intimacy. It is this essay, also, that has delighted those who are fascinated by Shaw's love-life, for here he revealed at least some of the details of his flirting with Morris's attractive daughter.

There is reason to believe, however, that the relationship was not always as smooth and placid as Shaw described in the 1930s. Morris obviously took delight in his conversation and his energy, and solicited articles from him after the establishment of *The Commonweal*. Yet these contributions, when they were forthcoming, were occasionally troublesome. In March of 1885, Shaw offered an article which commented on contemporary sex customs and practices. The article speculated in a provocative manner on the future of marriage and sexual practices after Socialism had been achieved.[2] Morris returned the article with apologies, remarking that he did not object to the contents himself (he did not specify what they were) but he felt that members of the League—which had only recently been organized—might be offended. Another letter, written on 4 May 1886, reveals that Morris was worried about the same kind of Shavian indiscretion more than a year later. 'My dear Shaw,' he wrote:

I would really be much obliged if you would write us an article: What I should like would be an economical one, tackling Jevons for instance. As to what we were talking about on Sunday I think it is better, except as a joke, not to have articles which go dead against our received policy. So though I would accept anything from you, I had rather not have to put a note at the bottom saying that I don't agree with it. So *please* the economical one.[3]

The image of Morris seeking to restrain his troublesome younger associate is no less interesting than his expression of interest in Jevonian economics. Shaw had published his first experimental article on the subject of Jevons *v.* Marx more than

[1] Ibid., p. xxxix.
[2] The document survives in the Shaw papers in the British Museum as Add. MS 50693.
[3] These letters are contained in Brit. Mus. Add. MS 50541 (provisional category).

a year earlier,[1] and Morris was obviously interested in his speculations at a time when he and the League were in spirited competition with Hyndman's Social Democrats.

In 1886 Morris read and admired Shaw's novel *Cashel Byron's
Profession*, which had been published in the Fabian-operated
journal *To-Day* because no other publishers wanted it. The praise
was reserved but warm: Morris obviously liked Shaw's portrayal
of character types and the undercurrent of social criticism.
'Whatever is attempted in "Cashel Byron" is done conscientiously
and artistically,' Morris wrote. He seems to have extended to
Shaw every courtesy and every opportunity for expression that was
consistent with the format and the objectives of *The Commonweal*.

Late in 1886 and in 1887, however, as the positions of the
various Socialist groups crystallized, the different points of view
of the Fabians and the Socialist Leaguers affected the relationship.
The Fabians watched the conflict within the Socialist League
with great interest and most of them objected to the anti-parliamentary stance of Morris's faction. When Shaw and some of his
colleagues formed the Fabian Parliamentary League in February
1887, partly in response to this controversy, he and Morris
inevitably came into conflict on fundamental questions of policy.[2]
Each came to apply to the other the derogatory pejorative 'anarchist' and each appears to have misunderstood the real position of
the other, at least for a brief period. In June 1887 Morris commented, in a private letter to a friend, that Shaw's 'real tendencies
are towards individualist-anarchism'.[3]

As the debate continued and became more intense, Shaw was
the more indelicate and aggressive. In September, the Reverend
Stewart Headlam wrote an article for *To-Day*—entitled 'A Plea
for Peace'—in which he made an appeal for unity and co-operation
among the competing Socialist groups. Shaw wrote an answer to
this proposal, entitled 'A Word for War', advancing a contrary
view.[4] He also used this occasion for a pointed slap at Morris.
Socialism had lost far too much in recent years from the wrong-
headedness of its friends to tolerate any such pleas for unity, Shaw

---

[1] Shaw, 'The Jevonian Criticism of Marx', *To-Day*, No. 13 (January 1885),
pp. 22–6.

[2] Shaw, *The Fabian Society*, op. cit., pp. 12–14.

[3] Quoted in Arnot, op. cit., p. 69.

[4] Stewart D. Headlam, 'A Plea for Peace', *To-Day* (September 1887),
pp. 78–81; and Bernard Shaw, 'A Word for War', Ibid., pp. 82–6.

argued. To make his point, he turned his sights on the Socialist League. The policy of abstaining from political activity he found to be particularly unwise, and in this connection he criticized both Joseph Lane and Morris. Lane, he believed, was primarily responsible, but Morris deserved much of the blame for the undesirable results of this policy:

. . . I can see plainly enough that he (Morris) has compromised the movement at a critical period in its development by giving the weight of his vote and countenance to that party in the League which is identified with rabidly individualistic Anarchism and advocacy of a violent overthrow of existing society.[1]

It must have stung Morris to have been thus upbraided by his young friend in the pages of a Fabian journal. He mentioned Shaw in a letter to Dr. John Glasse of Edinburgh, written 23 September 1887, with an obvious tone of frustration. Shaw and the Fabians were presenting difficulties, he said, by presenting themselves as the only sound body of Socialists in the country. Morris conceded that their work was useful and that they had the right to seek reform in parliament, if they wanted to try that means, but he wanted the Socialist League to remain free of such an encumbrance. He felt certain that Shaw and his associates would 'fall into the error of moving earth and sea to fill the ballot boxes with Socialist votes which will not represent Socialist *men*'.[2] Neither Shaw nor Morris wanted Socialist unity enough to compromise on this point in 1887.

This criticism by Shaw and the comment by Morris came just a few weeks before the events of 'Bloody Sunday', 13 November, which chastened both men and reminded them of the futility of violence. Their differences on strategy remained, but there was now more reason to emphasize their common aversion to direct physical combat. Shaw wrote to Morris in a light-hearted vein, observing that 'it was the most abjectly disgraceful defeat ever suffered by a band of heroes outnumbering their foes a thousand to one'.[3]

It was in the aftermath of 'Bloody Sunday' that Shaw wrote 'The Transition to Social Democracy' in Morris's home and composed 'The Impossibilities of Anarchism' in its original form.

[1] Ibid., p. 86.   [2] The letter is reproduced in Arnot, op. cit., pp. 85-7.
[3] Shaw, *Collected Letters: 1874–1897*, p. 177.

The moderate tones of these essays—by contrast with some of the vitriolic attacks he made on the non-Fabian Socialists a few years earlier—invites the speculation that his belligerence might have been restrained by 'Bloody Sunday'. The differences between Shaw and Morris now seemed less important than they had when the former wrote 'A Word for War'. As Morris's troubles within the Socialist League became greater, Shaw seems to have been less eager to spar with him. But the differences remained, and when the *Fabian Essays* appeared in print, Morris still had access to the columns of *The Commonweal*. Early in 1890, not quite a year before he broke with the League, the weary artist published a review of the *Essays*.[1]

This volume, Morris lamented, 'is hardly constructed to last longer than the coming into power of the next Liberal government'. It dealt only with matters of tentative or temporary interest. The basic principles and goals of Socialism, he felt, had been ignored. It was the response that might have been expected from one with anarchistic leanings, who wanted a complete and rapid transformation of society. Sidney Webb is treated as the offender and the unfortunate influence in this matter, because of his emphasis on the mechanism of reform, rather than its end.

Morris was badly mistaken about the durability of the *Fabian Essays*; they were still respected, living documents three-quarters of a century after the initial publication. But in his treatment of Shaw, he was almost prophetic:

. . . Mr. Shaw does not love opportunism for its own sweet self; for in his second lecture he definitely proclaims his shame of the course to which, as he thinks, circumstances have driven him; perhaps he only needs a little extra dose of Parliamentary tactics to disgust him so much as to force him to drop them altogether. Judging from the eloquence of the concluding part of his first paper, we can hardly suppose that that disgust will drive him into despair of the whole movement, and so deprive us of the services of one of the clearest heads and best pens that Socialism has got. As aforesaid, his criticism of the modern capitalist muddle is so damaging, his style so trenchant, and so full of reserves of indignation and righteous scorn, that I sometimes wonder that *guilty*, *i.e.* non-Socialist, middle-class people can sit and listen to him. If he could only forget the Sydney Webbian permeation tactic, even without putting any other in its place, what an advantage it would

<hr/>

[1] *The Commonweal*, Vol. 6 (25 January 1890), pp. 28–9.

be to all of us! He would encourage his friends thereby; and as to his enemies—could he offend them more than he does now?

Shaw's disillusionment with moderate Socialism was to come within a few years, but not quite as quickly as Morris's; the older man would not live to see his younger colleague's disenchantment with the Fabian ideal.

Morris's departure from the League and his softer attitudes towards theoretical and tactical questions after 1890 brought an end to his bickerings with Shaw. Their joint effort—together with Hyndman—to achieve Socialist unity in 1893 seems to have been rather frustrating for both, but not because their positions were as far apart as they had seemed to be in 1886. The two men were engaging in discussions on a wider range of subjects in the 1890s, 'reaching-out' to each other, as Stokes has so appropriately said, to enlarge their mutual appreciation of each other's works.[1] At times, Morris expressed his sense of futility to his younger colleague.

The Morris–Shaw correspondence in the British Museum includes one poignant letter written by Morris on 11 October 1894, about two years before his death. It is an example of the despair and resignation that enveloped the failing artist in his last years.

One last word as to the art (I beg pardon A R T) business. I cannot say that I see any hope for art catching on to modern (unregenerate) conditions of life, and even if we get out of our present muddle of stupidities into a demi-semi reasonable utilitarianism in something like a conceivable space of time, it will still take a long time (say 500 years) to develop any art out of it. Did you ever reflect on the extreme slow-ness with which events move since the Middle Ages. In the 60 years of my life e.g. nothing *essential* in public matters has happened except (if anything is to come out of it) the present talk about Socialism—think in contrast of 60 years in the Middle Ages—Albert Durer's life e.g. (50 years that was—worse luck!). . . .[2]

Written with a shaking clumsy hand, embodying the doubts that were so often expressed near the end of his life, this letter must have evoked Shaw's sympathy.

The culmination of Shaw's relationship with Morris came in

[1] Stokes, 'William Morris and Bernard Shaw: A Socialist-Artistic Relation-ship', op. cit., pp. 194–208.
[2] Brit. Mus. Add. MS 50541 (provisional category).

1895, when he wrote his famous counter-attack to Max Nordau's
Degeneration. This widely-circulated volume, written by a
Hungarian-born physician and erstwhile art-critic, had attacked
some of the modern art and artists that Shaw most admired—
including the music of Wagner, the drama of Ibsen, and the poetic
and visual creations of Morris and other pre-Raphaelites. Having
seen all these promising new artists assailed and dismissed by
Nordau as 'degenerates', Shaw responded to an invitation from
Benjamin Tucker, the editor of the New York anarchist newspaper
Liberty, to write a review, and the product was characteristically
Shavian. It was long, it was devastatingly satirical and insulting to
Nordau, and it constituted an elaborate counter-statement on
what art ought to be. It embraced, in large measure, a view of art
that Morris had been expounding in his lectures for nearly twenty
years, and it devoted much more space to a defence of Morris's
art than any attack from Nordau seemed to warrant.[1] This was an
enthusiastic eulogy, probably written in the expectation that
Morris had only a short time to live. Less than a year and a half
later, he was dead, and Shaw—then gaining fame as a drama critic
for the *Saturday Review*—wrote a tribute that was even more
laudatory than the one he had prepared for Stepniak a few months
earlier. Morris 'was a complete artist, who became great by a pre-
eminent sense of beauty', Shaw wrote, giving praise to his character,
his sensitivity, and his integrity, but little attention to his Socialism.[2]
He believed Morris could have created a Kelmscott Theatre
comparable to the remarkable Kelmscott Press had he chosen to
turn his energies in that direction. 'I feel nothing but elation when
I think of Morris,' Shaw wrote. 'My intercourse with him was so
satisfying that I should be the most ungrateful of men if I asked
for more. You can lose a man like that by your own death, but not
by his. And so, until then, let us rejoice in him.'[3]

For the remainder of his own long life, Shaw regretted that the
British Socialists of the 1880s and 1890s had not learned more

---

[1] The review was originally entitled 'A Degenerate's View of Nordau', and
was reprinted with revisions in 1908 as *The Sanity of Art*. It is most readily
available at present in Shaw, *Selected Non-Dramatic Writings of Bernard Shaw*,
op. cit., pp. 347–77. The special emphasis on Morris is well discussed in Stokes,
'William Morris and Bernard Shaw', op. cit., pp. 176–80.

[2] 'William Morris as Actor and Dramatist' in the *Saturday Review* of 10 October 1896, as reprinted in *The Collected Works of Bernard Shaw*, Vol. 24, p. 221.

[3] Ibid., p. 227.

from Morris; they admired him as a great man and used him as much as the controversies and his resources would allow, but they derived almost nothing from his aesthetic vision. 'Morris brought to the professed Socialists of the Leagues and Federations a conception of life which they never assimilated, and concerning which they could teach him nothing,' Shaw wrote about two years after Morris's death.[1] Part of Shaw's disappointment with the Fabian Society stemmed from the fact that its members were too 'Philistine' to publish some of the creative work of William Morris. In later years, when Shaw was at odds with his fellow Fabians or with members of the Labour movement, he would occasionally throw Morris's name at them, suggesting that he had been right after all in his abhorrence of conventional politics. In 1903, when he was still a member of the Fabian executive but had experienced many disappointments in the movement, he edited and reissued Morris's well-known 1893 essay 'Communism', which contained some admonitions for the Fabians. Shaw edited the manuscript slightly to improve some of the clumsy portions of Morris's language, and he made it clear that he was reviving the document because he had doubts about whether some Fabians really wanted the social revolution to be accomplished.[2] By 1930, when he wrote a Preface to the Fabian Essays for the third time and when his impatience with Fabian Socialism was even more acute, Shaw was correspondingly more respectful of the militant point of view that Morris had held for a relatively short time and that Shaw had then so vigorously opposed:

The distinctive mark of the Fabian Society among the rival bodies of Socialists with which it came in conflict in its early days, was its resolute constitutionalism. When the greatest Socialist of that day, the poet and craftsman William Morris, told the workers that there was no hope for them save in revolution, we said that if that were true there was no hope at all for them, and urged them to save themselves through Parliament, the municipalities, and the franchise. Without, perhaps, quite converting Morris, we convinced him that things would probably go our way. It is not so certain today as it seemed in the eighties that Morris was not right.[3]

[1] From a review in *The Daily Chronicle* of J. W. Mackail, *The Life of William Morris*, reprinted in Shaw's *Collected Works*, Vol. 29, p. 217.
[2] 'Communism' was issued as Fabian Tract No. 103.
[3] The Preface to the 1931 Reprint of the Fabian Essays is reproduced in *The*

When Shaw wrote his best-known tribute to his long-departed friend a few years later—'William Morris as I Knew Him'—he restated and enlarged upon some of his earlier compliments. He testified that Morris's stature had grown in his mind with the passing of the years, and although he acknowledged some of his old comrade's shortcomings, he obviously thought of him as the greatest innovator and creator of the era. He had written, in *Sigurd the Volsung*, 'the greatest epic since Homer', and he had led his contemporaries in many other fields. Shaw could, at this time, even find some redeeming qualities in the long, rambling prose romances that Morris had written and published for his own pleasure in the last years, but then by this time—in the middle 1930s—he was himself an old man and was writing plays that might be regarded as the dramatic equivalent of Morris's late literary efforts.

SHAW'S SOCIALISM IN THE 1890s

We have seen that the year 1890 marks an approximate turning-point in the Socialist hopes and expectations of the subjects of this study. Stepniak tried his hand at revolutionary creative writing, made his trip to America, and organized the *Free Russia* movement during or within a few months of this year. This is approximately the time that Kropotkin was reassessing the possibilities of an early and swift transformation of society and was elaborating the ideas expressed in *Mutual Aid*. Morris, as we have seen, became disenchanted and uncertain of himself and curtailed his own Socialist activities substantially after 1890, possibly having an important but delayed influence on the young Irishman who had become England's most loquacious Socialist propagandist.

On 28 July 1890, shortly after the publication of the *Fabian Essays*, Shaw wrote to a friend: 'My hours that make my days, my days that make my years, follow one another pell mell into the maw of Socialism; and I am left ageing and out of breath without a moment of rest for my tired soul.'[1] While this is a good summary of Shaw's preoccupation with Socialism at the end of the 1880s, he—like several of his contemporaries—changed directions in the next few years.

Collected Works, Vol. 30, *Essays in Fabian Socialism*, pp. 315–27. The quotation is at pp. 319–20.   [1] Shaw, *Collected Letters: 1874–1897*, p. 238.

In the British Museum's magnificent collection of Shaw papers there is evidence suggesting that Shaw was thinking of writing a history of the Socialist movement in about 1890.[1] There are twenty-four pages of rough notes in outline form showing that Shaw was interested in Lassalle and in Marx's activities in the First International. Some of the jottings also suggest interest in the English Socialists before 1870. The editor of the Fabian Essays may have been contemplating a work on the mid-century antecedents of the contemporary movement; it is impossible to determine the design or purpose he had in mind. But there are some hints about the conclusions he was reaching about the movement and its objectives. Social Democracy—a term he often used to indicate the entire Socialism movement—was 'far above the heads of the people'. The public had failed to grasp the simple economic demonstrations and a 'synthetic conception' of a social state. Women seem unable to free themselves from conventional social positions and morality. In short, the Socialist message appeared to be missing its target.

Little wonder that the energetic Shaw was seeking other media and other devices to attack bourgeois society in 1890. He was already established as a reviewer of London's music and of the fine arts, and now he turned to the drama, attracting substantial attention for the first time with his exegesis of the works of Henrik Ibsen. *The Quintessence of Ibsenism*, published first in 1891, originated as a series of lectures for the Fabian Society. Shaw's brilliant summary of Ibsen's dramatic message, emphasizing his repeated attacks on the ideals and illusions of society, was too esoteric for most of the 'Philistine' Fabians, but it was a premonition of Shaw's own career in dramatic literature, which began the following year.

Shaw's first three plays—the 'Unpleasant Plays'—were written before his disenchantment with Socialism was far advanced. *Widower's Houses* (1892), with its discussion of the exploitation of the poor by a capitalist landlord and the corruption of the middle-class youth by this process, and *Mrs. Warren's Profession* (1894), containing the famous frank consideration of prostitution, are the work of a man who was still dedicated to conventional Socialist propaganda. These plays are examples of Fabian permeation into the theatre. As Eric Bentley has demonstrated, while Socialism is

[1] Brit. Mus. Add. MS 50724.

not directly advocated in these plays, it is an 'unstated corollary'.[1] Shaw, like Ibsen, was attacking the morality and the illusions of contemporary society by portraying some of their ugly consequences. The other Unpleasant Play—*The Philanderer* (1893)—was another experiment in Ibsenian commentary on society without an implicit Socialist argument.

Shaw's fourth play, *Arms and the Man*, also owes little to his Socialism, but it embodies an attack on the existing social values from another direction. It is the earliest of the 'Pleasant Plays', and it seeks to puncture the illusions of patriotism, military heroism, and romantic love by the weapon of ridicule. The interesting point about this work in the present context is Shaw's debt to Stepniak. The energetic Russian may have contributed more than he intended and more than he realized to the play; Shaw might well have used more than Stepniak's testimony about Bulgarian customs. The role of Sergius Saranoff, the comical patriot-idealist, was presumably suggested to Shaw by the attitudes and adventures of R. B. Cunninghame Graham, the Radical M.P. and inveterate adventurer. At least Shaw reported later that this was the case. But it may not be coincidental that the name of Sergius Saranoff is almost an echo of that of Sergei Stepniak, and that the stage figure—like the flesh-and-blood Russian—found his own initial, super-romantic position somewhat unrealistic in the workaday world. It is odd, if Shaw did draw part of his portrait from Stepniak or from his reputation, that he did not make reference to the fact. But Saranoff may well have been inspired by several sources in addition to Cunninghame Graham, and Shaw's respect for Stepniak may have caused him to avoid identifying the Russian with the ridicule that the play directed towards Saranoff.

In any case, Shaw had little enthusiasm for the liberal-nationalist revolutionary zeal that Stepniak represented. He took no substantial interest in the Irish Home Rule agitation, for example. The social protest movement had evolved beyond the liberal or radical stage in Britain, and the older forms were being superseded by Socialism. And that Socialism itself was evolving Shaw observed in his next play.

Candida, written late in the same year as *Arms and the Man*, is the only one of the 'Pleasant Plays' in which Socialism is con-

[1] Eric Bentley, *Bernard Shaw*, p. 104.

sidered directly, and the variety under consideration receives rather devastating treatment. The Socialism of the Reverend James Morell is so tame and respectable that it is an object of ridicule, and Morell is weak enough to be humiliated by both a boyish poet and his wife. Shaw's play gives little quarter to the polite Christian Socialism that Morell represents.

Yet there is an aspect of this treatment to which Shaw draws attention in the Preface to the 'Pleasant Plays'. It is interesting that relatively few students of Shaw have taken advantage of a clue that was offered them in the Preface when they have analysed *Candida*. The Preface is characteristically wordy and in places obtuse, but Shaw weaves in some statements that anticipate many of his later positions on evolution and human creativity.

It does not fulfil the mission of a good playwright, Shaw says, simply to write of 'Christian Socialism' in its prosaic struggle against 'vulgar Unsocialism'. To be worthy of 'quintessential drama'—that is, obviously, drama like Ibsen's that seeks to attack the illusions of society— '. . . it must be shewn at its best in conflict with the first broken, nervous, stumbling attempts to formulate its own revolt against itself as it develops into something higher'.[1] Part of Shaw's purpose was to portray a form of Socialism that was out-of-date, superseded by impulses that represent a higher achievement in the evolutionary struggle. Morell, then, is a study in the evolution of Socialism as well as being a revelation of the weaknesses of one *genre* of it.

Shaw had been as much influenced by Darwin—or perhaps Lamarck—as anyone writing for the London stage in this period, and he recognized clearly that Socialism itself was subject to the process of evolution. Like the youthful artist who wins the intellectual victory over Reverend Morell, Shaw was possessed of insights that could not be gratified or explored within the Socialist format of his day. Although *Candida* did not deal with Fabian Socialism, the message of the play is as applicable to the Fabians as to the Christian Socialists whom Shaw has tried to portray.

The two later 'Pleasant Plays' tell us little of changes coming in Shaw's Socialism. *The Man of Destiny* (1895) did experiment with another hero—in this case the young Napoleon—shown in an unheroic context, but Shaw dismissed it in his 1898 preface as 'hardly more than a bravura piece to display the virtuosity of the

[1] Shaw, *Collected Works*, VIII, p. ix.

two principal performers'.[1] *You Never Can Tell* (1896) has nothing to offer to a study of Socialism; Shaw himself dismissed it as one of his 'potboilers' in later years. By this time, the budding dramatist was thoroughly fascinated by the theatre for its own sake and for its wider social potential, and he was experimenting with his newly-revealed talent. He was one of London's outstanding dramatic critics, and he was trying to reform the theatre by assaulting its favourite illusions and by introducing an unconventional ethic.

The first well-developed product of this attitude was his play of 1896, *The Devil's Disciple*. Dick Dudgeon, an advocate of the 'diabolonian ethics', is an evil man by the standards of society. As an apologist for Satan's cause against the ecclesiastical and political establishment of colonial New England, he should be the villain of the melodrama, but when he is mistaken for a clergyman and is about to be hanged as a traitor, he will not reveal his true identity in order to save himself. And Shaw took unusual pains to show that it is not conventional romance or love for the clergyman's fair lady that prompts this noble decision. It is simply a revolutionary impulse, and perhaps the sense that he is sacrificing his life 'for the world's future', that explains his action.[2] Dudgeon is the hero of the play not because of any conventional virtues but because he is a heretic, and his conduct inspires the conversion of the clergyman whom he had tried to save to the revolutionary cause.

The play, in short, is an experiment with the kind of ethical reasoning that Stepniak had described in his books of the 1880s, and it is similar to that new morality that Kropotkin and Bax, among others, had tried to define a few years earlier. Shaw, of course, as a disciple of Ibsen, tried to produce a hero who is free of the romantic illusions, so the result is less sentimental. He had written a dramatic piece that, while not specifically a Socialist play, shared the evolving ethics of the Socialist movement as well as the anti-idealism of Ibsenism and the 'hackneyed' tricks of British melodrama.

Meanwhile he continued to put his many observations on

---

[1] Shaw, *Collected Works*, VIII, p. xi.

[2] Archibald Henderson, *George Bernard Shaw: Man of the Century*, pp. 551–552, notes that this line was not in the original version of the play, but was inserted later, probably at the suggestion of an actor.

Socialism into essay form. Even as he was writing *The Devil's Disciple* in the autumn of 1896, a New York periodical published one of his offerings that carried the suggestive title 'The Illusions of Socialism'.[1]

Shaw regarded this as one of his best essays on Socialism, but it has been given scant attention by biographers and scholars, presumably because it has not been widely available until recently. It is not one of his typical, sarcastic, destructive essays; on the contrary, it is unusually solemn for a work of Shaw, neither burdened nor brightened frequently by his usual wit and cynicism. It is primarily aimed at the Marxists, whose assumptions about their own scientific pre-eminence and moral superiority constitute some of the illusions that Shaw had in mind. On one level, the essay is an argument for Fabian policies as opposed to the dogmatic and idealistic variations of the so-called scientific socialists. Parenthetically, he also touched on the illusions of the philosophical anarchists.

All men and organizations are influenced by illusions; some are necessary to encourage men to action. But some illusions are foolish and destructive; for example, the assumption by some Socialists that they are morally superior to their foes. Some enthusiasm and passion are elementary, but Shaw obviously had little stomach for the fervour and theatrical enthusiasm that most of the revolutionary writers—including Stepniak, Kropotkin, and Morris—had described:

What incidents are to a drama, persecutions and salvational regenerations are to a religion. Accordingly we have, in the religious illusion of Socialism, a profuse exploitation of the calamities of martyrs exiled, imprisoned, and brought to the scaffold for 'The Cause'; and we are told of the personal change, the transfigured, lighted-up face, the sudden accession of self-respect, the joyful self-sacrifice, the new eloquence and earnestness of the young working man who has been rescued from a purposeless, automatic loafing through life, by the call of the gospel of Socialism.[2]

---

[1] Initial publication was in *The Home Journal*, 21 and 28 October 1896, but it did not get into print in England until the next year in Edward Carpenter's *Forecasts of the Coming Century by a Decade of Writers* (Manchester, 1897), pp. 141–73. It has recently been reprinted in Laurence, *Selected Non-Dramatic Writings*, pp. 406–26.

[2] Shaw, in Carpenter, op. cit., pp. 157–8; in *Selected Non-Dramatic Essays*, p. 416.

Shaw was as cool towards this kind of romantic Socialism as he was towards typical melodrama, and it is interesting that he produced this essay during the same season that he was writing *The Devil's Disciple*. There was a large body of work that qualified for this generalization: he must have thought of such examples as Morris's *Pilgrims of Hope* and Stepniak's volumes as he wrote these lines. But he was primarily concerned with those dreamers, such as some Marxists and anarchists, who had 'Calvinist' illusions about the objectives and the procedures of Socialism. And he contrasted with these the calm, sane expectations of the Fabians.

Yet Shaw recognized that each branch of the Socialist movement regarded itself as most realistic and scientific, while considering its rivals confused, and he acknowledged that Fabianism itself was not free from illusions. It is a matter of opinion whether the Fabians are more scientific and hard-headed than their rivals. Shaw's opinion is clear; he still pronounced the Fabian message with conviction and insisted that social change would come gradually and unevenly. He was still devoted to democracy and to the principle of permeation, and he saw the boundary between the moderate Socialists and the liberals or progressives as an unclear one.

There was yet another article written in the same vein during that same season, prompted by the congress of the International that was held in London that summer. Published under the title 'Socialism at the International Congress', it gave Shaw another occasion to comment on some of the fantasies and myths of the movement. His special targets on this occasion were Hyndman and the German militant Wilhelm Liebknecht, whom he believed had showed themselves to be hypnotized by their Marxian dreams. Political accomplishments, he argued, would always lag behind the imaginations of the Socialists, and it was only reasonable to anticipate this:

... in order to bring a social movement to a fruitful issue, it is necessary to propose—and to propose with entire conviction—ten impossible results for every one possible one. Christianity had to propose a communist millenium to secure the feudalism of the Middle Ages; the Reformation had to propose Anarchism to clear the ground for modern individualist Capitalism; ... And, no doubt, as realised Christianity is to the Christianity of the Gospels and of Tolstoi, so will realised Socialism be to 'the New Moral World' of Robert Owen.[1]

It followed for Shaw that while such dreams had their place in the Socialist movement, they were only dreams and they should not dictate tactical policy. The English Fabians and the German Social Democrats were making progress step by step, and they should recognize that this had to be so. He disapproved of the fact that the German Social Democrats, who were regularly gaining strength at the polls and winning concessions from their government, continued to cling to their militant positions:

Unfortunately, they are still dominated by the old revolutionary tradition; and instead of assuring the normal world that they have come to their senses, they nervously reassure the revolutionary sects that they are as mad as ever. Liebknecht still covers every compromise by a declaration that the Social-Democrats never compromise: . . .[2]

At the conclusion of his article, the enterprising playwright who was just then experimenting with melodrama, offered an analogy from his current experience:

In nothing is the middle-class origin of the Socialist movement so apparent as in the persistent delusions of Socialists as to an ideal proletariat, forced by the brutalities of the capitalist into an unwilling acquiescence in war, penal codes, and other cruelties of civilisation. They still see the social problem, not sanely and objectively, but imaginatively, as the plot of a melodrama, with its villain and its heroine, its innocent beginning, troubled middle, and happy ending. They are still the children and romancers of politics.[3]

Thus Shaw brought new arguments into use in his continuing quarrel with the Marxists. Meanwhile, elsewhere in London, one of the leading German Social Democrats, having reached the same conclusion from a different observation point, was about to shock his colleagues with the same kind of arguments, which they came to call 'revisionism'.

[1] George Bernard Shaw, 'Socialism at the International Congress', *Cosmopolis*, III, September 1896, p. 659.
[2] Ibid., p. 667.
[3] Ibid., p. 673.

VI

BERNSTEIN

From Radicalism to Revisionism

MOST biographers and analysts of the work of Eduard Bernstein argue—contrary to Bernstein's own assertion—that the famous German Revisionist owed a heavy intellectual debt to Fabianism. It is customary to point to a letter that Eleanor Marx-Aveling wrote to Kautsky in 1898 calling attention to the possibility that the Fabians would use Bernstein for their own purposes, or to other later statements, largely from English Fabians, who claimed Bernstein as one of their disciples. Bernstein, not a man to deny his intellectual debts, continuously insisted in his later years that this was not the case. 'The opinion which has gained wide currency that I was converted to my Revisionism by the model of English Fabianism is wholly erroneous,' he wrote in 1924.[1]

Bernstein's statement is pertinent; it invites examination of other possible sources of his heretical views on Socialism. It is generally accepted that Bernstein did not have much contact with English Socialists before the death of Engels in 1895, and by that time his challenging ideas had taken shape and were soon to emerge in print. In his reminiscences, he indicated that he had little occasion to meet Englishmen or to learn about their country during his early visits in 1880, 1884, and 1887. On those occasions, he had been primarily involved with technical conversations with Engels (and in 1880 with the ailing Marx). Although his third visit coincided with events of 'Bloody Sunday', he had no real opportunity to learn about English Socialism first-hand. During this visit, he recalled, he had become acquainted with Hyndman— with whom his relations were never cordial—and with 'the magnificent William Morris'.[2]

---

[1] Eduard Bernstein, 'Entwicklungsgang eines Sozialisten', op. cit., p. 23.
[2] Eduard Bernstein, *Aus den Jahren meines Exils*, p. 185; *My Years of Exile*, p. 171.

After he moved from Switzerland to England in 1888, it was some time before he met many Englishmen, and there is no evidence that the Fabians had any primary claim to his attention. The Englishmen whom he came to know best in his early years came to the home of Engels—Edward Aveling, Eleanor Marx, and the ubiquitous Ernest Belfort Bax, whose acquaintance he had already made in Zurich in 1876. Later, he was invited to speak before Fabian meetings and the Hammersmith Socialist Society, but his work on behalf of the German Social Democratic cause kept him away from most of the activities of these groups during his early years in London. He met Shaw at the British Museum on occasion; his disbelief in the theory of the class struggle and his low opinion of the proletariat made an impression on the German exile, but he was not favourably disposed towards Fabian ideas during his first London years.

Bernstein was a receptive person, and there was much in the London intellectual climate that could contribute to a non-doctrinaire point of view. Bernstein had neither the training in Hegelian reasoning nor the rigid commitment to ideology that were so important to some of his fellow-Marxists. He was open-minded enough to take pleasure in attending the National Liberal Club, where he could meet members of the respectable middle-class society—many of them reformers of a different kind. He also met Socialists of various shades at the Socialist Supper Club, which gathered each fortnight in some private room, often in and around Soho. He met and respected some of the leading Christian Socialists of the time, including the Reverend Stewart Headlam, the Reverend Thomas Hancock, and the Reverend William Morris. He admired many British periodicals, the English language, and the English workingman's practical, utilitarian point of view. He liked the English spirit of compromise and toleration. Some of these features, of course, were embodied in Fabianism, but Fabianism was only one segment of the English scene, and not the one which he admired most. He was like Stepniak, Kropotkin, and Shaw in rejoicing in the unusual intellectual opportunities that London offered. Although he was not at large in the city to the same extent as these men were, Bernstein had the same peripatetic instincts. He did not ignore the groups that were criticizing the Marxists; there is a letter in the archives of the International Institute of Social History in Amsterdam written by—or at least on behalf of—Bernstein to the Socialist League in October 1888, asking that his copy of *The Commonweal* now be sent to him at his London address, rather than to Zurich, and requesting several back numbers.[1] It can be inferred from this that Bernstein had been reading the paper earlier and that he was trying to keep abreast of developments in Morris's group, and perhaps in other organizations. On the other hand, Bernstein found himself sharply criticized by Hyndman in the pages of *Justice* within a few months of his arrival in London,[2] and after that his relations with the Social Democratic Federation were never very cordial.

BERNSTEIN'S HISTORICAL VENTURES

Bernstein continued to give most of his political and journalistic talent to the party during his years in London, even though the expiration of the anti-Socialist legislation in 1890 removed the need for the publication of the *Sozialdemokrat* in exile. He wrote often for *Die Neue Zeit* and other Socialist journals, and, from 1890 onwards, his time was increasingly devoted to historical research and writing related to the background of the Socialist movement, and this took him regularly to that most-cosmopolitan of libraries—the Reading Room of the British Museum.

His first significant task was the collecting and editing of the works of an old Socialist enemy of the Marxists—Ferdinand Lassalle.[3] Published in 1892–3 in three volumes, this set of writings provided an occasion for Bernstein to think of other approaches to the social problem than that offered by the masters of Marxism. Bernstein reacted unfavourably to Lassalle's basic approach and wrote a critical introduction to the works in 1891, showing that he disapproved of the dictatorial methods and attitudes that Lassalle had embraced in his later years, and he objected to Lassalle's willingness to co-operate with Bismarck as a means of attaining his objectives. Bernstein believed Lassalle's economic

---

[1] Socialist League Correspondents, 1837, International Institute of Social History Collection, Amsterdam. The letter was written in English in the name of the German Publishing Co. (E. Bernstein), publishers of the *Sozialdemokrat*. It may have been his editorial duties that prompted such interest.

[2] *Justice*, VI (June 15 1889), p. 3.

[3] Ferdinand Lassalle, *Ferd. Lassalle's Reden und Schriften*: Neue Gesammt-Ausgabe. Mit einer biographischen Einleitung herausgegeben von Ed. Bernstein. 3 vols. (Berlin, 1892–93).

theories to be out of date and his nationalism to be too intense. But there were ideas in Lassalle, such as the advocacy of universal suffrage and the independence of ethical systems from economic conditions, that Bernstein would eventually share.[1] Bernstein admired Lassalle's enthusiasm and gave him credit for having performed an important service in giving the German labouring class a political consciousness and a social programme. His writings had a great 'missionary effect', Bernstein acknowledged, suggesting perhaps he had been aroused and convinced in ways that he had not expected.[2]

This editorial project brought Bernstein early attention not only among his fellow Social Democrats for whom it was prepared, but also in England. During the next two or three years, they were extensively used by the young Bertrand Russell, who made a study of the German Socialists that resulted in a series of lectures at the London School of Economics. These lectures were assembled and published as Russell's first book in 1896, and the section dealing with Lassalle borrowed heavily from Bernstein's work.[3] Russell at this point was still expressing the views of an 'orthodox Liberal', and his critique of Marxism was harsh, although his respect for Social Democracy as a social movement was obvious. Russell drew conclusions from his examination of German Social Democracy that the most important parts of the programme were the demands for political democracy and economic collectivism, and he saw much promise for the movement if it could abandon some of its Marxian rigidity and rely upon liberal political procedures. In short, he anticipated the 'revisionist' arguments of Bernstein on several important points, and his observations obviously did not remain unnoticed by the studious Bernstein.

After finishing this work, Bernstein turned to another, more challenging project, again drawing on the resources of the British Museum. He undertook a study of the English revolutions during the time of the Stuart kings. He apparently turned to the seventeenth century because of his interest in British institutions and

---

[1] For an excellent brief summary of Bernstein's relationship to Lassalle's thought, see Gay, op. cit., pp. 77–83. For Bernstein's revised attitude towards Lassalle more than a decade later, see Eduard Bernstein, *Ferdinand Lassalle und seine Bedeutung für die Arbeiterklasse* (Berlin, 1904).

[2] Lassalle, *Reden und Schriften*, Vol. I, pp. 182–5.

[3] Bertrand Russell, *German Social Democracy* (London, 1896; New York, 1965), pp. 41–68.

because that period seemed to offer inviting topics for Marxian analysis. The Marxist interpretation runs through the whole study, but this is not the most interesting feature of the book. It is evident that Bernstein developed an intellectual admiration for some of the people whom he discovered, and he treated them and their ideas with a scholarly affection that went beyond the typical class-struggle analysis.[1]

He took special interest in some of the revolutionaries who had been either harshly treated or completely ignored by previous historians of the revolutions. He has received praise from professional historians for pointing out the importance of Gerrard Winstanley, the spokesman for the lower-class Diggers. Bernstein summarized and analysed the grievances that Winstanley called to the attention of Cromwell during the period of the Commonwealth. He examined the liberal-republican suggestions of Pieter Cornelius Plockboy, the Netherlander who wrote pamphlets for the movement shortly before the Restoration. He praised the Levellers and the Quakers, and he commented on the seventeenth-century contributions to nineteenth-century English Socialism.

He reserved his highest praise for John Bellers, the prolific Quaker whose contribution to the literature of the English Revolutions had come rather late, beginning only in 1695. Marx and Engels had previously mentioned him in *Das Kapital* and Bernstein followed their lead in examining his work, but he found there much more to appreciate. Bellers had advocated 'Colleges of Industry' or 'Civil Fellowship' Communes, an international confederation of nations with peacekeeping responsibilities, a reform of hospital and penal facilities, and plans for discouraging corruption of members of parliament. He also sought the moral elevation of the poorer classes.

Each of these men, as Bernstein represented them, had been seeking reform within the existing political framework and the changes that each proposed could be achieved by peaceful means. It is suggestive of Bernstein's personal tastes—and this foreshadows his Revisionism—that these moderate advocates of reform appear in a better light than the more militant John

---

[1] The main German edition appeared under the title *Sozialismus und Demokratie in der grossen englischen Revolution* (Stuttgart, 1908). The English language translation is *Cromwell and Communism: Socialism and Democracy in the Great English Revolution* (London, 1930, reprinted, New York, 1963).

Lilburne. Bernstein saw that the reformers eventually sought not to destroy the state but to make it the instrument for advancing the welfare of all. Just as the attitude of the English revolutionaries towards the state had matured, culminating in the refined ideas of Bellers, so Bernstein undoubtedly recognized his own ideas undergoing transition. 'In 1648 and 1649,' he wrote, 'it was possible to believe in the feasibility of a democratic revolution, inasmuch as the democratic sections of the nation were then under arms; but in 1688 or 1695 such an expectation was clearly an illusion.'[1] Likewise, the conditions that had made Bernstein an uncompromising radical in his days as editor of the illegal *Sozial-demokrat* in the 1880s no longer existed in the 1890s. The comparison is not explicit, but it is obvious that Bernstein had thought a good deal about the change in tactics that had occurred among the subjects of his study as the revolutionary movement matured.[2]

So there is internal evidence that his studies of English revolutionary history contributed to his tendency towards evolutionary socialism. The examination of the comparative utopian schemes of the seventeenth century and of the evolution of those schemes made him less disposed to regard any single formula or dogma as a final gospel. Socialism got a good history from Bernstein's studies of the English revolutions, but it also got a man who had developed a taste for heresy.

THE FRUITION OF 'EVOLUTIONARY SOCIALISM'

The years of Bernstein's work on Lassalle and on the English revolutionaries coincided with the period of his closest collaboration with Engels. It was during these years, also, that his friendships with such people as Bax and Stepniak flourished, partly because the home of Engels was open to all of them. It is probable that the social gatherings at the Engels residence on Sunday nights gave Bernstein an opportunity to comment on and to test some

---

[1] Bernstein, *Sozialismus und Demokratie*, p. 365; *Cromwell and Communism*, p. 282.

[2] Bernstein kept his interest in Bellers for many years, and on 12 October 1918, when Germany was on the verge of defeat in the First World War and the prospect of a league of nations was being widely discussed, Bernstein delivered a paper in which he referred favourably to Bellers's suggestions on the subject. Eduard Bernstein, *Völkerbund oder Staatenbund: Eine Untersuchung* (Berlin, 1919).

of his emerging ideas on Socialism, and to hear the conclusions of his colleagues. Bernstein remained sufficiently orthodox, however, to retain the respect of Engels, who designated him and Bebel as trustees of his literary remains.

Bernstein had become increasingly troubled by the Marxian message as he became more familiar with it. Like many other thoughtful students, he had observed some serious problems in the Marxian arguments as developed in the first two volumes of *Das Kapital*, and he had awaited the completion of the third volume with interest. When Engels issued it in 1894, having worked on it with great dedication for several years, Bernstein was among the first to recognize the gaps and inconsistencies in the arguments. He felt a sense of disappointment when the work was completed.[1]

Marx's predictions that capitalism would become increasingly centralized and that the proletariat would become increasingly impoverished were obviously not being fulfilled in the mid-1890s. Increased prosperity—especially in Germany—had been shared by the proletariat, and the class struggle had become less violent rather than more intense. It seemed unrealistic to expect catastrophic change in the near future, and both the historical English example and the contemporary German Social Democratic experience suggested an evolutionary transition. At the time of Engels' death in 1895, and when Bernstein spoke at Stepniak's funeral a few months later, praising his dead friend for his willingness to break with tradition, he was himself already in the process of changing his position.

The series of articles that advanced his 'Revisionist' ideas was called 'Problème des Sozialismus'. It appeared in the pages of *Die Neue Zeit* in 1896 and 1897, and within a short time the international Social Democracy was engaged in one of its most famous controversies. Vera Zasulich, whom Bernstein had met occasionally at the Engels' home, had alerted Georgi Plekhanov in Geneva, and he was one of the first to denounce the deviation. Rosa Luxemburg, the brilliant and passionate voice of left-wing Social Democracy for Germany and Poland, was among the earliest of his fellow party-workers to denounce him. Even while Bernstein was still in exile—he remained in England until 1901—his ideas provoked bitter debates as Kautsky published them and as party

[1] Eduard Bernstein, 'Entwicklungsgang eines Sozialisten', op. cit., p. 22.

congresses discussed them in Germany. As the conflict became more intense and emotional, Bernstein became even more heretical under attack, and with surprising frequency his arguments paralleled those of some of his colleagues in England—including the anarchists.

In October of 1898, Bernstein transmitted to the party congress in Stuttgart a letter that eventually went into his classic work on Revisionism. The letter might well have been a paraphrase of some of the previously-cited statements in *Fabian Essays:*

I have at no time had an excessive interest in the future, beyond general principles; I have not been able to read to the end any picture of the future. My thoughts and efforts are concerned with the duties of the present and the nearest future, and I only busy myself with the perspectives beyond so far as they give me a line of conduct for suitable action now.[1]

Such an announcement, of course, gave support to the conclusion that Bernstein had indeed become a Fabian in tactics, and it has often been cited by those seeking to define or to argue against Bernstein's position. He was actually much more willing to speculate about the future of Socialism than his critics acknowledged, often talking about the 'general principles' in terms that defined his expectations. *Die Voraussetzungen des Sozialismus und die Aufgaben der Sozialdemokratie* is not only an exegesis of Marxian doctrinal errors but also a definition of the ideals that Bernstein felt should guide the movement.

About half way through the book, Bernstein attempted a definition of Socialism. It is, he said

... a movement towards—or the state of—an order of society based on the principle of association (genossenschaftlichen Gesellschaftsordnung). In this sense, which also corresponds with the etymology of the word (*socius*—a partner), the word is used in what follows.[2]

Like most beginning definitions of an abstract term, this one is broad and vague, and it reveals little without the elucidation that

---

[1] Eduard Bernstein, *Die Voraussetzungen des Sozialismus und die Aufgaben der Sozialdemokratie* (Stuttgart, 1899), p. VIII. In the English language translation, *Evolutionary Socialism: A Criticism and Affirmation*, translated by Edith C. Harvey (London: 1909; reissued New York, 1963), p. xxix. One must be cautious in using the English translation, since some sections of the German original are omitted.

[2] Bernstein, *Voraussetzungen*, p. 84; *Evolutionary Socialism*, p. 96.

follows. But it is worthy of note that at this point, we are not preoccupied with economic factors or material conditions of life. Bernstein soon considered those aspects of the social relationship, but he began with cordial social relationships as the basis of society.

For Bernstein, such a principle of association did not mean a dictatorship. On the contrary, a harmonious social association or partnership worked best where the principles of democracy were applied. His concept of democracy embraced the theme of Mill's *On Liberty* relative to minority rights within a political system where majority rule prevails.

To-day we find the oppression of the minority by the majority 'undemocratic,' although it was originally held to be quite consistent with government by the people. The idea of democracy includes, in the conception of the present day, a notion of justice—an equality of rights for all members of the community, and in that principle the rule of the majority, to which in every concrete case the rule of the people extends, finds its limits. The more it is adopted and governs the general consciousness, the more will democracy be equal in meaning to the highest possible degree of freedom for all.[1]

And democracy also means universal suffrage, Bernstein argued; this is the political alternative to violent change. It is only a part of the social partnership, but once implemented, it tends to draw other parts after it.

In good Marxian fashion, Bernstein looked askance at utopian communal experiments, and he recognized the limited value of co-operative associations exclusively for purposes of production. But, in much the same way as Kropotkin, he was interested in the potentialities of the co-operative associations that he saw functioning in Britain. The kind of association that he admired and conceived should have a comprehensive programme, but violence was not part of it. Those Socialists who anticipated the immediate seizure of power by means of a civil war had not demonstrated to his satisfaction that co-operation among the various segments of society could be established soon after the destruction of the old system of ownership. On the contrary, the historical record suggested to Bernstein that disruption of the economy and failure of social co-operation was likely to follow a period of violence.

---

[1] Bernstein, *Voraussetzungen*, p. 123; *Evolutionary Socialism*, pp. 142–3.

This he saw as an important reason for abandoning the programme of violence that was assumed in the first part of the Erfurt programme.

In this, of course, Bernstein was a long way from the position of the Communist Anarchists, but he reached other conclusions that are strikingly similar to those that had been expressed by Kropotkin. He hoped that as society evolved towards the Socialism of his preference, small and medium-sized industrial and agricultural organizations would become most important, rather than the centralized, monopolistic economic units that Marx had anticipated as society moved through the capitalist phase towards Socialism. A 'differentiation' in capital and labour—new classes and types of plants and producers—was appearing and increasing both the possibilities and the conditions under which men laboured. Municipalities were becoming increasingly active in assuming political responsibility, and in productive roles. Bernstein's hopes and observations here coincided with both those of the Fabians of the 1890s and those of Kropotkin in *Fields, Factories and Workshops*, and they complemented those of Stepniak's later non-fiction works. All expected to see the smaller social and economic units flourish as society assumed its new form. Bernstein's Social Democratic colleagues, of course, noticed most quickly the resemblances to Fabianism, which were obvious because Fabianism was most widely publicized in Great Britain.

Doctrinaire Marxists were highly shocked by the whole thrust of Bernstein's thought as expressed in *Die Voraussetzungen*; especially offensive was his moderate attitude towards liberalism. To the extent that liberalism is a defensive weapon of the capitalists, Bernstein said, it must be opposed. But as an historical movement it was the ancestor of Socialism and there were features of the liberal tradition that should be preserved. The rights and freedoms that had been won from autocratic governments constitute one part of the beneficial legacy of the movement. Another part, in Bernstein's view, was the concept of individual economic responsibility to society.

Although Bernstein stated the argument somewhat differently, he approached the basic question to which many Socialists addressed themselves: how was society to be assured that individuals would accept personal responsibility for performing social duties once the capitalist system of organization and property had been removed? In grappling with this problem, Bernstein went further in his speculations than most of the utilitarian-minded Fabians, and he wandered, almost in spite of himself, into the field of ethics. He did not possess the expansive optimism of Kropotkin, Morris, or Stepniak, but he had to assume, with them, that there would emerge a new sense of individual responsibility to society. Bernstein partially embraced the ideas of the Manchester School and in places he echoed liberal sentiments:

. . . . Without responsibility there is no freedom; we may think as we like theoretically about man's freedom of action, we must practically start from it as the foundation of the moral law, for only under this condition is social morality possible. And similarly, in our states which reckon with millions, a healthy social life is, in the age of traffic, impossible if the economic personal responsibility of all those capable of work is not assumed. The recognition of individual responsibility is the return of the individual to society for services rendered or offered him by society.[1]

But he quickly went beyond into a zone where he was not far from the Communist Anarchists. This individual responsibility is not to be enforced by an oppressive bureaucracy, but by locally arranged units. Bernstein knew he was moving through a thicket and the path was not clear, but the general objective emerges:

Socialism will create no new bondage of any kind whatever. The individual is to be free, not in the metaphysical sense, as the anarchists dreamed—*i.e.*, free from all duties towards the community—but free from every economic compulsion in his action and choice of a calling. Such freedom is only possible for all by means of organisation. In this sense one might call socialism 'organising liberalism', for when one examines more closely the organisations that socialism wants and how it wants them, he will find that what distinguishes them above all from the feudalistic organisations, outwardly like them, is just their liberalism, their democratic constitution, their accessibility.[2]

The dismissal of the anarchists was standard liberalism and standard Marxism, but obviously he had in mind the individualist anarchists when he referred to their lack of responsibility to the community. When he spoke of 'organising liberalism' he meant 'an

---

[1] Bernstein, *Voraussetzungen*, pp. 130–1; *Evolutionary Socialism*, p. 151.
[2] Bernstein, *Voraussetzungen*, p. 132; *Evolutionary Socialism*, pp. 153–4.

elaborately organised self-government with a corresponding economic, personal responsibility of all the units of administration as well as of the adult citizens of the state'.[1]

This is vague enough to allow several interpretations, and reference to the original German-language text does little to lift the fog, but against the background of other statements which precede and follow, Bernstein is proposing something like the locally-oriented and voluntary units of the anarchists, perhaps hardly more 'organized' than Kropotkin would have tolerated.

The comparison is worth pursuing, because Bernstein's text specifically invites it. He showed that Marx, in *The Civil War in France*, had moved away from the rigid position expressed in *The Communist Manifesto* and had recommended a programme bearing 'the greatest similarity to the federalism of Proudhon'.[2] And Bernstein proceeded to quote at length some of the federalist ideas of the famous French anarchist, having legitimatized his position by comparing it favourably with Marx on the question of municipal or communal self-government. His remarks about the 'principle of association', then, contained some elements that carried him towards the position of Kropotkin.

Bernstein was not ready to admit that central authority could be dismissed soon, of course, because he saw too many social and economic operations that were beyond the scope of the locally-oriented bodies. Yet he expected local authority to grow and the role of the national assemblies and bureaucracies to decline as society evolved towards Socialism.

Even as he made these predictions, he insisted that he was not trying to anticipate the form of the future society. He said that he was talking only about the tendencies—the necessary democratic spirit—that would guide society towards its future goal.

THE QUESTION OF ETHICS

Almost in spite of himself, Bernstein became involved in a complex and protracted debate on the subject of ethics, a topic that had attracted so many of his Socialist contemporaries. He invited some of the trouble, to be sure, by challenging in the

---

[1] Bernstein, *Voraussetzungen*, p. 133; *Evolutionary Socialism*, p. 155.
[2] Bernstein, *Voraussetzungen*, p. 134; *Evolutionary Socialism*, p. 156.

earliest pages of the *Voraussetzungen* the validity of economic determinism in the realm of ideology:

Modern society is much richer than earlier societies in ideologies which are not determined by economics and by nature working as an economic force. Sciences, arts, a whole series of social relations are to-day less dependent on economics than formerly, or, in order to give no room for misconception, the point of economic development attained to-day leaves the ideological, and especially the ethical, factors greater space for independent activity than was formerly the case. In consequence of this the inter-dependency of cause and effect between technical, economic evolution, and the evolution of other social tendencies is becoming always more indirect, and from that the necessities of the first are losing much of their power of dictating the form of the latter.[1]

This, of course, was heretical enough to annoy the orthodox Social Democrats, but Bernstein compounded the offence by appealing to Kant rather than Hegel during the debate over revisionism.

Bernstein had been mildly interested in and opposed to Kantian thought as a young Marxist, but he had no background in systematic philosophy. What started the controversy was one of his statements in *Die Neue Zeit* to the effect that Socialists could learn something from Kant's questioning, critical method.

As Peter Gay has carefully demonstrated, Bernstein's suggestion that Social Democrats turn 'back to Kant' was not directly related to the question of ethics.[2] When he suggested, at the end of *Voraussetzungen*, that the critical spirit of Kant would be more healthy than the repetitive 'cant' based on a Hegelian formula, he was not thinking about the categorical imperative or other abstractions. He never became a follower of Kant's teachings in a formal sense and he did not have a clear understanding of Kant's theory of knowledge. 'He called on Kant,' Gay concludes, 'but he remained a common-sense philosopher.'[3]

It may have been Bax, as much as anyone else, who suggested the line of argument that Bernstein eventually adopted on ethics. Having often seen Bax at the home of Engels, Bernstein may even have heard the two men argue about whether ethical ideas must necessarily be rooted in material conditions of life. And Bax had written an essay in the 1880s that Bernstein may have known about when he responded to his critics in the *Voraussetzungen*. The essay

---

[1] Bernstein, *Voraussetzungen*, pp. 10–11; *Evolutionary Socialism*, pp. 15–16.
[2] Gay, *The Dilemma of Democratic Socialism*, pp. 141–51.   [3] Ibid., p. 151.

carried the title 'On Some Forms of Modern Cant. A Contribution to the Phenomenology of Cant', and it defined cant as the
ostentatious assumption of a virtue or vice that one does not actually
possess, or boasting of a quality that one happens naturally to have.[1]

There were, of course, other ideas available to one of Bernstein's
scholarly, eclectic inclinations. Jean Jaurès, who rose to prominence
among the French Socialists during the 1890s, published in French
his Latin academic thesis which touched precisely on this problem.
The work was entitled 'The Origins of German Socialism', and in it
he argued that modern Socialist thought had evolved from Luther
through Kant, Fichte, and Hegel to Lassalle and Marx. Jaurès
tried to show that factors other than material conditions and productive arrangements contributed to German Socialist thought. In
an un-Marxian manner, he offered an impressive demonstration that
the sense of justice and the collective spirit that modern German
socialism embodied could be traced to the teachings of Luther,
and he attributed great importance to the idealism of Kant and
Hegel. Jaurès did not deny that material conditions were important in bringing about German Socialism, but he did insist upon
a balance between material and idealistic factors, and he proposed
the independence of moral thinking from economic considerations.[2]

Whatever the origins of Bernstein's ideas on the subject, his
critics in the late 1890s over-emphasized his reliance on Kant's
philosophical system, which was seen by the Marxian faithful to
be tinged with bourgeois or pre-bourgeois features. Georgi
Plekhanov, the leader of the Russian Marxists, was one of the first
to attack Bernstein on this front, and he did so in bitter, insulting
terms. He sent his articles to *Die Neue Zeit*, but Kautsky deleted
some of the more vitriolic passages before publication.[3] Plekhanov's rage obviously had an impact on the author of Revisionism.
The final section of the *Voraussetzungen*, entitled 'Ultimate Aim
and Tendency' and subtitled 'Kant against Cant', is largely a
counter-statement directed against Plekhanov. The anger of the

---

[1] Bax, *The Ethics of Socialism*, pp. 90–8. There is also another Bax article at
pp. 129–37 in this volume entitled 'That Blessed Word' that discusses the
tendency to make certain ideas sacrosanct.

[2] Jean Jaurès, *Les origines du socialisme allemand*, translated from the Latin by
Adrien Veber. New Preface by Lucien Goldmann (Paris, 1960). First translated
and printed in 1892.

[3] Plekhanov's reaction to Bernstein is thoroughly discussed in Samuel H.
Baron, *Plekhanov: The Father of Russian Marxism* (Stanford, 1963), pp. 164–85.

Russian had fortified Bernstein's belief that Social Democracy required a Kant who would judge existing doctrine in a critical spirit and demonstrate that 'apparent materialism is the highest— and therefore the most misleading—ideology . . .'[1]

So it was an internal Socialist feud—magnified by the fact that Plekhanov and others had chosen to attack Kantian thought—that largely accounted for Bernstein's appeal to Kant. The categorical imperative might have served his purposes well, had he chosen to pursue this line. Kant's precept that a man should act only on the basis of a principle that he can desire to be universal law, is fundamentally a call for an individual sense of duty, derived by rational means. Bernstein's expressions on the subject of ethics complemented this idea, and he might have built a stronger abstract argument had he looked more closely at Kantian literature. Of course, in the journalistic and political arena where he faced his critics, arguments of that kind would have been scorned, and in any event Bernstein did not have the intellectual inclination to move in that direction.

One senses something of the Old Testament idea of the 'chosen people', or perhaps of the Protestant ethic that was so effectively described by his fellow countryman and contemporary, Max Weber, in the discussions of Bernstein. He regarded work as a virtue, and he saw the proletariat as a kind of 'elect' segment of society, not in the strict Marxian sense but almost in a spiritual sense. At one point he wrote:

Just because I expect much of the working classes I censure much more everything that tends to corrupt their moral judgment than I do similar habits of the higher classes. . . . A class which is aspiring needs a sound morale and must suffer no deterioration. Whether it sets out for itself an ideal ultimate aim is of secondary importance if it pursues with energy its proximate aims. The important point is that these aims are inspired by a definite principle which expresses a higher degree of economy and of social life, that they are an embodiment of a social conception which means in the evolution of civilisation a higher view of morals and of legal rights.[2]

Like Shaw, Bernstein has set for himself the task of not only dispelling the illusions of his comrades but also of accelerating

---

[1] Bernstein, *Voraussetzungen*, p. 187. Reference to Plekhanov has been deleted here and at a few other places in the English translation.

[2] Bernstein, *Voraussetzungen*, pp. 186–7; *Evolutionary Socialism*, p. 222.

their evolution towards more advanced ethical standards and social forms. The writing that he had done in England, culminating in the *Voraussetzungen*, was to be regarded as his definitive statement, but he produced many additional arguments after he returned to Germany in 1901.

THE LATER HERESIES

When Bernstein returned to Germany in 1901, with the legal threats against his person and his freedom removed, he continued to meet the disparagement of his critics with vigorous counter-arguments. In the spring, only a few months after he had settled again in his homeland, he delivered a lecture evaluating the claims of Marxism to be 'scientific' (*wissenschaftlicher*). While it might be based on some scientifically collected and systematically arranged information, its essential conclusions and value judgements could not be regarded as scientific because they were subjective and therefore biased. No 'ism' can be a science, Bernstein concluded, and therefore it should continuously be subject to criticism and review in the Kantian spirit.[1] Thus he gave new dimension to his heresy, emphasizing as Shaw had often done that Marxism had no unique claim to scientific validity.

This and similar speeches and pamphlets kept Bernstein prominent in the party for a number of years, and his election to the Reichstag in 1902 also added to his reputation. He was not a vocal member of that body however, preferring to make his most serious statements elsewhere. Socialists usually tried to keep their intra-party differences outside the Reichstag, but in their congresses, their periodicals, and their books, party members produced a great volume of doctrinal argument. Kautsky, increasingly annoyed and finally antagonized by Bernstein's deviations from orthodoxy, became one of his leading adversaries. He wrote a number of harsh pieces that temporarily severed their friendly relations. Kautsky even wrote a small book in 1905 partly to neutralize the effect of Bernstein's contentions about ethics and his appeal to Kant, although its purpose and target were not limited to this.[2] The basic differences between the two, however,

[1] Eduard Bernstein, *Wie ist wissenschaftlicher Sozialismus möglich?* (Berlin, 1901).
[2] Karl Kautsky, *Ethik und materialistische Geschichtsauffassung* (Stuttgart, 1906).

were less fundamental than they believed in the years of the Revisionist controversy. Careful examination of their basic attitudes has since convinced leading students of German Socialism that their disagreements were largely matters of tactics and semantics, since each believed in universal suffrage, parliamentarism, and political liberties for the masses.[1] In the first few years of the new century, however, the polemics were bitter and Bernstein found himself frequently chastised at the hands of his fellow party-members.

During his first years back in Germany, he edited a monthly journal called *Dokumente des Sozialismus*. This periodical mirrored Bernstein's scholarly and historical approach to the Socialist movement and offered a range of documents to its readers. A bibliographical section often contained references to works outside the Social Democratic movement, including those of Kropotkin and other anarchists. In the articles and short notices Proudhon was represented, and there were a number of articles on Robert Owen. The work of Marx and Engels and commentaries on them appeared frequently, but they did not predominate. It was an attempt to give German Social Democracy a periodical of high intellectual quality and variety.

Bernstein found some of the works of his British contemporaries suited to his purposes. In 1902 he revived and published a translation of Shaw's well-known attack on Marxism, 'Bluffing the Value Theory'.[2] About a year later, he published a German version of William Morris's 1893 lecture entitled 'Communism', which was not strictly compatible either with his own inclinations or with orthodox Marxism.[3] Yet the publication of it was consistent with his contention that Socialists needed Kantian critics.

There were several notable issues in subsequent years that placed Bernstein outside the mainstream of his party. The SPD became increasingly cautious as it became more deeply involved in the German political arena and as its political successes continued. It has often been pointed out that Revisionism prevailed in fact as party policy, even though it was not formally acknowledged

---

[1] Milorad Drachkovitch, *Les socialismes français et allemand et le problème de la guerre: 1870–1914* (Geneva, 1953), pp. 189–91. See also Erich Matthias, 'Idéologie et Pratique: Le Faux Débat Bernstein-Kautsky', *Annales: Économies, Sociétés, Civilisations*; 19(1), (1964), pp. 19–30.

[2] *Dokumente des Sozialismus*, II (November–December 1902), pp. 78–87.

[3] Ibid., III (November 1903), pp. 502–13.

by the party's congresses and most of its spokesmen. The party revealed its essential conservatism both by anti-revolutionary conduct at home and by the equivocal positions of its spokesmen at international congresses before 1914. Shaw had been basically correct as early as 1896 when he wrote that the SPD leaders often compromised even while denying that they did so. In spite of his desire for compromise, Bernstein could not always endorse the kind of policies that his fellow party leaders were willing to endorse in order to assure it.

When German Social Democracy became embroiled in its famous debate over the theory of the 'general strike' after 1903, Bernstein found himself opposed to the party's consensus, and this debate pushed him into an odd, partial alliance with the party's extreme left wing and the anarchists. Implicit in his Revisionism was the idea that the trade union movement, with its demands for immediate and practical reforms for the working classes, was important in the evolution of a better society. (While Bernstein was emphatic that his Revisionism was not derived from Fabianism, he was willing to admit that he had learned much about the trade union movement from the Webbs.)[1] He gave substantial attention to this movement and to its role in society, and since trade union leaders in Germany became increasingly cautious as their stake in society grew, Bernstein found support among them for his anti-revolutionary political theories.

The question of strikes, however, brought about an important variation. The first years of the new century produced several examples of labour unrest outside Germany. General strikes occurred or were called in Belgium, the Netherlands, Sweden, and Austria, and the Second International put the question of the general strike on the agenda for discussion at its Amsterdam Congress of 1904. This congress looked much more favourably on the mass strike as a political tactic than its predecessors had done, stimulating still more discussion in German Social Democratic circles. There was an unsuccessful but apparently spontaneous strike in the Ruhr coal mines early the following year. Then came the revolutionary events in Russia, adding more fuel to the flames and giving more evidence to those who wanted to see direct,

---

[1] Bernstein, 'Entwicklungsgang', p. 23; also see 'Zur Geschichte des Revisionismus', an undated 7-page typescript in the Bernstein archives, A43, International Institute of Social History, Amsterdam.

proletarian action against existing authority. In the wake of these developments, anarchists and Social Democrats of the extreme left felt encouraged and strengthened, and the party was forced to deal openly with the issue of the general strike for the first time at its congress at Jena in the summer of 1905.[1]

In the course of this expanding debate, Bernstein advanced the argument that the political mass strike might be used as a defensive tactic, to be employed if the fundamental rights already won were threatened, as many Socialists thought them to be in 1905. He wrote a tract in which he attempted to distinguish between his position and that of the revolutionaries who would try to use the general strike as the first step to forcible seizure of power. He hoped that the day of the barricades was past, but if the existing government should try to restrict the right of suffrage or to impose a new anti-Socialist law, then the proletariat should stand ready to stop work and thus to prevent the normal functioning of society. Obviously such a tactic carried the danger of physical combat and defeat, but Bernstein was ready to accept the risk if the political threat were great enough. He was, in short, ready to adopt a modification of the anarchist syndicalist programme. He found himself sharing with German anarchists and with Luxemburg the idea that the mass political strike had a place in party planning.[2] He felt that a general strike should only be called for specific, limited objectives, not for the total transformation of society, and here he was in substantial disagreement with the extreme left, but the moderates in the party and in the trade union leadership made little distinction on this count.

Bernstein also stressed the ethical implications of a general political strike. It should be employed when the morality of the action is clear—when it is evident that the strikers have right on their side; otherwise there is the danger that necessary public support would not be forthcoming. The mass strike was 'an economic weapon with an ethical object'.[3]

---

[1] Two good discussions of the debate within the party may be found in Carl E. Schorske, *German Social Democracy: 1905–1917* (Cambridge, 1955), pp. 23–45; and J. P. Nettl, *Rosa Luxemburg* (London, 1966), pp. 296 ff.

[2] Eduard Bernstein, *Der politische Massenstreik und die politische Lage der Sozialdemokratie in Deutschland* (Breslau, 1905). Bernstein also contributed a number of articles to *Sozialistische Monatshefte*, the leading organ of the Revisionists, on this subject in 1905 and 1906.

[3] Eduard Bernstein, 'Politischer Massenstreik und Revolutionsromantik', *Sozialistische Monatshefte*, X(XII), 1 (1906), 19, as cited in Gay, op. cit., p. 234.

Bernstein's alliance with the militant left was short-lived. The party seemed to move towards the left at the Jena meeting, embracing the principle of the general strike in ambiguous terms, but in the following year at the Mannheim Congress, it moved in the opposite direction, in effect capitulating to the conservatism of the trade union leadership. As this happened, the revolutionary left, for whom Luxemburg was the most effective spokesman, became more convinced than ever that the party was drifting into parliamentarianism or Revisionism. Bernstein, meanwhile, continued to reflect and write occasionally on his specialized concept of the political strike, but with little new result.

This series of episodes reveals again that it is misleading to think of Bernstein simply as a right-wing Socialist, eager to collaborate with the liberals. His thought, while basically consistent, is sufficiently eclectic to defy precise categorization.

In the field of foreign policy, Bernstein also charted his own course. He was essentially a pacifist and an internationalist, but he was also a moralist and an evolutionist, so his arguments were occasionally variegated. On the question of imperialism, he took a position in 1900 that resembled that of Shaw in his famous *Fabianism and the Empire*, published in the same year. While exploitive colonial practices were evil, imperialism should not be condemned as a whole, he argued. Countries that are advanced culturally and economically have a right to carry civilization and trade to regions of inferior development, and he believed it was proper for European countries to impose their will against certain reactionary regimes, as the British did in the Boer War. On the other hand, in 1902 Bernstein condemned German policy towards the Ottoman Empire. Kaiser William II's support of the Sultan's regime during the last years of the century, in the face of the Armenian massacres and international pressures for reform, seemed to Bernstein to be contrary to the best interests of civilization. Germany had an unenviable record in foreign affairs; she had often been the conqueror and never the liberator.[1] He was to hold a similar attitude towards his native country through the years of the First World War when such a position corresponded rather closely with that of the revolutionary left.

Like most of his Socialist colleagues, Bernstein deplored the armaments race and the hysteria that accompanied it. One of his

[1] Angel, op. cit., pp. 318–20.

best known pre-war papers, 'The English Peril and the German People', challenged the current propaganda against Britain. It was widely believed—and many Socialists accepted the notion—that the United Kingdom was the leading enemy of the German Empire, and that war between the two powers was a probability. It was not simply Bernstein's pro-British sympathies that emerged in this short document, which appeared in 1911; he also recognized that some segments of society—including munitions makers, unscrupulous writers, and certain politicians—were benefiting from the growing international tension. He saw that many of his countrymen had become so anti-British that they overlooked evils and provocations on the part of Germany. He criticized German foreign policy and the conduct of the Kaiser, and he deplored the growing militarism of the state, all in language that was blunt even for a Socialist.[1] The SPD was of course committed to an anti-war policy, but its members were not immune from the mass fear that the government and the press encouraged. Bernstein's essay did nothing to change the course of events; when Germany and her neighbours went to war in the summer of 1914 it was with the support of the SPD and Bernstein, who succumbed to the kind of fear against which he had warned in 1911.

In the confusing days of late July and early August 1914, Bernstein, like most other political figures of Europe, saw his theories overrun by events.[2] The party had traditionally opposed appropriations for military purposes, and since the Stuttgart Congress of the Second International in 1907, it was officially pledged to oppose the war efforts of the government in the event of hostilities. The SPD leadership and press had condemned government action in supporting Austria until the last days of July, and there had been mass anti-war meetings under party

[1] Eduard Bernstein, *Die englische Gefahr und das deutsche Volk* (Berlin, 1911). Bernstein maintained correspondence with some of his former English friends in subsequent years. Among his papers are letters from Ramsay MacDonald and Graham Wallas. International Institute of Social History, Bernstein Archives, D438 and D809.

[2] The events of these days have been subjected to extensive discussion and debate. A basic German study is Eugen Prager, *Die Geschichte der U.S.P.D.: Entstehung und Entwicklung der Unabhängigen Sozialdemokratischen Partei Deutschlands*, 2nd edn. (Berlin, 1922). Good short accounts in English are available in Schorske, op. cit., pp. 285–91 (see also the bibliographical essay on pp. 344–5); in Landauer, op. cit., pp. 505–9, 1097–9; and A. Joseph Berlau, *The German Social Democratic Party: 1914–1921* (New York, 1949), pp. 67–91.

sponsorship throughout the country. But by 2 and 3 August when the SPD Reichstag delegation met to decide whether to vote for war credits, the mood had changed. Patriotic zeal for the father-land was rampant, and there was a clear possibility that the govern-ment would take police action against the dissenters, even to the extent of suspending liberties and reimposing Bismarckian anti-Socialist laws in the event of opposition. Some Socialists obviously welcomed the prospect of competing with their former class enemies in militant nationalism. On 4 August Hugo Haase, the party chairman, reluctantly announced the party's decision in the Reichstag. He referred to the threat from the Russian autocrat, 'stained with the blood of the best among his own people', who now seemed ready to destroy Germany. Bernstein, like his colleagues, responded to the facts as he knew them on that day by voting for war credits. The 110 SPD delegates voted as a block as usual.

Yet the decision left some men troubled and confused, and just before the final vote came it was learned that Germany had violated Belgian neutrality. For Bernstein, this was the first in a series of revelations that raised questions about Germany's role in the war. As additional information became available in the next few weeks about the Empire's conduct of diplomatic affairs in the final weeks before August, he recognized that more was involved than national self-defence. As most of his countrymen became more chauvinistic, Bernstein struggled with his conscience and with the ethical standards that he believed to be essential for mature socialism.

Within weeks after the beginning of hostilities, he was speaking against the irrational conduct of intellectuals and party colleagues who had thrown themselves completely into the war effort. He wrote a number of articles on this theme, calling upon the Socialist leadership and press not to abandon their principles for so-called national unity. The party should assert its right to express opinions about the conduct of the war and to try to do the work of peace even in wartime, he asserted.[1] As the weeks passed it became clear that once again he was taking a line different from most of his

[1] One of Bernstein's articles in this vein appeared in the *Leipziger Volkszeitung* on 3 November 1914 and was subsequently translated and published in the *New York Sunday Call*. Bernstein Archives G460, International Institute of Social History, Amsterdam.

fellow revisionists, who overwhelmingly supported the government. He was soon denied the right to publish his articles in *Sozialistische Monatshefte*.

The question of emergency war credits appeared again on 2 December 1914; disturbed and disheartened, but still not ready to violate party discipline, he voted a second time for the appropriation. In March of 1915, he and thirty other members of the SPD left the chamber rather than vote for the third war credits measure. Meanwhile, he had raised questions about the war objective of Germany and about the moral position it had assumed.

One of Bernstein's prominent statements was a pamphlet on the international labour movement and the war, written early in 1915 and published the following year.[1] It pointed out the substantial differences between the present conduct and the past policies of the SPD. It was as though men had drunk great quantities of the waters of Lethe on 4 August 1914, Bernstein said, and had forgotten everything they had written and said before that time. He reminded his colleagues of the pledge they— and other European Socialists—had ratified at Stuttgart in 1907, promising not only to resist the outbreak of war but also to work for a speedy end if war did come, and to make use of the crises caused by the war to rouse the people and thereby to hasten the end of capitalistic class rule.[2] He cited a similar pledge made at Copenhagen in 1910, and then he presented some of the pertinent documents relative to the outbreak of the war. He recapitulated the Socialist anti-war statements made during the last few days before the beginning of hostilities, and offered evidence that the German Empire had not conducted itself with honour. He drew the conclusion that Germany—and German Social Democracy— did not have a very enviable record in the eyes of foreign observers. Among the foreigners whose anti-German attitude he cited was that of the respected Peter Kropotkin.

Bernstein had not been a close friend of Kropotkin, but he obviously admired his integrity and learning, and it was unpleasant to see him regarding Imperial Germany as a greater evil than Tsarist Russia.[3] Nearly two years later, when Kropotkin left England to return to Russia and share the long-awaited revolution,

---

[1] Eduard Bernstein, *Die Internationale der Arbeiterklasse und der europäische Krieg* (Tübingen, 1916).

[2] Ibid., p. 6.   [3] Ibid., pp. 49–50.

he wrote a letter of farewell to his English friends which was published in *The Times*. A clipping of this letter found its way into Bernstein's hands and into the final collection of his papers. Kropotkin rejoiced that Russia had joined hands with Western civilization against the forces of aggression that were attempting to stop progress. The words obviously offered Bernstein new confirmation for his argument:

. . . I earnestly hope that the efforts now made to lure the Russian nation into the wake of the German servants of Conquest will not succeed. The great bulk of the Russian nation see that such a step would bring back the misrule of a pro-German Tsar and the reconstitution of the Holy Alliance in the shape of the Three Emperors' Union. And I feel sure that Russia will continue to fight so long as the Germans themselves do not recognize the criminal mistake they have made in favouring the 'World Empire' schemes of their rulers.[1]

Bernstein had already become nearly as categorical as this in his own statements. One of the most famous documents to which he signed his name was an article, published in June 1915, entitled 'The Need of the Hour'. Co-signers of the manifesto were Kautsky and Haase, who like Bernstein had become appalled at the policies that the German government was adopting. It argued that Germany was turning the conflict into a war of conquest.[2] Bernstein now believed that German Socialism would certainly sacrifice its moral influence entirely unless it was willing to oppose such a war.

In December, after fighting against the prevailing attitude for more than a year within the party, after incurring occasional censorship at the hands of the government and frequent insults from party colleagues, he reached breaking-point. Together with nineteen fellow-party members, he voted against a war credits measure. This constituted a violation of party discipline of serious proportions, and three months later a formal split occurred. Haase was officially expelled and Bernstein, among others, joined him in leaving the party.

It was one of the great ironies of Bernstein's life that he, more than any other single individual, had shown German Social

[1] Bernstein Archives, G300, International Institute of Social History. The letter appeared in *The Times* (8 June 1917), 6 : 3. Presumably Bernstein had the letter soon after it was published.

[2] 'Das Gebot der Stunde' is reprinted in Prager, op. cit., pp. 72–4.

Democracy the wisdom of co-operating with the existing regime
to obtain desirable social objectives. Now, the party that he had
helped to accommodate to the German political structure was
helping the regime to pursue ends that Bernstein found repulsive
to the international spirit and the principles of Socialism.

Following his departure from the Party, Bernstein broadened
his criticism considerably; his Kantian critical methods and his
rigorous ethical standards carried him well beyond the immediate
problems of the war, although nearly everything he wrote had
some bearing on it. He composed one essay, for example, to
challenge the widely-held notion that Germany was the victim
of a conspiracy of encirclement and another contending that
German foreign policy had been managed for the privileged
classes, not for the nation at large.[1] It was not his practice to speak
often in the Reichstag, but on 29 March 1917 he delivered an
address there that attacked the existing regime on many fronts.
He condemned not only its pre-war militarism but also its refusal
to use international courts of arbitration, its violations of international law, its recent programme of unrestricted submarine
warfare, and a number of other acts and omissions that he regarded
as wrong.[2] Of course he came to know well the indignities that a
man may suffer if he speaks out against his government at a time
when its leaders are bent on aggressive war. At such times, the
self-righteous authors of official policy have little patience for the
moral arguments of those whose horizons extend beyond political
boundaries and beyond the current battle.

In the summer of 1917, Bernstein talked about Germany's war
guilt and discussed the future policy the country would have to
adopt to make restitution. He advocated the self-determination of
peoples, full restitution for Belgium and acknowledgement of its
independence, a plebiscite for Alsace and Lorraine, the establishment of an independent Poland, and the creation of a league of
peoples. He was proposing these ideas to a largely unreceptive
nation several months before Woodrow Wilson formulated the
Fourteen Points.

When the defectors from the SPD formed the Unabhängige

---

[1] Bernstein, *Die Wahrheit Über die Einkreisung Deutschlands* (Berlin, 1920),
and *Die parlamentarische Kontrolle der auswärtigen Politik* (The Hague, 1916).

[2] The speech is summarized briefly in A. Joseph Berlau, *The German Social
Democratic Party: 1914–1921* (New York: 1949), pp. 149–50.

Sozialdemokratische Partei Deutschlands (USPD) in 1917, Bernstein once again stood out as a dissenter among dissenters. Most of his fellow rebels belonged to the left-wing of the party and some of them, including the Sparticists led by Luxemburg and Liebknecht, advocated violent civil war and proletarian rule. He was not comfortable in his new alliance, but he hoped to guide USPD towards a constructive post-war policy.

The events of November, 1918, presented unprecedented challenges. With the fall of the Empire and the proclamation of a Republic, Bernstein sensed a great opportunity and a serious danger. The SPD and the USPD temporarily joined hands to form a government and to face the problems of the defeated country. The elderly revisionist—now nearly seventy years old and stripped of much of his former political prestige because of his controversial past—tried to bring his polemical talents to the service of the new government. He accepted a position as Assistant Secretary of State for the Treasury and he became an advocate of compromise within the fractured Socialist movement.

The co-operation between the SPD and the USPD was not destined to last beyond the end of the year. The hostilities that had developed during the war were too intense and the USPD had too many hard-line revolutionaries to permit a durable reconciliation. Bernstein's speeches and newspaper articles of this period reveal his sensitivity to the dangers of the militant Left—including the Sparticists who led the way in forming a Communist Party on the Bolshevik model at the end of the year—and from the still vigorous military establishment on the reactionary end of the political spectrum. He argued for the preservation of many features of capitalist ownership and distribution to avoid chaos in the current crisis.[1] But such ideas were not compatible with his continued membership in the USPD for more than a few months. When leaders of the SPD, as government officers, found it necessary to use military units to forestall rebellion, most Independents could not condone it. Bernstein, although troubled,

---

[1] An excellent example of his attitude shortly after the war can be seen in *Was ist Sozialismus* (Berlin, 1919), published from a speech he delivered on 28 December 1918. For a summary of his activities in the post-war years see Angel, op. cit., pp. 403 ff. The best account in English of this period is Berlau, op. cit., pp. 214 ff. See also Bernstein's own account, *Die deutsche Revolution: Geschichte der Entstehung und ersten Arbeitsperiode der deutschen Republik* (Berlin-Fichtenau, 1921).

supported the SPD in this. He deplored the killing of Luxemburg and Liebknecht during the civil disorders of January 1919—murders that cast a shadow over the authorities that arrested them in the name of the Socialist provisional government—but he stood by the government, the SPD, and later the Weimar Republic through all the vicissitudes that followed.

His support of the SPD and the Republic, however, did not imply full acquiescence in the prevalent policies, and he continued to be a gadfly, preaching ethical sermons that were often repulsive to his audiences. In June 1919, he went before a congress of the SPD—to which he had returned—when the newly revealed terms of the Versailles treaty were arousing hostile German reactions. Once again he told his audience what it did not want to hear—that most of the provisions of the treaty were acceptable and necessary, that Germany should recognize honestly the German government's war guilt, and that she should work to win the respect of other peoples.[1] The reaction to his remarks took a form that must not have surprised him by this time; he was nearly shouted down and was verbally attacked by a host of critics. Arguments from an ethical basis and from empirical evidence had no more appeal in 1919 than they had had in the previous few years.

During the last dozen years of his life, Bernstein was not a significant force in German Socialism. He served in the Weimar Reichstag from 1920 to 1928, but his past controversies and his advanced years made him better known as a curiosity than as a party leader. Most of his writing dealt with reminiscences or with party history; he made no substantially new contributions to the theories or the literature of Socialism. His work of this period reveals his concern about the ugly anti-Semitism that was reviving in Germany. Undoubtedly his own Jewish ancestry made him sensitive on this point. He noticed with alarm the growing strength of the Communists and the Nazis at the end of the 1920s. Among his papers is a document, apparently written in the late 1920s or early 1930s, in which he tried to evaluate the major events of the previous decade, and it is obvious that post-war developments in Hungary and Bavaria had impressed him. The seizures of power in those regions by Communists in 1919 had been followed by

[1] *Protokoll über die Verhandlungen des Parteitags der Sozialdemokratischen Partei Deutschlands.* 1919 (Berlin, 1919), pp. 240-9; 277-81.

brutalities committed by the reactionaries, and the cause of social reform had been retarded. The violence of the Russian Revolution and civil war had been a prelude to Stalin. These developments appeared to confirm Bernstein's conviction that class warfare could only harm the political and moral advancement of society.

A few years later Communist historians would be writing that Bernstein's Revisionism had softened and weakened German Socialism to the point that the triumph of militarism and Naziism in post-war Germany was made possible, but Bernstein did not live to see this occur. On 18 December 1932, less than a month before his eighty-third birthday and less than two months before Adolph Hitler came to power, he died. He was thus spared the pain of seeing his nation grotesquely transformed and his party mutilated by a movement that represented the exact opposite of his ethical standards.

VII

KROPOTKIN

The Years of Frustration

IN many respects the last years of Kropotkin's life resembled the final period of Bernstein's political activity. The Russian Prince had a longer period of exile and a shorter period of dis-illusionment and disappointment than Bernstein did, but in each case the final period was marked by quarrels with colleagues and each man saw his cherished ideals ignored or defeated. Their final years were saddened by the events they witnessed in their native countries. Their paths never crossed again, but from time to time they ran parallel.

The anarchists understandably took an interest in Bernstein's revisionist ideas when they were fresh and most controversial. When *Freedom* published a review of the *Voraussetzungen*, it found reason for self-congratulations on the part of the anarchists, suggesting that Bernstein had taken some of his anti-Marxian arguments from anarchist sources. The reviewer—probably Max Nettlau—was eager, however, to make it clear that Communist Anarchists did not share Bernstein's ideas about the alternatives to Marxism. His proposals for accommodation with the existing economic order were totally unacceptable; he was 'the apologist of the Social Democratic degeneration'.[1] Kropotkin appears to have sent part of this review to *Les Temps Nouveaux*, the leading anarchist weekly in Paris, to which he contributed regularly. When it appeared in that newspaper, it was accompanied by an editorial note from Kropotkin that revealed his admiration for Bernstein's criticism. Kropotkin, like many others, immediately assumed that Bernstein was indebted to the Fabians, but he seems to have

---

[1] The review is signed N. It appears in *Freedom*, XIII (December 1899), pp. 81–2; and XIV (January–February 1900), pp. 2–3. It was reprinted as N. 'German Social Democracy and Edward Bernstein', *Freedom Pamphlets* No. 12 (London, 1900), pp. 12–23.

regarded this as less important than the convincing assault on Marxian theory. Bernstein's critics had accused him of apostasy and had showered him with invectives, but they had not effectively answered him, because he could not be answered by the so-called 'Scientific Socialists', Kropotkin asserted.[1] The short statement is free of objections to Bernstein's theories, a surprising fact in view of the different attitudes of the Communist Anarchists and the Revisionists, and in view of Kropotkin's long-standing, anti-German bias.

Unlike Bernstein Kropotkin believed the Socialist movement to be misguided because of its orientation towards political activity within the existing capitalist context. As early as 1895, he had written that the development of Socialism had halted and that the German Social Democrats, by their compromises with the German state, shared the blame for this situation.[2] Yet in the late 1890s Bernstein's criticism of Marx seemed to be a ray of light.

The Communist Anarchists obviously were not welcome at the congresses of the Socialist International after the middle 1890s; the Marxists who controlled the Second International passed resolutions at Zurich in 1893 and in London in 1896 which sought to weld the trade union movement to Socialism without embracing the anarchist ideas that some trade unionists held, while at the same time paying lip service to the doctrine of revolution. The whole procedure, which as previously noted aroused Shaw's objections, also stimulated Kropotkin's wrath. In a series of articles composed for *Les Temps Nouveaux* late in 1896, he emphatically demonstrated that an Anarchist of his convictions could no longer hope to identify with the Second International.[3] His reasons of course were different from Shaw's and Bernstein's, but his distaste for the pretensions and illusions that he identified among the Social Democrats—and particularly the Germans—was much the same.

Yet Kropotkin held tenaciously to illusions of his own. He was eager to believe that the principles of anarchism were spreading through society. During his American tour of 1897, he told a

[1] *Les Temps Nouveaux*, V, 27 January–2 February 1900, p. 2.

[2] Kropotkin, 'La crise du socialisme', *Les Temps Nouveaux*, I, 26 October–1 November 1895, pp. 1–2.

[3] *Les Temps Nouveaux*, II, 15–21 August 1896, p. 1; 29 August–4 September, pp. 1–2; 12–18 September, pp. 1–2; 19–25 September, pp. 1–2; and 10–16 October, pp. 1–2.

New York City audience that he believed even the English churches were coming to share some of his ideas.[1] In his *Memoirs of a Revolutionist*, written for *The Atlantic Monthly* following his first appearances in the United States, he reaffirmed his belief that the Socialist principles for which he stood—'of no-government, of rights of the individual, of local action and free agreement'—had made substantial progress in the previous twenty years.[2] Kropotkin did not lose his optimism, even as he became discouraged with the trends within the Left. In his opinion the errors of the Social Democrats did not affect the validity or strength of Socialist ideals.

In spite of the title that his memoirs carried, at the end of the century Kropotkin was somewhat reluctant to be identified as a revolutionary. When the editors of *The Atlantic Monthly* assigned the well-known title to his reminiscences, they apparently did not consult the author, and he tried to get them to change it to 'Around One's Life'. But he made his request too late, and the editors' decision stood.[3] Kropotkin was occasionally willing to call himself a 'revolutionist', but perhaps like some of his London contemporaries he had become convinced that one could be more effective if he did not carry a pejorative label.

Memoirs of a Revolutionist was to become his best-known book. It had a few of the qualities of an adventure story, a bit of the appeal of the travelogue, and a kind of grace that was almost Victorian. Several reviewers compared it favourably with the reminiscences of Tolstoy and some mentioned its similarity to Stepniak's books. Indeed much of the book was devoted to an exposure of the Russian social system and a discussion of the plight of the peasants, and it constituted an extended justification for his own political conduct. It contained, however, little that could be construed as anarchist propaganda.

Partly because of its success, in 1901 Kropotkin was persuaded to make a second trip to the United States for additional lectures. He spoke at Lowell Institute in Boston, at Chickering Hall in New York City, at Harvard University, the University of Illinois,

[1] *The New York Times*, 23 November 1897, 3: 6.
[2] P. Kropotkin, *Memoirs of a Revolutionist* (Boston and New York, 1899), p. 501.
[3] Kropotkin's comment to this effect may be found in a letter to Georg Brandes in the *Correspondance de Georg Brandes, II, L'Angleterre et la Russie* (Copenhagen, 1956), p. 132. The letter is dated 22 September 1898.

the University of Wisconsin and before several groups of fellow anarchists. His primary theme in Boston was Russian literature, a subject that had recently won new attention in America.

The volume that resulted from this series of lectures won Kropotkin additional acclaim. Although it does not now appear to have outstanding merit as literary criticism, it was admired as an introduction to Russian literature at a time when there were few good competitors. The first edition, appearing in 1905, was timely because of the events of that year in the Tsarist empire, and it seemed to offer new insights into the Russian mind. Kropotkin himself, in a letter to his friend Georg Brandes, called it 'a page of collective autobiography'.[1] The book was not primarily a polemic against the Tsarist regime, but inevitably its discussions of the troubles of writers constituted an attack on the autocracy, and it introduced some Western readers to little-known figures in Russian literature who had felt the burdens of censorship and official punishment.[2] It belonged, in short, to the *genre* that Stepniak had popularized a few years earlier.

The visit to America in 1901 proved to be Kropotkin's last, because shortly after it had ended, the assassination of President William McKinley occurred, and public reaction against anarchism included a legal ban against the immigration of anyone holding anarchist views. Inevitably, some writers tried to associate the event with Kropotkin's activities, but no proof was produced by any responsible source. There is no evidence that Kropotkin advocated violence, and he customarily stressed that he would not propose any action that he was not prepared to undertake himself. In addition, he was clearly anticipating the evolution of Russian institutions towards constitutional monarchy.[3]

The well-known periodical *North American Review* opened its pages to the famous Russian and gave him a new opportunity to comment favourably on the constitutional agitation of his countrymen. In one article, written early in 1901, he contended that there had been social pressure for a constitution for forty years and that

[1] Brandes, op. cit., p. 193. The first edition was P. Kropotkin, *Russian Literature* (New York, 1905). It was republished in 1915 under the title that became better known, *Ideals and Realities in Russian Literature*.
[2] See, for example, the reception and interpretation accorded it in *The New York Times* supplement Saturday Review of Books, 8 July 1905, p. 449.
[3] One of his speeches to this effect is reported in *The New York Times* for 30 March 1901, 8: 7.

there was still a strong popular wish for an imperial representative assembly.[1] While he was careful not to advocate a specific governmental form as his own preference, he showed an interest in a Canadian-type of federalist system that had been proposed earlier by the Grand Duke Constantine. The article brought a rejoinder from the highest ecclesiastical officer in the Russian Empire, Konstantin Pobedonostsev, head of the Holy Synod of the Russian Orthodox Church and one of the Tsar's leading advisors. He undertook to discredit not only Kropotkin but also the representative form of government that Kropotkin had predicted for Russia.[2] Then the editors gave Kropotkin a chance of answering. Once again he praised the efforts of Russian liberals, but with reservations. 'If I speak of the coming Constitution, it is not because I see in it a panacea. My personal ideals go far beyond that. But, whether we like it or not, it is coming.'[3]

By the end of 1904, it was obvious that Russia was confronting a major crisis. The failures of the Tsarist establishment in the Russo–Japanese War and the growing internal dissension provided new ammunition for Kropotkin, who by now had become as vigorous in the production of anti-Russian propaganda as Stepniak had been at the peak of his activity in Britain. He took a warm interest in the activities of the Zemstvo representatives who were agitating for a constitution and Western-style political rights. As he watched Russia advancing towards representative institutions and freedoms of the Western variety, he came to hope that the transition could be made relatively peacefully.[4] His anarchistic purism was slowly mellowing in the wake of developments.

Most anarchists and anarchist sympathizers who have written about Kropotkin have overlooked the extent to which he tolerated and even encouraged constitutional aspirations in Russia. The revolutions of 1905 and 1917 each caused him to embrace constitutional experimentation, although tentatively and with reservations. In 1905 he was disillusioned and returned to a relatively

[1] Prince Kropotkin, 'The Present Crisis in Russia', *North American Review*, Vol. 172 (May 1901), pp. 711–23.

[2] Constantin Pobiedonostseff, 'Russia and Popular Education', *North American Review*, Vol. 173 (September 1901), pp. 349–54.

[3] Prince Kropotkin, 'Russian Schools and the Holy Synod', *North American Review*, Vol. 174 (April 1902), p. 527.

[4] See his article 'The Constitutional Agitation in Russia', *The Nineteenth Century*, Vol. 57 (January 1905), pp. 27–45.

austere anarchism; in 1917 after the October Revolution, he turned his attention to non-political matters. When these variations are recognized, Kropotkin can be seen as a more thoughtful and less rigid personality than his admirers and biographers have generally acknowledged.

The 1905 revolution aroused in him, for the first time in many years, the expectation that he would soon be going home. He felt he still might have a physical role to play in spite of his years—he was now past sixty—and he was willing to take his chances on the barricades, if necessary.[1] Events moved too rapidly, however, and the counter-revolution triumphed before he could make arrangements to go. On the basis of information coming from Russia, he continued to write for periodicals that had long published his works and he undertook to interpret events that were often confusing to Westerners. Writing on 21 November 1905, after the October Manifesto had extended the promise of a representative Duma, Kropotkin gave voice to his native optimism and treated the developments as a fulfilment of his predictions. Workers of the towns and peasants of the countryside had demonstrated 'such a wonderful unanimity of action, even where it was not concerted beforehand, and such a reluctance from useless bloodshed, that we may be sure of their ultimate victory'.[2] The violence that had occurred was solely the responsibility of the 'defenders of autocracy'. The peasants and workers had relied upon the device of the peaceful general strike, but they had been assaulted by armed troops. Revolts in various parts of the Empire presaged its eventual reconstruction in smaller, autonomous units. The authoritarian regime was fighting back irrationally, he argued, but the future was clear:

Why do they continue repression and provoke new massacres, when *they will have to recognise in a few months hence universal suffrage as the basis of representative government in Russia, and the legislative autonomy of Poland as the best, the only possible means for keeping the two countries, Russia and Poland, firmly linked together*, just as they were compelled, after having set all the country on fire, to recognise that the honest recognition of Finland's autonomy was the only means of maintaining her bonds with Russia?[3]

[1] Woodcock and Avakumović, op. cit., pp. 365–6.
[2] P. Kropotkin, 'The Revolution in Russia', *The Nineteenth Century*, Vol. 58 (December 1905), p. 882.   [3] Ibid., The emphasis is Kropotkin's.

Compared with Kropotkin's main anarchist works, this acceptance of the institutions of representative government, and the indication that there was something desirable in Russian political ties with non-Russian areas of the Empire shows a substantial variation. Kropotkin had adjusted his hopes and expectations considerably, and he was now much nearer to the position of the Revisionists and the Fabians on political tactics than he ever admitted. One does not detect any substantial alteration in his economic position; private property was still anathema and capitalism was still an evil. He continued to stress that reform would have to be economic as well as political if it were to be meaningful, and he persistently warned against excessive centralization. But representative government—at least until the end of 1905—no longer seemed to be the enemy that he had previously regarded it to be.

The articles that Kropotkin wrote in Russian for his fellow countrymen who were engaged in the rebellion, provide the best guide to his evolving ideas on the subject of representative government after 1905. He had become more deeply involved in the Russian anarchist movement in exile as social tensions in Russia became more obvious in the first years of the century. He was a regular contributor to *Khleb' i Volia*, a monthly newspaper founded in the summer of 1903 and smuggled regularly into Russia. The founders had taken the Russian-language title of Kropotkin's *The Conquest of Bread* for the masthead of the periodical. Although *Khleb' i Volia* had only survived for slightly more than two years, ceasing publication in the fall of 1905, the Russian anarchists managed to produce a successor, *Listki 'Khleb' i Volia'*, from 1906 to 1910, where one can see a struggle between Kropotkin the romantic revolutionist and Kropotkin the foe of irrational violence. Some of his articles from this period are reminiscent of those written by Morris in the late 1880s and early 1890s. The Russian revolution was not going to be content with merely substituting a representative parliament for the Tsarist autocracy; it was not going to make the mistakes that the German rebels had made in 1848, settling only for an impotent representative body that would satisfy the bourgeoisie and the Social Democrats. In 1906 Kropotkin believed that the peasants and workers of Russia would act according to the principles that he had enunciated in *The Conquest of Bread*, seizing land and factories and achieving an economic transformation of society simultaneously with the political change.[1]

Every Parliament, every Duma, every Constituent Assembly *in its very essence* is a bargain between parties of the future and parties of the past. That is why it cannot take any kind of revolutionary measures. The most revolutionary parliament can only affirm and legalize that which is already accomplished by the people. The very most that it can do is to extend (on paper, at least) to the whole country that which already exists in a considerable part of the country. And even that happens only under pressure from without. . . .[2]

Kropotkin did not, however, take the classic anarchist position that the Duma would inevitably be the oppressor of the people. Although anarchists had no role to play in it and should make no compromises with political blocs, it would be a mistake merely to ignore the business conducted there. Kropotkin saw the possibility of pressing popular demands upon the attention of the representatives, and it was implicit in his argument that if sufficiently pressed, a legislative body would acquiesce in revolutionary change. If the people merely waited for legal change, the result would be the 'death of the revolution', so they must remain active and alert, and anarchists had a duty to work among them. Kropotkin was by this time concerned about the isolation of the anarchist movement from the main stream of the revolutionary movement, and he hoped to give his colleagues more practical guidelines for their conduct. It would be a betrayal of anarchism simply to oppose contemporary institutions because they were not purely anarchist in form, he argued.[3]

He adopted a similar cautious but flexible attitude on labour organizations. Although he believed that unions might play a major role in initiating the new order—they could become instruments of a general strike and they constituted the kind of voluntary association that he admired—there was also the danger that unions might be the tools of political organizations. They might come under the influence of those who wanted to co-operate with the existing order, of Social Democrats, for example. If a union requires its members to support the Social Democrats or otherwise to embrace a compromise with an existing regime, then

[1] P. Kropotkin, 'Revoliutsiia Politicheskaia i Ekonomicheskaia', *Listki 'Khleb' i Volia'*, 30 October 1906, pp. 3–6.
[2] Ibid., p. 4.   [3] Ibid., pp. 5–6.

anarchists should establish their own organization, but they should try to carry on their propaganda among workers within existing unions when there was a chance of preventing exploitation by those with conventional political objectives.[1]

Kropotkin had predicted during the early stages of the 1905 revolution that victory for the people would be delayed and that the autocracy would launch many counter-offensives to oppress the people, but for some time he refused to believe that the cause had been substantially defeated. Not until mid-1907 did he acknowledge that something had gone seriously wrong.[2] Earlier he had talked of a 'calm before the storm', a rising anger that would soon manifest itself in new action by the people. But the Stolypin programme of immobilizing the Dumas, of placating some of the discontented groups with proposed reforms, and of suppressing other rebellious elements was obviously proving effective by summer, and Kropotkin had an explanation ready at hand. The centralist ideas that he associated with both Teutonic despotism and Marxian Socialism had undermined the effort.

During the preceding years the German ideas of Governmental centralisation and of discipline had been actively propagated among the Russian revolutionists, while at the same time the ideals of the Socialists dwindled to a disheartening commonplaceness. The result now made itself felt. Our revolutionists knew how to march heroically to death, but they did not know how to extricate and uphold the ideas of the revolution . . .[3]

In addition to the anarchist propaganda that he composed during this period, he wrote a tract specifically for Britain on the brutalities of the Tsardom. *The Terror in Russia: An Appeal to the British Nation* had the endorsement of more than twenty members of parliament and an impressive group of spokesmen for the press, the universities, and the churches.[4] It resembled Stepniak's early books in organization and subject-matter, with chapters on the

---

[1] P. Kropotkin, 'Nashe Otnoshenie k' Krest'ianskim' i Rabochim' Soiuzam' ', *Listki 'Khleb' i Volia'*, 14 November 1906, pp. 3–5. See also his article 'Syndicalisme et parlementarisme', *Les Temps Nouveaux*, Vol. 12 (13 October 1906), pp. 1–2.

[2] 'Assez d'illusion', *Les Temps Nouveaux*, vol. 13 (20 July 1907), pp. 1–2.

[3] *Freedom*, Vol. XXI, August 1907, p. 1.

[4] Prince Kropotkin, *The Terror in Russia: An Appeal to the British Nation*, issued by the Parliamentary Russian Committee (London, 1909). Among the sponsors was Ramsay MacDonald.

prisons, the exile system, the officially-sanctioned atrocities, abuses in tax collection and administration, and similar subjects.

This work appeared in 1909, the same year as the publication of *The Great French Revolution*. For more than two decades he had been intermittently studying and lecturing on the developments of the 1780s and the 1790s, gathering materials for an anarchist volume on the subject.[1] He believed, like many revolutionists, that this was the great model for modern Socialist movements, and he recognized that many errors of the revolutionists of the 1790s had been repeated in 1905. Furthermore, he remained convinced that earlier historians had consistently emphasized the wrong things—individual personalities and politics—thus giving incorrect impressions of the era. In view of his frustrations of the post-1905 period, it was logical for him to work diligently on a historical subject that he believed to have potential utility.[2]

One who was familiar with Kropotkin's earlier work could have easily anticipated the emphasis he would give to the events of the French revolutionary era. The main factors that had been neglected in previous studies, he argued, were the role of the peasants and the city masses and the economic considerations. It was the masses, not the middle class politicians whom most historians have honoured, who made the Revolution and recorded its great achievements.

. . . Although the educated middle classes did undoubtedly profit by the conflicts with the Court and the *parlements* to arouse political ferment, and although they worked hard to disseminate discontent, it is nevertheless certain that the peasant insurrection, winning over the towns also, made the real basis of the Revolution, and gave the deputies of the Third Estate the determination, presently to be expressed by them at Versailles, to reform the entire system of the government in France, and to initiate a complete revolution in the distribution of wealth.

Without the peasant insurrection, which began in winter (i.e. of 1788–89) and went on, ever growing, until 1793, the overthrow of royal

---

[1] There is an article in *The Nineteenth Century*, Vol. 25 (June 1889), pp. 838–851, in which he presented the same fundamental arguments that are developed at length in *The Great French Revolution*.

[2] P. A. Kropotkin, *The Great French Revolution: 1789–1793*, translated from the French by N. F. Dryhurst (London, New York, 1909). French and German language editions appeared in the same year, and a Russian language edition a few years later.

despotism would never have been effected so completely, nor would it have been accompanied by so enormous a change, political, economic and social. . . .[1]

Kropotkin had much more respect for the revolutionary potential of the peasantry than did the Orthodox Marxists, and he tried to show that there was no Social-Democratic 'Collectivism' behind the revolutionary movement. Yet he seems to have made extensive use of the works of Jaurès and Aulard, and there are places where Kropotkin's thesis overlaps with that of the Marxists. The class-struggle interpretation found a prominent place in this work, and the frequent attribution of full-blown political and economic programmes to an entire class suggests that he found a few Marxian arguments persuasive. He relied more heavily, however, on the works of Louis Blanc and gave the well-known events some special interpretations.

He rejected the frequently-repeated doctrine that high principle and courage had characterized the actions of some of the leaders of the Third Estate, the Assemblies, the Convention, the Jacobin Club, and other institutions. In most cases, these groups had to be prodded and threatened by the aroused masses to move the Revolution along; they followed—and did not lead—the revolutionary current. Laws drawn up by the Constituent Assembly and the Convention were basically dead-letters; they accomplished nothing unless the people forced action. The only institutions that proved efficient and worthy of the times were the Communes and other voluntary co-operatives. The Paris Commune especially distinguished itself in Kropotkin's eyes, organizing food distribution, cultivating waste land, manufacturing and engaging in activities to support the French armies fighting against foreign enemies. The principles of anarchism 'had their origin, not in theoretic speculations, but in the *deeds* of the Great French Revolution'.[2]

It was the enemies of the Revolution, as Kropotkin saw it, who prematurely involved France in war, who conspired to undermine its communistic objectives, and who provoked the Terror. The mass of the people, generally motivated by instinctive wisdom and alertness, finally succumbed to the plotting of their enemies and to exhaustion, and the reactionary forces of Thermidor managed

[1] P. A. Kropotkin, *The Great French Revolution, 1789–1793*, pp. 44–5.
[2] Ibid., p. 184.

to reassert themselves. There had been some serious errors. The Revolution had unwisely allowed a strong government to be created by the Convention and it had failed to go far enough with its egalitarian programme; church land had been distributed to individuals when it should have been socialized. The revolution had only gone part-way, and thus was doomed to fail.

The only individual of the Revolutionary era whom Kropotkin consistently found worthy of high praises was Marat, who had not fared well under the scrutiny of most previous historians. He saw Marat not as the blood-thirsty villain of the bourgeois histories but as a 'devoted friend' and beloved spokesman of the people; his function and his personality had been grossly distorted. In Kropotkin's opinion he had possessed the most nearly perfect understanding of the dangers of the revolutionary epoch. He had worked for the relief of the poor and had opposed indiscriminate use of the Terror. 'He was the only one, we may say, of the revolutionary leaders who had a real understanding of events and power of grasping them as a whole, in their intricate bearings on one another.'[1]

Kropotkin argued his case with a skill that brought him grudging compliments from British and American reviewers, some of them historians. It was generally acknowledged that his work had made a contribution to the understanding of the economic aspects of the Revolution and that he had offered a corrective to the typical overemphasis on politics. Considering the state of monographic literature in this field at the time, and in view of the fact that Kropotkin had to do nearly all his research in Britain (he was not allowed to enter France until 1905, and then had little opportunity to consult documents there), he produced a respectable scholarly work that offered many fruitful suggestions.

Yet Kropotkin did not quite meet the standard that he had set for historians more than a decade earlier when he wrote *Mutual Aid*. He frequently asserted that co-operative instincts had prevailed among the masses and that they had eagerly shared the burdens of the Revolution, but his history is disappointing as a revelation of the principles of mutual aid at work. One reaches the conclusion that Kropotkin saw what he wanted to see in the evidence, and that all the French events under his scrutiny were coloured by contemporary Russian affairs. When he wrote of the

[1] Ibid., p. 451. Other contemporary admirers of Marat were Bax and Jaurès.

decadence of the French nobility and the plight of the French
peasantry in the last years of the *ancien régime*, he obviously had
in mind duplicates of the Russian aristocracy and peasantry of
the late nineteenth century. His unconventional depiction of
Louis XVI as a crafty, scheming, firm despot—rather than the
soft and indecisive monarch of popular history—invites the
speculation that he was drawn from the Romanovs whom Kropotkin had known. Kropotkin indicated in more than one place that
Russian events were following the French pattern closely, and
like many of his contemporaries he believed it was axiomatic that
the revolutionary experience was cumulative. In his conclusion
he asked:

Which of the nations will take upon herself the terrible but glorious
task of the next great revolution? One may have thought for a time that
it would be Russia. But if she should push her revolution further than
the mere limitation of the imperial power; if she touches the land
question in a revolutionary spirit—how far will she go? Will she know
how to avoid the mistake made by the French Assemblies, and will she
socialise the land and give it only to those who want to cultivate it with
their own hands? We know not: any answer to this question would
belong to the domain of prophecy.

The one thing certain is, that whatsoever nation enters on the path of
revolution in our own day, it will be heir to all our forefathers have done
in France. The blood they shed was shed for humanity—the sufferings
they endured were borne for the entire human race; . . .[1]

In the course of defining his attitude towards the revolution of
1905 and its aftermath, Kropotkin proved himself to be somewhat
out of step with many of his anarchist colleagues, including some
of his fellow Russians. A work like *The Great French Revolution*,
of course, brought praise and admiration, but the more ephemeral
material written three or four years earlier had produced some
important differences in attitude. Kropotkin's relative moderation,
his dislike of terror as a tactic, the gradualism that was implicit
in most of his remarks about representative institutions—all these
features of his writings brought occasional adverse comments
from nominal allies. At least two other major varieties of anarchism
—both favouring unrestrained terror—had come to life in Russia
and among the exile groups in 1905. Kropotkin's Anarchist-
Communism was distinguished from Anarchist-Syndicalism and

[1] P. A. Kropotkin, *The Great French Revolution, 1789–1793*, pp. 581–2.

Anarchist-Individualism, and the latter two groups were more conspicuous than that associated with the *Khleb' i Volia* movement.[1] Kropotkin, in short, found himself on the right wing of the Russian anarchist movement.

In this sense, he might be regarded as the Bernstein of the anarchists. A forthright and prolific writer, he was willing to follow his ideas where they led and to incorporate current political observations into his thought. Although in the final analysis he remained committed to his anti-capitalist, anti-statist doctrine, within the general outline of his philosophy he demonstrated considerable flexibility. Bernstein's assumption that existing institutions could be used to achieve the peaceful transition to Socialism and Kropotkin's belief that in the final analysis physical force would be necessary in the struggle were obviously far apart, but it is significant that each regarded the use of force as an evil. Both held the idea that it would be wrong for a small, revolutionary élite to try to seize power by violence; both saw physical combat as a defensive weapon, to be used by the masses if the regime in power initiated the violence. Both Bernstein and Kropotkin assumed that a reformer or a revolutionary had an ethical obligation to restrain hate and irrational violence, and this was not true of most of those who called themselves anarchists or Orthodox Marxists.

WAR AND REVOLUTION: 1914–1921

Differences between Kropotkin and most other vocal anarchists became more obvious as war approached, and when it finally came, the old Prince virtually broke away from the majority of his comrades by supporting the Entente cause against the Central Powers. In the eyes of most members of his own *Freedom* group, Kropotkin disgraced himself by his attitude; the most widely-held anarchist view was that the war should be opposed categorically, and no support should be rendered to any government engaged in it.

Kropotkin had feared the coming of war for thirty years and had written scores of articles deploring governmental policies that seemed to be leading to it. He had repeatedly shown himself to be

[1] For a discussion of these groups, see Paul Avrich, *The Russian Anarchists* (Princeton, 1967).

a pacifist, but he allowed one substantial reservation. If a nation, like France—where revolutionary transition seemed possible—were to be attacked by another power where the revolutionary potential was small, then the revolutionaries should not merely fold their arms and give *carte blanche* to the invaders. A decade before the outbreak of the war, Kropotkin was arguing in these terms against some of the French Syndicalists. Kropotkin believed that the social revolution might begin as a result of the war, but defence of the motherland after the fashion of 1793 would be necessary.[1] His pro-French and anti-German biases made him almost an instinctive opponent of the Central Powers long before the war began.

The war was only a few weeks old when the split between the pacifist and pro-Entente factions within the anarchist movement became wide and bitter. Kropotkin wrote a letter to *Freedom* in October 1914, arguing that it was vitally important that Germany be defeated.[2] Some of his comrades took issue with his stand the following month. Soon Kropotkin lost the privilege of presenting his ideas in *Freedom*—the paper that he had founded and sustained nearly thirty years earlier—because his position was too heretical for the conventional anarchists. When his erstwhile colleagues published an 'International Anarchist Manifesto on the War' the following winter, Kropotkin refused to sign it because of its opposition to the Allied war effort.[3] Instead, he and about a dozen others who shared his views drafted and published a separate manifesto, calling for a fight to the end against German militarism. Errico Malatesta, a respected voice in the movement and longtime friend of Kropotkin, now accused him and his colleagues of trying to put anarchists into the service of warmongers.

Kropotkin did not take pleasure in the fact that many whom he desired least to please—the leaders of the existing social and political order in Britain—admired his stand. Yet the threat of Teutonic militarism seemed so great that resistance to it warranted a virtual crusade; he believed everyone with the strength to fight and the will to defend the best in European civilization should help to crush the foe. Kropotkin's prose from this period is

---

[1] *Les Temps Nouveaux*, XI, 28 October 1905, p. 1.

[2] *Freedom*, XXVIII, October 1914, pp. 76–7. *Les Temps Nouveaux* suspended publication with the outbreak of hostilities in August.

[3] *Freedom*, XXIX (March 1915), p. 21.

passionate almost to the point of hysteria. The old Russian became more isolated and more bitter as the war dragged on.

The events of March 1917 seemed like a prophecy fulfilled. Kropotkin's reaction to the overthrow of Nicholas II was a renewal of his native romantic enthusiasm. He allowed himself to believe once again that his vision was being fulfilled in his own lifetime. He received an invitation to return to Russia soon after the establishment of the Provisional Government, an invitation that was hardly necessary. He had been making plans for the trip almost from the moment of the *coup* in St. Petersburg.

It had been more than forty years since he had fled from the Tsarist police, and he had been living in England for more than three decades. It required several weeks to settle his affairs, to arrange his passage and to make his departure. Finally, in June, he wrote his farewell to the British people in *The Times* and set sail amid a flurry of publicity that continued his anti-German, pro-Allied propaganda. His old colleagues at the *Freedom* office, who had tried to ignore him during most of the war, tossed a modified insult at him after his departure:

In bidding farewell to Kropotkin on his return to Russia, we can but hope that by contact with the Russian workers he may realise the errors of his attitude on the war, and with them work in the building up of that Anarchist society of which he was such an enthusiastic exponent prior to the war. His numerous Anarchist books and pamphlets will be read and remembered long after his patriotic backsliding in this war has been forgotten.[1]

The revolutionary situation in Petrograd in 1917 was not the kind that Kropotkin had anticipated in *The Conquest of Bread*, with embattled revolutionaries behind their barricades, co-operating selflessly against clear-cut authoritarian enemies. Here was a country in chaos, threatened along a thousand-mile battlefront by German and Austro–Hungarian armies and challenged within by militant rebels from both the Left and the Right. Kropotkin was a witness to the Bolsheviks' attempted *coup d'état* in July and the other disruptive developments of the summer. In public addresses and articles he reiterated his conviction that the war against Germany must be pressed to victory and he lent moral support to the efforts of Alexander Kerensky to hold the provisional

[1] *Freedom*, Vol. XXXI (July 1917), p. 32.

government together. Kerensky offered him a cabinet office early in August, but Kropotkin, consistent with his anarchist principles, declined. He remained busy with speeches and meetings, however, in spite of his age and ill health.

Kropotkin's only major role in the Revolution was his famous —or as his critics believed, infamous—appearance at the Moscow State Conference late in August. Kerensky had called the Conference in an effort to rally all revolutionary groups behind the Provisional Government, and some of the aged heroes of the Revolution had opportunities to appear. Here Kropotkin made a speech that his leading biographers have found unfortunate and inconsistent with his lifelong attitudes. He not only appealed for a continuation of the war, but he argued that Western countries were moving gradually towards Socialism and that the conduct of David Lloyd George was an indication of this trend. He called for support of the projected Constituent Assembly, and he made favourable references to the federalist system of government of the United States. His boldest statement was a call for a republican regime for Russia, a proposal that was unusual in that situation because the Provisional Government and most of those present were still formally committed to a Constitutional Monarchy. Many in the audience liked the suggestion of a republic; he received a long ovation on this point.[1] But there were slurs and insults from the Russian anarchists and the revolutionary Left. This moderation was 'fatal' to his prestige and effectiveness, his biographers have concluded. 'It was a classic example of the danger of compromise, and was used by the Bolsheviks to rob Kropotkin of much of the devotion that still existed towards him, and also to discredit further the whole anarchist movement, which did not support him on such issues.'[2]

Whether Kropotkin's conduct was so unfortunate or so damaging to the anarchist cause, as Woodcock and Avakumović argued, is an open question. It is doubtful whether the anarchists would have had more success even if Kropotkin had not supported the war effort and even if he had not proposed a republican government at the Moscow State Conference. In any event, Kropotkin's action was basically consistent with the ideas that he had been expressing from time to time for the previous twenty years, and his

[1] For a Reuters report of the occasion, see *The Times* (London), 30 August 1917, 8a.   [2] Woodcock and Avakumović, op. cit., pp. 400–1.

remarks should not have come as a surprise. Certainly anyone who had read his essays of the 1905-9 period or his history of the French Revolution could have anticipated such an argument. He had not isolated his scholarship or his political commentary from current events, as some anarchists did, and he could not ignore the historical evidence that he had consulted. When he argued for continued participation in the war, he remembered the embattled France of 1792, fighting to preserve its achievements against foreign kings and armies. He knew that it would mean humiliation for the Revolution to surrender, and military success would enable the Constituent Assembly to move more boldly. In his seventy-fifth year, after a lifetime of waiting, he had obviously concluded that it was necessary to hold what had been won as a basis for future change.

The weeks rolled on and brought November, with its momentous but relatively quiet sequel. Kropotkin had long feared and often criticized the Bolsheviks, not only because they were Marxist and authoritarian in principle, but because they seemed to represent the Terroristic tradition of the French Revolution that he disliked. After they came to power, Kropotkin participated for a time in Moscow anarchist activities. He objected to Lenin's methods both in a face-to-face interview and in letters that became known in the West. The Bolshevik practice of taking and holding hostages as a means of restraining potential opposition particularly infuriated him. After June of 1918, he lived in Dmitrov, a village about forty miles north of Moscow and out of contact with the main stream of events. His failing health and the restrictions of the Bolshevik regime made it increasingly difficult for him to play a role in public affairs.

Less than three years of life remained to him after he moved to Dmitrov, and conditions proved to be difficult for the old rebel and his devoted wife and daughter. They suffered the privations that were common in Russia between 1918 and 1921, but Kropotkin preferred not to accept special rations that the Bolshevik regime offered him. He had little contact with the Western countries, and erroneous reports circulated in Britain and America to the effect that he had been imprisoned by the Bolsheviks. His only important formal communication with the West was a letter to Brandes written from Dmitrov in April, 1919.[1] It was widely reproduced

[1] Brandes, op. cit., Vol. II, pp. 225-9.

in left-wing publications. The letter contradicted the reports of his arrest, but its main purpose was to offer an analysis of the current Russian situation. Pursuing his often-used analogy between the French Revolution and the Russian affairs, he characterized the Bolsheviks as neo-Jacobins, using methods that would eventually lead to a 'furious and wicked reaction'. The Allied intervention in the Russian civil war, however, was simply contributing to this tendency, generating hostility and stimulating chauvinism among the Russian people, creating hardship instead of offering necessary bread and building materials. The Allies, in short, were assuming the role that Austria and Prussia had played against revolutionary France in 1793, and thus contributing to the internal oppression.

Several friends from the West managed to visit him, including the journalist George Lansbury, editor of the London *Daily Herald*. He found the old man 'scornful and condemnatory of the Soviet Government and all its methods', but confident that the Russian nation would 'win its salvation' if the outside world would cease to molest it.[1] Emma Goldman, who like Kropotkin had returned to her homeland from abroad in the hope of seeing an anarchist society born, was another visitor who recorded his frustrations; she saw him twice in 1920. The Bolsheviks were crushing the revolutionary impulse in their struggle to retain power, Kropotkin told her, but he did not feel it appropriate to speak out against the new authoritarian dictatorship while Russia was under attack from the Allied interventionists and while Russian people were suffering from the Allied blockade. The old man had not lost his optimism, and he believed that contemporary errors would be corrected in the future.[2] And in the hope that he could serve this cause, he was working once again on his study of revolutionary ethics. He never finished that project, because in February of 1921 he died. His funeral became the occasion for the last public anarchist function in revolutionary Russia.

THE HALF-FINISHED ANARCHIST 'ETHICS'

It was largely the violence and immorality of the ascendant Bolshevik movement that caused Kropotkin to turn to his study

[1] George Lansbury, *What I saw in Russia* (London, 1920), pp. 28–30.
[2] Emma Goldman, *My Disillusionment in Russia* (Garden City, N.Y., 1923), pp. 53–6, 153–9.

of ethics again in the last years of his life. On several occasions in the previous thirty years he had written brief pieces or worked at an 'anarchist morality', but it required first-hand evidence of revolutionary brutality—and perhaps also the involuntary isolation of a place like Dmitrov—to make him give sustained attention to the subject.

The *Ethics* that was finally published from his incomplete manuscript shortly after his death is an intriguing fragment. Some critics and admirers of the book have lamented the fact that he did not live to develop the case that he wanted to present for a scientific system for anarchist morality. The main lines of the argument seem to be clear, however, in the existing portion. This is primarily a history of ethics, which presumably was to have been followed by a dialectical demonstration of the moral system.

Kropotkin had reached some of his basic conclusions as early as 1890, when he wrote the pamphlet entitled *Anarchist Morality*. The portion of the *Ethics* that he was able to complete does not depart in any substantial measure from that early tract, which contains many of the same arguments as *Mutual Aid*. First, man like the animals is instinctively communal; the 'golden rule' is the pattern of nature. This aspect of man's nature may be obscured or retarded by prejudice, but it is fundamental. Second, justice, in the anarchist view, means a recognition of the equality of all men and a removal of the inequality that present society imposes. Third is the argument—which Kropotkin attributes to the contemporary French philosopher Marie Jean Guyau—that many men possess an instinct and a capacity to serve their fellows far beyond their obligations and their own personal interests. This excess of the emotional and intellectual energy necessary for survival is the stuff of human progress as well as the basis of the natural, anarchistic morality.[1]

While Kropotkin set forth his basic ethical argument in 1890, he recognized that it was one thing to assert a theory of morality and another thing to demonstrate its scientific validity. As a devotee of science, he felt certain that philosophy, like any other field of learning, could be subjected to scientific examination and demonstration. (In this respect, Kropotkin had a different faith and more expansive expectations than Bernstein, who—as we have

[1] Marie Jean Guyau, *Esquisse d'une morale sans obligation, ni sanction* (Paris, 1890), 2nd edn.

seen—did not believe Socialism could become a *'wissenschaft'*
because it involved moral judgements. It was those judgements
themselves that could be validated or rejected by the scientific
method, in Kropotkin's view.) But this was not a simple matter.

Kropotkin made a clumsy start on this project in 1901 when he
published an essay—or more accurately a collection of notes and
observations—entitled *Modern Science and Anarchism*.[1] This tract
does not represent any substantial advance or variation on his
earlier writings, but it shows him attempting to make Communist
Anarchism the logical culmination of the intellectual-technical-
scientific advances of the eighteenth and nineteenth centuries.
His conclusion was that the new 'scientific' discoveries of the late
nineteenth century had provided new techniques of measurement,
new electrical principles, and new understandings of mechanics
to revolutionize knowledge, ultimately applicable to the realm of
social affairs. The essay is almost pure positivism, but Kropotkin
did not give unreserved praise to Comte. Although Comte was
on 'the proper way' to a science of human societies, his system did
not reach its fulfilment because he did not develop a morality
based on biology. Now, he believed, biological evidence was
sufficient to do this.

But once again Kropotkin had made an assertion and not a
demonstration, and the problem was getting more complicated.
At about the turn of the century, Nietzsche's attacks on the
Christian ethic, his assumptions about a perpetual conflict
between the most advanced men and their societies, and his
speculations on the coming 'supermen', were attracting attention
among the intellectuals, and Kropotkin was aware that this
philosophy had an important appeal. Nietzsche was especially
exciting to some of the so-called Individualist-Anarchists and
those in whom the urge to violence and destruction was strongest,
or at least so it seemed to Kropotkin. In any event, here was a
rival ethic that was also being regarded as anarchistic, and Kropotkin felt a need to criticize it.[2] Nietzsche's ideal of the 'blond beast'

[1] Peter Kropotkin, *Sovremennaia Nauka i Anarkhizm'* (London, 1901). It
was issued in English in Philadelphia in 1903, but the standard English edition
is *Modern Science and Anarchism* (London, 1912).
[2] Kropotkin, 'Une lettre inédite de Pierre Kropotkine à Max Nettlau',
International Review of Social History, IX (1964), Pt. 2, pp. 268–85. This letter,
summarizing his attitude towards Nietzsche's ethics, was written on 5 March
1902.

was a 'false individualism', involving the slavery or servility of some to gratify the egoism of the 'beast'. It is a brutal kind of individualism, related to that of bourgeois society, that demands exploitation and suppression, and therefore it is self-defeating; the domineering 'individualist' is the slave of those whom he dominates, and is therefore not an individualist at all. The true individualist is he who establishes his special identity by distinctive contributions to or on behalf of the larger community. Thus Kropotkin dismissed categorically Nietzche's moral philosophy, but it seemed to him to remain one of the serious challenges of the new century.

Kropotkin seriously undertook his work on ethics soon after the turn of the century and produced two articles, 'The Ethical Needs of the Present Day' and 'The Morality of Nature', for the *Nineteenth Century* in 1904 and 1905. These essays formed the basis for chapters in the book on which Kropotkin was working at the time of his death, and they added little to his previous ideas. His involvement in the propaganda and other activities arising from the 1905 Revolution apparently diverted him from his project. He reported to a friend again in 1913 that he had resumed his study of ethics. He did not make any substantial progress, however, until 1918. By this time, events had convinced him that a new ethics incorporating his theories was 'absolutely necessary'. It was not that books could produce intellectual movements, he wrote, but they could clarify ideas and help to produce a higher morality at a time when human thought was 'struggling between Nietzsche and Kant . . .'[1]

The first four chapters are reminiscent of *Mutual Aid*; they contain the material that he had previously written. The fifth chapter begins the history of ethics in Western civilization, with a level of criticism and exposition that showed him to be competent in yet another field of learning.

The Russian scholar had a qualified respect for some ancient Greek philosophers—beginning with the Sophists—because in their analysis of morality, they departed from the religions and superstitions of their predecessors and considered them as institutions of human social origin. The rejection of any ethical system

[1] The English language edition, which was carefully prepared with the assistance of material that Kropotkin issued in the West, is *Ethics: Origin and Development*, authorized translation from the Russian by Louis Friedland and Joseph R. Piroshnikoff (New York, 1924), pp. xii–xiii.

based upon theology or metaphysics was central to Kropotkin's thought, and he believed the Sophists had taken the first step in this direction. Subsequent Greek philosophy, however, did not continue the advance. Plato gave the ethical speculation a wrong direction when he sought the origins of morality outside the universe—in the 'Idea'. Both Plato's 'other-worldly' assumptions and his authoritarian political theories seemed to Kropotkin to have been an insidious influence in European thought.

The Greek whose work Kropotkin most admired was Epicurus, because his writings contained the germs of a modern morality. The idea that 'the primary and natural good' is based in the quest for happiness commended itself to the anarchist because it seemed to provide one of the ingredients of a naturalistic morality; there was an instinct for happiness that would serve as a guide to conduct.[1] Yet Kropotkin would not rely merely on a simple 'eudemonistic' explanation for the origin of morality, since he recognized that selfish as well as socially desirable conduct could result from the quest for personal satisfaction and happiness.

In dealing with Jesus and Christianity, Kropotkin's analysis is reminiscent of Voltaire and the Enlightenment. It expresses admiration for the simplicity, the charity, and the egalitarian message implicit in Jesus' teaching—and attributes some of the same qualities to the Gautama Buddha. Then follows the familiar argument that Jesus' moral code was contaminated by the church, which introduced sacraments and the priesthood and accepted the Eastern idea of a struggle between good and evil. The church became a government of the chosen, dedicated to rooting out error and sin, and thus an instrument of persecution rather than a force for equality and charity, and it placed the source of ethics in the Christian God.

It remained for the Renaissance writers to suggest again an ethical standard based on nature and man. The works of Bacon, Descartes, Grotius, and Spinoza won a large measure of Kropotkin's respect for their contributions to a rational, non-metaphysical ethical system. He evaluated most of the important European philosophers in turn, judging each according to his personal standard. He had especially high praise for Shaftesbury, who was 'the first to point out the existence of mutual aid among animals', and who had recognized the origin of moral conceptions

---

[1] Kropotkin, *Ethics: Origin and Development*, pp. 103–9.

in inborn social instincts.[1] Shaftesbury seemed to be developing an ethical system liberated from outside authority, from narrow eudemonism, and from utilitarianism. And furthermore he had answered Hobbes, whose *Leviathan* was understandably a pernicious work in the eyes of a philosophical anarchist. Kropotkin dissected the arguments of Hobbes but gave him his due for helping to remove ethics from the metaphysical realm.

Thus the study advanced, becoming almost a catalogue of ethical theories in the latter chapters. The eighteenth-century philosophers and the makers of the French Revolution had contributed the concept of justice—the second important ingredient of the anarchist morality. Justice, or equality, as an aspect of ethics was then formalized in the philosophy of Proudhon, whom Kropotkin praised most warmly.

The crowded canvas of the nineteenth century obviously troubled Kropotkin and one senses that he did not have the energy to develop the theme here as he would have liked to do. Basically, he gave attention and recognition to Darwin, Comte, Spencer, and the socialist movement. In both the third chapter and near the end of the book, Kropotkin returned to the theme that Darwin had at one time reached a sound conclusion—that the instinct for social self-preservation was stronger than the instinct for individual self-preservation and that the drive for sociality and co-operation within a species was greater than the tendency towards individual competition. But Darwin's message was narrowed and diverted by some of his followers, especially Kropotkin's old foe, Huxley, who 'proved to be quite incapable of following his great teacher in the realm of moral thought'.[2]

Comte had helped provide a new basis for serious scientific thought with his positivism, and socialism had helped to consolidate the advances made by the eighteenth century and to enlarge nineteenth-century ethical thought with its teaching of political and social equality.

... we have in socialism a great moral current, and from now on no new systems of ethics can be built without in some way considering this teaching, which is the expression of the striving of the working masses for social justice and equity.[3]

[1] Ibid., p. 171.
[2] Ibid., p. 282.
[3] Ibid., p. 231.

To the instinct for mutual aid and the drive for equality, it was necessary to add the idea of self-sacrifice to complete the new ethics, and Kropotkin dwelled on this third ingredient in his final pages. His last complete chapter (the Conclusion was not finished when he died) is devoted to the ethical speculations of Guyau. It appears that Kropotkin was rushing to the end, relying upon the words and ideas of Guyau to convey the arguments he had hoped to develop in the second volume.[1]

Generally speaking [Kropotkin wrote], it is safe to say that in his treatise on the bases of morality without obligation and without the sanction of religion, Guyau expressed the modern interpretation of morality and of its problems in the form it was taking in the minds of educated men towards the beginning of the twentieth century.[2]

Kropotkin found in Guyau the argument that man possesses more powers than are necessary for his own personal needs, and these extra energies are willingly given to the service of others. Man is endowed with a 'moral fecundity', a willingness and a natural drive to yield his extra energies and talents for non-selfish causes. And this often involved struggles and risks not oriented towards one's personal welfare.

All great discoveries, explorations, and advances by humanity had required such risk and dedication. At times, the risk was 'intellectual' or 'metaphysical', rather than physical; some measure of risk is involved when a new hypothesis is advanced, as Kropotkin well knew. Usually the risk does not require jeopardizing one's life for others or for the higher cause, but in those cases when the ultimate self-sacrifice is required, the act becomes 'one of the most precious and most powerful forces in history'. Thus martyrdom for a social cause has special ethical significance.

In his final and rather eloquent statement on the nobility of personal sacrifice for the social cause, Kropotkin embraced a type of individualism, a kind of Nietzscheism in reverse, although he would have denied he was doing so. He believed he was proceeding from his scientific assumptions and by rational means, but he had ended his search by putting his faith in men of superior dedication to the cause of humanity. In fact, Kropotkin's ethics with its emphasis on the commitment to change and with its affirmation of integrity and justice in the face of oppression and brutality,

[1] The chapter is *Ethics: Origin and development*, pp. 322–32.
[2] Ibid., pp. 330–1.

bears a resemblance to some of the existentialist thought of the subsequent generation. Kropotkin, of course, was an optimist and presumably did not have the sense of the absurd or the experience of despair that many of the existentialists felt, but like some of them, he was engaged in a quest for meaning in the face of a chaotic world. His philosophy contained echoes of the Russian nihilism and of the *narodnik* thought of his youth, but it was also a rather crude anticipation of the most characteristic European philosophy of the mid-twentieth century.

VIII

SHAW

Beyond Socialism

By the end of the 1890s, Shaw had completed his education in Socialism and was far advanced in his experimentation with drama. He was better known at this time for his Socialism than for his playwriting, at least in London, because his articles, tracts, and street-corner speeches were more successful among the left-wing sympathizers than his earlier plays had been with theatre managers. It was not until after the turn of the century that Shaw began to receive substantial recognition in Britain for his talent as a dramatist.

Shaw tried to put the theatre at the service of the revolution in much the same way that Kropotkin tried to use history and philosophy for that purpose. Although Shaw occasionally wrote 'potboilers', apparently for money and for the pleasure of creating situations and conversations, most plays carried some serious social message. He regularly insisted that his purpose was deadly serious and that his objective was the total transformation of society. His important plays after 1898 were experiments with unusual social and political ideas, and the prefaces to them were usually overloaded with propaganda.

Shaw, like Kropotkin, seems to have approached the threshold of existentialism in some of the dramatic creations of his mature years. Indeed Robert Brustein, in his provocative *The Theatre of Revolt*, has represented Shaw as being engaged in a 'profound and bitter existential revolt' which he fails to penetrate sufficiently to give classic stature to his drama or to make his philosophy significant.[1] Shaw did not recognize the darker side of rebellion, in Brustein's view; his persistent optimism blinded him on this score. Thus he did not produce a philosophy or a point of view

---

[1] Robert Brustein, *The Theatre of Revolt* (Boston, Toronto, 1964), pp. 183–277.

which—like existentialism—speaks to the generation of the middle
of the twentieth century.

Many scholars have pointed out the dichotomy between Shaw's
artistic creations and his propaganda. He obviously engaged in
quests in his dramas that did not completely fit his political
purposes. Much more than he was willing to acknowledge, he was
engaged in art for its own sake and for the pleasure it gave him;
he acknowledged this quite readily near the end of his life. Like
his friend Morris who believed that works of art should be useful
but who took the greatest pleasure in producing books, tapestries,
printing-type, and romances that were merely decorative, so Shaw
followed his whims and impulses in producing some of his pieces
for the theatre, and most of his plays are much less revolutionary
in the conventional sense than are the prefaces that he attached to
them. Thus Shaw as a Socialist and as a social commentator is not
consistent; his unfriendly critics over the years have made much
of this truism.

The inconsistency can be explained in part by the fact that after
he became sceptical about the various types of Socialism that he
had known in London before the turn of the century, he found it
possible to embellish revolutionary ideas in his imagination and
to put them into dramatic form for three-dimensional investiga-
tion. And in doing so, he could recast the characters, the organizations, and the ideals that he had studied between 1882 and 1900
in various forms. He could even put the capitalists, the military
hero, the dictator—traditional foes of Socialism—under artistic
scrutiny and give them the advantage of his remarkable polemical
talents. He invented an amalgam of biology and religion which he
eventually offered in *Back to Methuselah*, and he dabbled in most
of the important controversies of his time. And he did all this
without completely abandoning Socialism. He remained emotionally and intellectually committed to the aspirations of the most
romantic Socialists, and usually could not abide criticism of any
brand of Socialism—from anarchism to Marxism to Fabianism—
without taking up his pen in defence of it. Yet he was unhappy
with all of the schools of Socialism that he had known in his
younger days, and he was alternately criticizing them, trying to
purify them, or attempting to make others understand what the
revolutionary tradition was all about. Much of the drama and the
propaganda that he wrote in the last half-century of his life was

the product of his search for new definitions and contexts or substitutes for the Socialism that he had learned in the 1890s.

Shaw's occasional revolutionary outbursts and insults against British politics often diverted attention from the fact that during the last fifty years of his life, he continued to issue moderate tracts of the Fabian variety, calling his readers to adopt specific reform policies. Several times he returned to the work of producing down-to-earth articles or handbooks that would inform the uninformed and demonstrate the respectability of Socialist policies. Some of the titles suggest the reasonable tone that he employed in this type of propaganda: *The Common Sense of Municipal Trading* (1904), *Common Sense About the War* (1914), *The Intelligent Woman's Guide to Socialism and Capitalism* (1928), and *Everybody's Political What's What* (1944). When in 1947, for the fourth time, he wrote a preface to the *Fabian Essays*, he seemed to take pride in their services to social stability:

Although this volume of essays is sixty years old, and I, its editor, am ninety, it is still alive doing its old work, which was, and is, to rescue Socialism and Communism from the barricades, from the pseudo-democracy of the Party System, from confusion with the traditional heterodoxies of anti-clericalism, individualist anti-State republicanism, and middle-class Bohemian anarchism: in short, to make it a constitutional movement in which the most respectable citizens and families may enlist, without forfeiting the least scrap of their social or spiritual standing.[1]

Shaw alternately admired the Fabian method and repudiated it. He deplored conventional politics yet he could not abandon them completely. Near the middle of his life, he tried his hand at regular politics and governmental administration. For six years from 1897 to 1904, he served as vestryman and borough councillor of London's district of St. Pancras, serving with distinction in the mundane business of governing a municipal unit. He even stood for a position on the London County Council, but he experienced defeat at the polls because of his unpopular views on church matters and his unorthodox political campaigning. During these years, his hopes for political reform—and specifically for the Socialist movement—seem to have diminished almost to vanishing point, and his frustrations can be seen clearly in his

[1] Shaw, *Fabian Essays*, 6th edn. (London, 1962), p. 295.

plays. Yet he continued to preach incessantly as the realist and the common sense philosopher.

CAESAR AND SUPERMAN

During his years as vestryman and borough councillor, Shaw wrote two of his major plays and one of the more interesting minor works. The latter, *Captain Brassbound's Conversion*, shows the common sense of a rather unsophisticated heroine—Lady Cicely Waynflete—victorious over conventional virtues and respectable political, commercial, and religious ideals of her associates. The two major plays—*Caesar and Cleopatra* and *Man and Superman*—present heroes who attempt to carry on their projects in a sane and orderly manner, but who are deflected by forces or conditions beyond their control.

Caesar, the world conqueror of ancient history and the hero of traditional drama, becomes under Shaw's pen a harassed politician who has great trouble coping with underlings and associates. We are reminded by a number of devices—including a prologue added later and a number of intentional anachronisms—that mankind has changed very little since the first century B.C. He wrote in the notes:

... the period of time covered by history is far too short to allow of any perceptible progress in the popular sense of Evolution of the Human Species. The notion that there has been any such Progress since Caesar's time (less than 20 centuries) is too absurd for discussion. All the savagery, barbarism, dark ages and the rest of it of which we have any record as existing in the past, exists at the present moment.[1]

What has commonly been misunderstood as progress in modern times is only an illusion, Shaw said in this context, and held out no hope for an early change. His cynicism, his Ibsenite observations, and his artistic impulses thus combined in a very un-Fabian conclusion—that common-sense policies will not be very effective in changing mankind.

Interwoven with the farcical situations is a deeply pessimistic message. The most that Caesar's intelligence and sanity can achieve is to make the best of recurring bad situations. He cannot stop the hideous cycle of war, treachery, and revenge in which

---

[1] Shaw, *Collected Works*, IX, p. 204.

his fellow Romans and the Egyptians are caught, and he recognizes at the end of the play that he will himself soon be the victim of it. Any hope of change is very remote. Caesar says:

... And so, to the end of history, murder shall breed murder, always in the name of right and honor and peace, until the gods are tired of blood and create a race that can understand.

It is not merely a feline Cleopatra who has turned Caesar from his objectives; it is an irrational civilization. In this play, for the first time, Shaw wrote comedy that transcended itself. It is the nearest thing to tragedy that he was to create until the appearance of *St. Joan* nearly a quarter of a century later. It is not insignificant that such a solemn commentary should appear in comic form at the very time that Shaw was losing his enthusiasm for the Socialism that had occupied his energies so completely for a decade and a half.

Man and Superman (1903) is an even more explicit testimonial to his disenchantment with progress and politics—and specifically with Socialism. It might even have been sub-titled 'More Illusions of Socialism'. In the same way that James Morell was a personification of what was wrong with Christian Socialism of the 1890s, Jack Tanner was a personification of what Shaw found to be amiss with Socialism generally after 1900. Shaw may have used his old foe Hyndman as the model for Tanner, but he represents more than Marxian Socialism. Tanner is a generalized revolutionist, made silly in his moderately revolutionary aspirations because there are such greater forces operating in the world.

Shaw was feeling his artistic wings as never before. He was not merely transcending Socialism; he was adapting the Don Juan legend and modernizing Mozart with the aid of Nietzsche and Bergson. In this company, the pretensions of Socialism appear rather trivial, and this was precisely Shaw's attitude. Jack Tanner is clearly never going to achieve his political objectives; whatever role he has to play in mankind's destiny will be the result of his marital union with Ann Whitefield. It is his highest duty to compromise his Socialist purity, to yield to the Life Force, and to do his bit towards breeding the future Superman. Caesar had anticipated that the gods might create a better race; Tanner acquiesces in the idea that mankind must slowly produce it by evolution. As Shaw despaired of Socialism, he put his faith in evolutionary biology or—as he was to call it in 1920—meta-biology.

Man and Superman bristles with satire against the Socialists in the text of the play. There is not only Tanner as an example of the ineffective revolutionary, but also the thief Mendoza and his bands of brigands. Mendoza is another of Shaw's diabolian figures, at war with the standard morality as well as with society. He is one more gentlemanly revolutionary, who tries to keep order among his squabbling Social Democratic and anarchist followers. He believes himself to be a practical man, free of illusions. He almost sounds Shavian. '. . . I am not a slave to any superstition. I have swallowed all the formulas, even that of Socialism; though, in a sense, once a Socialist, always a Socialist.' This is both a boast and a confession. Mendoza proves to be a victim of romance, but he is superior to the quarrelsome, ridiculous Socialist-brigands whom he is trying to lead. His colleagues are types rather than person-alities. The Rowdy Social-Democrat, the Sulky Social-Democrat, the Anarchist, and the French revolutionary are all parodies of branches of the left-wing movement.

Then, as if to underscore his discontent, Shaw attached the bitter *Revolutionist's Handbook* to the end of the work. This strange blend of Fabianism and Nietzscheism is gratuitous; it is not necessary to the drama and it belabours his point. But it is impor-tant as a summing-up of his views on Socialism after almost exactly twenty years in the movement, and it reinforces, in tract form, the points that Shaw had represented in comedy.

The *Handbook* begins in the Fabian spirit, defining the Revolu-tionist simply as 'one who desires to discard the existing social order and try another'. No reference to violence or chaos intrudes here; a popular election in England is an opportunity for revolu-tion. 'Revolution is therefore a national institution in England; and its advocacy by an Englishman needs no apology.' This is Shaw the preacher of 'common-sense' politics. Yet before he has released the reader from the brief preface, there is a counter-statement:

AND YET

Revolutions have never lightened the burden of tyranny: they have only shifted it to another shoulder.[1]

---

[1] Shaw, *The Collected Works*, Vol. X, p. 175.

What is needed, Tanner/Shaw believed, is a new kind of total revolution. The method of the Fabian and the method of the dynamitard and assassin are both 'fundamentally futile', the readers of *The Revolutionist's Handbook* are told:

. . . we may as well make up our minds that Man will return to his idols and his cupidities, in spite of all 'movements' and all revolutions, until his nature is changed.[1]

Here is Caesar's conclusion again; Shaw was not afraid of redundancy and operated on the assumption that men would not understand unless he made his main points repeatedly in provocative terms. And then he drove it home as emphatically as possible;

The only fundamental and possible Socialism is the socialization of the selective breeding of Man: in other terms, of human evolution. We must eliminate the Yahoo, or his vote will wreck the commonwealth.[2]

Such negative sentiments are stuff of which destructive policies are made, and there is much in the *Handbook*—particularly in the 'Maxims for Revolutionists'—that suggests an anarchistic position:

Democracy substitutes election by the incompetent many for appointment by the corrupt few.

Equality is fundamental in every department of social organization.

Property, said Proudhon, is theft. This is the only perfect truism that has been uttered on the subject.

Civilization is a disease produced by the practice of building societies with rotten material.

Criminals do not die by the hands of the law. They die by the hands of other men.

The assassin Czolgosz made President McKinley a hero by assassinating him. The United States of America made Czolgosz a hero by the same process.

There are a number of other similar utterances that can be picked from the handbook. This does not prove, of course, that the assumptions of Tanner/Shaw coincided with those of the anarchists on all points, but in his despair he came to share some of the same convictions about the futility of achieving a better society on present foundations. The renegade Fabian, like Kropotkin at a later stage of his own development, yearned for the total transformation of society by means of superior individuals. Though Kropotkin took pride in his 'scientific' analysis and Shaw

[1] Shaw, *The Collected Works*, Vol. X, p. 198.   [2] Ibid., p. 210.

in his 'common sense' approach to contemporary problems, each turned to the charismatic figure to provide the only progress that was meaningful. Yet each continued to be a product of his past commitments. Shaw had remained a Fabian in method and had become an anarchist in objectives; he tried to be both Bernstein and Kropotkin.

This dichotomy between method and objective has been partly responsible for the varied reactions of critics and scholars. It has been analysed in various ways. Emil Strauss has shown with admirable clarity that *Man and Superman* is the climax of a long process of Shaw's disillusionment. 'The comedy itself completes the process of disillusion and conversion by showing the hero swallowed up by the world which he understands, despises and which—quite in vain—he wants to revolutionize.'[1] The only sphere remaining to one who suffers such defeat is that 'of thought and dreams, of contemplation'. The *Don Juan in Hell* dream-scene gives *Man and Superman* its philosophical dimension and its quasi-religious significance. Chesterton said that Shaw especially in *Man and Superman* had become 'a complete and colossal mystic'.[2] As usual, the playwright's old intellectual adversary offered a productive suggestion, but being susceptible to mystical attractions himself, perhaps he exaggerated. It would be more to the point to say that Shaw was the most cosmopolitan of disenchanted Socialists. He had examined and found wanting the promises of contemporary philosophy, modern science, religion and democracy, as well as the varieties of Socialism, but he tried to salvage something from each of them. But he had only started to do this when he had finished *Man and Superman*.

The concept of the superman is not a very manageable one in the drama. Once the idea of superior individuals—destined and entitled to guide mankind to its new stature—has been adopted as a working hypothesis, it becomes a challenge to define his qualities. Shaw did not immediately accept the challenge, although he occasionally played with the idea of the transformation of man in subsequent plays. Arthur Nethercot asserted in his careful analysis of Shavian characters that there are 'no real Supermen in any of Shaw's plays, with one possible, but dubious, exception'.[3]

[1] Strauss, op. cit., p. 47.   [2] Chesterton, op. cit., p. 167.
[3] Arthur H. Nethercot, *Men and Supermen: The Shavian Portrait Gallery* (Cambridge, 1954), p. 287.

This exception is indeed questionable; it is the youth Raphael, who has feathers like a bird, in the *Far Fetched Fables* that Shaw composed at the age of ninety-two. As Nethercot correctly suggests, he is more like an embodied spirit than a superior variety of humanity. It is not easy to identify any character in Shavian drama as an intentional representation of the Superman, but there are several tentative sketches.

The peripatetic Irishman was not willing to spend all his time on even such a hopeful concept as the Superman. In *John Bull's Other Island*, it was the plight of his homeland—for which he revealed a sentimental affection that he would not allow his intellect to acknowledge—that came under scrutiny. This play, written and performed soon after the completion of *Man and Superman*, reasserts Shaw's contempt for existing values and ridicules the capitalist entrepreneur, but we have no Socialist in the scene as comic-hero. The dissenting figure is hardly even a rebel; the saintly defrocked priest Mr. Keegan is a half-mad remnant of medieval Christendom—the opposite of a Superman. He talks to the animals and lives in a dream world most of the time. Yet he possesses a keen wit and has a sensitive understanding of the objectives of the investor Broadbent, who has entered Ireland to impose 'progress'. Shaw must have recognized that one direction to take in opposition to the prevailing values system was to follow the fantasies of Father Keegan; William Morris had done something of the sort in the 1890s. (In fact, the perceptive Irvine thought he recognized a correlation between Morris's socialism and Keegan's vision of heaven.) But Shaw would not stay long in this realm at this stage of his career as a playwright. The Irish rebellion did not impress him greatly; there were too many immature romantics in the ranks, and Shaw had long since lost interest in that kind of hero. The analysis of the Life Force and the search for the qualities of the Superman required him to turn to matters more central to the issues of his time.

THE PROBLEM OF 'MAJOR BARBARA'

No single play by Shaw has provoked more varied critical comments than *Major Barbara*. There is no consensus on Shaw's objective or on whether the views of his diabolian hero, Andrew Undershaft, should be read as those of the author. Nor is there

agreement about whether Undershaft and his capitalist values are
the victors or the vanquished in the intellectual struggle against
the Salvation Army Christianity of his daughter Barbara and the
poetic-humanist values of his future son-in-law, Cusins. That the
play is an allegory is obvious to most, but there are several possible
readings of the symbols and results. The 'First Aid to Critics' with
which Shaw began his preface has not provided an unequivocal
clue as to his final purpose.

Perhaps the most commonly held view is that the munitions'
maker Undershaft is triumphant and that he suggests a capitalist
Superman. This 'profiteer in mutilation and murder' persuades
Cusins to be his successor in the management of the munitions
industry and Barbara enthusiastically accepts the decision. Emil
Strauss concluded that Shaw was compromising completely with
capitalism when he wrote this play. *Major Barbara*, he decided,
is *Mrs. Warren's Profession* redone, with victory more obviously
on the side of the realistic money-maker.[1] The Marxian-oriented
Alick West carried this analysis even further, treating *Major
Barbara* as the final stage of Shaw's surrender to capitalist-
oriented Fabianism.[2] West yearned for the 'unspoken play' that
lies beneath the surface—that Shaw's creative instincts always told
him to write, but that his Fabianism made impossible. Shaw
always disarms his rebels, West asserted, imposing on them
the solutions that his Fabianism requires, and that means acquiesc-
ing in capitalism.

Irvine, whose criticism is the most consistently satisfactory,
offered the opposite thesis—that 'both *Major Barbara* and its
Preface imply the theory of class war in its most drastic form'.
Shaw had lost his faith in democratic processes and had taken
refuge 'in the Marxian dialectic of force'.[3] It is possible to analyse
the poet Cusins as a symbol of the proletariat struggling for the
power with which to destroy capitalism; the film version of the
play produced in 1940 implemented this idea.[4] Eric Bentley
represents still another important school of criticism, believing
that Shaw intended Cusins to be victorious.[5] He wins both the

[1] Strauss, op. cit., pp. 55–8.
[2] Alick West, *A Good Man Fallen Among Fabians* (London, 1950).
[3] Irvine, op. cit., pp. 262–3.
[4] Bernard F. Dukore, 'The Undershaft Maxims', *Modern Drama*, IX (May
1966), pp. 90–100.
[5] Bentley, *Bernard Shaw*, pp. 166–7. For a complementary argument, see the

father's wealth and power and the idealistic daughter's hand, hopefully combining the two and possessing the power to make war on war. This latter analysis seems most acceptable in view of Shaw's intellectual and emotional preferences, and it is consistent with his Socialist frame of mind at this stage of his career.

Major Barbara is the result, in dramatic form, of Shaw's representation of a potential Superman in an economic setting. Could it be that the successful capitalist is an instrument of the Life Force, providing the means of eliminating inferior individuals according to a Neo-Darwinian principle and setting the stage for further evolution? Shaw conceived him assuming that the most realistic, Machiavellian capitalist might be an instrument of the Life Force and a potential Superman. Undershaft, whose doctrine of salvation is 'money and gunpowder', is identified in the Preface as 'only the instrument of a Will or Life Force which uses him for purposes wider than his own'. Just as Shaw saw Socialism evolving from lower to higher forms in the previous decade, so he speculated on the evolution of capitalism. Undershaft's wealth has provided the possibility of an idyllic community—Perivale St. Andrews—where physical want has been eliminated, but its residents need spiritual nourishment; 'their souls are hungry because their bodies are full', Undershaft says, conceding that there are crucial problems of life beyond materialism.

It is not conventional politics and morality—personified by Undershaft's silly son or his self-righteous ex-wife—that holds the hope for the future. It is the combination of Undershaft's power and wealth, Barbara's transformed and secularized Christianity, and Cusin's poetic idealism that promises to produce the improved society. As early as the second act, Undershaft announces this to Cusins. 'We three must stand together above the common people,' he says; 'how else can we help their children to climb up beside us? Barbara must belong to us, not to the Salvation Army.'

Shaw then was not regarding either Christianity or capitalism as the implacable enemies, as many of his fellow Socialists were inclined to do. Nor was he even proposing a doctrinaire Socialist solution to the problem. He had not suddenly returned to the Marxian assumptions that he had put aside nearly twenty years

evaluation of Ozy, 'The Dramatist's Dilemma: an Interpretation of *Major Barbara*', *The Shaw Bulletin*, II (January 1958), pp. 18–24.

earlier; he did not expect that the proletariat would achieve its destiny through a class struggle. Like his fellow Fabians and the Revisionists, he was looking for the instruments of reform within the existing social format but now he conceived of accomplishing this by the introduction of superior individuals possessed of the finest attributes and greatest power of the time.

The impression that Shaw did not intend to make Undershaft triumphant has been strengthened by an examination of his alterations in the text in the later editions. The original printed edition of 1907 obviously gave most readers the impression that the capitalist had prevailed. In revisions for the 1931 standard edition, however, Shaw inserted a number of stage directions and other changes, the total effect of which was to strengthen the positions of both Barbara and Cusins *vis à vis* Undershaft. Most of the adjustments are subtle, but their intention was clearly to make the capitalist less domineering, more cruel, and thus less attractive.[1]

Evidence to support this interpretation can be easily extracted from the play. Cusins clearly recognizes his challenge and the opportunity for transforming the power that heretofore has been so wantonly used. 'I want to make power for the world,' he tells Barbara, as he justifies his decision to her in the final act. The power for good necessarily embraces the power for evil.

I now want to give the common man weapons against the intellectual man. I love the common people. I want to arm them against the lawyers, the doctors, the priests, the literary men, the professors, the artists, and the politicians, who, once in authority, are more disastrous and tyrannical than all the fools, rascals, and impostors. I want a power simple enough for common men to use, yet strong enough to force the intellectual oligarchy to use its genius for the general good.[2]

It is the threat of the terrorist then that forces the leaders to act responsibly and on behalf of society. Again a brand of anarchism

[1] For an excellent summary of these changes, see Bernard F. Dukore, 'Toward an Interpretation of "Major Barbara" ', *The Shaw Review*, VI (May 1963), pp. 62–70.
[2] *The Collected Works*, XI, pp. 346–7. This version in the speech (1931) is slightly different from the one that Shaw published in the first printed version of the play in 1907. Originally, the last line read 'I want a democratic power strong enough to force the intellectual oligarchy to use its genius for the general good or else perish'.

and Fabianism complement each other. There is no Socialist message, except a negative one, and it touches upon the failures of even some of those Shaw admired most. In the Preface one reads:

Rich men or aristocrats with a developed sense of life—men like Ruskin and William Morris and Kropotkin—have enormous social appetites and very fastidious personal ones. They are not content with handsome houses: they want handsome cities. They are not content with bediamonded wives and blooming daughters: they complain because the charwoman is badly dressed, because the laundress smells of gin, because the sempstress is anemic, because every man they meet is not a friend and every woman not a romance. They turn up their noses at their neighbors' drains, and are made ill by the architecture of their neighbors' houses. . . .

So far, however, their attack on society has lacked simplicity. The poor do not share their taste nor understand their art-criticisms. They do not want the simple life, nor the esthetic life; on the contrary, they want very much to wallow in all the costly vulgarities from which the elect souls among the rich turn away with loathing. It is by surfeit and not by abstinence that they will be cured of their hankering after unwholesome sweets. What they do dislike and despise and are ashamed of is poverty. To ask them to fight for the difference between the Christmas number of the Illustrated London News and the Kelmscott Chaucer is silly: they prefer the News. The difference between a stockbroker's cheap and dirty starched white shirt and collar and the comparatively costly and carefully dyed blue shirt of William Morris is a difference so disgraceful to Morris in their eyes that if they fought on the subject at all, they would fight in defence of the starch. 'Cease to be slaves, in order that you may become cranks' is not a very inspiring call to arms; nor is it really improved by substituting saints for cranks. Both terms denote men of genius; and the common man does not want to live the life of a man of genius: he would much rather live the life of a pet collie if that were the only alternative. But he does want more money. Whatever else he may be vague about, he is clear about that . . .[1]

Shaw is unnecessarily garrulous here, and his lumping of Kropotkin with Morris and Ruskin seems to have been a whim that reveals his tendency to think of the two men together among the noble Socialists; it is not a very precise or informative reference to them. However, the point is that Undershaft, in the short run, is right to the extent that he puts highest priority on the elimina-

---

[1] Shaw, Collected Works, Vol. XI, pp. 218–19.

tion of poverty, even at the risk of violence. His brand of capitalism will be superseded when a new order can offer aesthetic and spiritual experience to the fattened workmen who have been rescued from slums. Cusins and Barbara, perhaps, can do this. For one who was always a bit unhappy because his Socialist colleagues could not embrace the artistic values of Morris and who regarded Morris the reformer as unrealistic, this combination must have been an engaging prospect. Shaw must have enjoyed putting a William Morris Labour Church in the imaginary Perivale St. Andrews.

One does not need to decide whether Undershaft or Cusins and Barbara are victorious in the final scene; Shaw left the matter open. Perhaps he did not know whether modern economic and technical power could be reconciled with the finer traditions of European civilization. But obviously he hoped that such a possibility existed.

Lurking always in the wings is the threat that murder and chaos are one alternative to such a combination. Undershaft is literally playing with dynamite, and he recognizes that he risks death constantly. As usual, Shaw treats the awesome possibilities with frivolity; there are the stupid antics of Lomax with his match and cigarette in a high-explosive shed to make the point. But the fact is that the destructive power might be turned against its makers and beneficiaries in a trice. This is the situation of the anarchist who traffics in death.

It may seem somewhat incongruous that he included in the Preface an apology for the anarchist who had recently thrown a bomb at a royal couple at a Madrid bullfight, killing twenty-three people and injuring thirty-nine. Yet there is a clear connection between this use of explosives by a terrorist and the manufacture of gunpowder by a capitalist millionaire. Undershaft has been recognized by a number of critics as a virtual anarchist, beyond and behind the law and despising established institutions, acting by his own moral standards. What is wrong with society can be attacked by the half-mad rebel who possesses the power to kill, but it can also be redeemed by the enlightened use of superior intellect combined with the vast technical and economic resources of modern industry. This is a central message of the play and its Preface.

Between 1905 and 1916, Shaw was busy with his dramatic

career, but he did not add anything substantial to his Socialist criticism or to his search for the Superman. He wrote nearly a score of plays and playlets between *Major Barbara* and *Heartbreak House*, but none of them are nearly as ambitious or as daringly experimental as the works that emerged just before and just after that decade. It is as though Shaw's creative force took a rest after *Major Barbara* until it was kindled again by the events of the war.

The works of this period have been called disquisitory plays, because some of them inquire into and discuss at length various social problems, and it is worth noting that all of them are at least partially related to the idea of producing superior men. The *Doctor's Dilemma* (1906) raises the issue of the morality of selecting some individuals for survival and the cost of leaving others to perish, a problem that is inevitable if conscious improvement of the species is to be undertaken. *Getting Married* (1907), *Misalliance* (1910), and *Overruled* (1912) all deal with various aspects of the mating process. *Androcles and the Lion* (1912) is a farcical adaptation of the old story in half-evolutionary, half-religious terms, and *Pygmalion* (1913) shows how a dirty flower-girl can be made into a lady.

There are, of course, the dozen others, occasionally interesting for their reassessments of the old problems and for showing how Shaw was thinking, but revealing little new about his revolutionary thought or his aspirations for mankind. It was the events of 1914 and their sequels that gave him the substantially new matter and new frustrations that he needed to move on from the level of *Major Barbara*.

COMMON SENSE AND HEARTBREAK HOUSE

In 1905, Shaw apparently believed that Cusins, the personification of European humanism, had a chance to manage the power of the modern world for good. The First World War finally shattered that hope, but not before the contentious Irishman had lectured Britain almost to distraction. *Common Sense About the War* and his other wartime essays were the journalistic rebel's comments on the situation, and *Heartbreak House* was his despairing response as an artist. The play won a lasting place in literature while the tracts suffered the usual fate of topical propaganda, but it is instructive to consider the two types of writing together.

'Heartbreak House is not merely the name of the play which follows this preface,' he wrote in 1919 as he began the inevitable introduction to his newest work. 'It is cultured, leisured Europe before the war.' And the message of the play was that the intellectuals with whom he had cast his lot had failed to meet the challenge. A decade after he conceived a poet and a modernized Christian succeeding to the position of the capitalist Undershaft, Shaw saw that this possibility had not been realized. 'In short, power and culture were in separate compartments.'[1]

Shaw was writing *Heartbreak House* when the war began, but he did not finish it until 1917 and then withheld it from the stage for reasons that he explained in the Preface. Sometime during this period, presumably during the early part of the war, he came to realize that Cusin's objective could not be achieved. 'Dare I make war on war?' Cusins had asked himself, echoing Undershaft's challenge. 'I dare. I must. I will.' But when the guns were firing, Shaw realized that he could not issue a play that preached the insanity and incompetence of Britain's leadership. 'You cannot make war on war and on your neighbor at the same time,' he wrote in 1919.[2] But at the beginning of the war he tried to do just that.

Common Sense was written when the war was only a few weeks old; it is dated November 1914. It is a remarkable document, and looking at it after the lapse of fifty years, one is tempted to say an admirable one. It is a call for sanity during a period of militant hysteria, and it includes a plea for a just and gentle peace for the enemy once he has been defeated. It proposed the idea of a league of nations in the post-war period, and it has been suggested that his proposal may have had some influence on Woodrow Wilson. It contains, of course, a generous measure of Shavian castigation for the idealists, the statesmen, and the patriots.

Shaw regarded the diplomacy that preceded the war as terribly inept, and he offered an incisive discussion of the conditions that had created the crisis. He took special delight in discussing the blunders of Sir Edward Grey and the Foreign Ministry. While he argued that the war now must be pushed vigorously to a decisive victory over Prussian militarism, he insisted that Britain should shed her pretensions of moral superiority. The Junker class was as much a part of British life as of German; British assumptions about her pre-eminent claims on the sea were no more proper

---

[1] Shaw, *Collected Works*, Vol. XV, pp. 3–5.   [2] Ibid., pp. 39–40.

than Prussian military vanity. The British were as brutal in war, as unethical in diplomacy, and as much in need of reform as the Germans.

For nearly a hundred pages he did his best to demonstrate the silly qualities of chauvinistic British patriotism. It was Shaw at his most Irish, caustic and flamboyant in his destructive criticism, and frequently offering recommendations for the future that were bound to offend because they assumed a large measure of British guilt. The tract—like several others that followed it during the war—is essentially the same in spirit as the criticisms of Bernstein during the same period; the main difference emerges from Shaw's use of sarcasm and ridicule. Shaw, like his German colleague, was bitterly criticized by his more patriotic fellows and not a few of them regarded him as insane.

One section offers a clue to Shaw's subsequent admiration of the Russian Revolution. Obviously Shaw did not foresee the events of 1917 when he wrote *Common Sense*, but he made some remarks that reflected his continuing regard for the Russian rebels and that anticipated his attitude towards the Bolsheviks at a later period. He regarded Tsardom and Russian militarism as a great danger for the future of Europe. Britain and France, he said, must not seek to crush Germany between themselves and the Russian Tsardom, because in the last analysis an authoritarian Russia represented a greater threat than German militarism. The British-French combination must defeat the Germans essentially by themselves, without substantial Russian aid, and must then be lenient in the peace negotiations if the Russian threat were to be minimized. 'The Russian Government is the open enemy of every liberty we boast of,' he wrote, repeating the lesson that Stepniak and his fellow exiles had effectively taught twenty years earlier.

After he had finished indicting imperial Russia, Shaw was moved to insert a special apology:

And here I must save my face with my personal friends who are either Russians or discoverers of the soul of the Russian people. I hereby declare to Sasha Kropotkin and Cunninghame Graham that my heart is with their Russia, the Russia of Tolstoy and Turgenieff and Dostoieffsky, of Gorki and Tchekoff, of the Moscow Art Theatre and the Drury Lane Ballet, of Peter Kropotkin and all the great humanitarians, great artists, and charming people whom their very North German Tsars exile and imprison and flog and generally do what in them lies to suppress and abolish. For the sake of Russian Russia I am prepared to strain every point in Prussian Russia's favor. I grant that the Nihilists, much as we loved them, were futile romantic people who could have done nothing if Alexander II had abdicated and offered them the task of governing Russia instead of persecuting them and being finally blown to bits by them. I grant that the manners of the Fins to the Russians are described as insufferable both by the Swedes and the Russians, and that we never listened to the Russian side of that story. I am ready to grant Gilbert Murray's plea that the recent rate of democratic advance has been greater in Russia than anywhere else in Europe, though it does remind me a little of the bygone days when the Socialists, scoring 20 votes at one general election and 40 at the next, were able to demonstrate that their gain of 100 percent was immensely in excess of the wretched two or three percent that was the best the Unionists or Liberals could shew. I am willing to forget how short a time it is since Sir Henry Campbell-Bannerman said: 'The Duma is dead; long live the Duma!' . . .

. . . if I doubt whether the Tsar would feel comfortable as a member of a Democratic League of Peace, I am not doubting the good intent of Kropotkin: I am facing the record of Kropotkin's imperial jailer, and standing on the proud fact that England is the only country in Europe, not excepting even France, in which Kropotkin has been allowed to live a free man, and had his birthday celebrated by public meetings all over the country, and his articles welcomed by the leading review. In point of fact, it is largely on Kropotkin's account that I regard the Tsar as a gentleman of slightly different views to President Wilson, and hate the infamous tyranny of which he is the figurehead as I hate the devil . . .[1]

This explanation was obviously gratuitous. Shaw did not have to apologize to the famous Russian for supporting the existing Tsarist regime, because in this situation the positions of the two men were similar. But the loquatious Irishman obviously has a special sympathy for Russian revolutionaries and was eager to take pains not to be misunderstood. Little wonder that he was to take a keen interest in Russian events in subsequent years.

Shaw's essays on the war, like some of the prefaces to his plays, are not orderly expositions. In places they are hardly coherent. He left the impression of a man battling his way through a thicket with a hatchet, unable to avoid slashing even at branches that were not in his way. He was obviously tempted to use hundreds of items from the daily war reports, and he could not tame his catholic

[1] Shaw, *Collected Works*, Vol. 21, pp. 84-6.

interests for the purpose of offering simple arguments on a carefully limited theme. He found the kind of illusions he deplored so rampant—patriotism, military heroism, ecstatic praise of democracy—and the opportunities for advising so profuse that he was tempted to write more polemical literature between 1914 and 1920 than he had done in any comparable period since the 1890s. Relatively few of his ideas are distinctively Socialistic, but they are the creations of a self-confident man and a rebel.

It was almost as though Shaw put his affirmative and constructive fury into his political articles during the war and unburdened himself of his despair in the only major play that he wrote in this period.

Heartbreak House is subtitled 'A Fantasia in the Russian Manner on English Themes'. Shaw was explicit in attempting to adapt Chekhovian techniques to an English setting and by implication to suggest that the form and the message were pertinent to both societies—indeed to all of Europe. The characters who appear in *Heartbreak House*, while nominally English, are meant to represent the kinds of people and attitudes that had led all of Western civilization to the brink of disaster. Captain Shotover, the visionary, half-mad, ancient sea captain of past years suggests a cosmopolitan tradition and a vanished glory that exists only in memory. His two daughters and their husbands represent the degenerate contemporary generation, dedicated to little except the pretensions of cultural and imperial leadership. Into this odd household comes young Ellie Dunn, full of hope and innocence—or, to be more Shavian—illusion. Her father, Mazzini Dunn, personifies a Liberal generation whose day and cause have passed into history; his noble ideas and instinctive urge to fight for freedom remains, but he has no programme, and he has been victimized by the capitalist, Boss Mangan.

The allegorical elements are as pronounced as those in *Major Barbara*, but most of the figures are inferior characters rather than the strong individuals who function at the centre of the earlier play. In *Heartbreak House*, lethargy and incompetence are prevalent, and no formula for redemption emerges, unless it is in the nihilistic finale that suggests triumph in threatened destruction.

When we become acquainted with Ellie early in the play, we learn that she has been fascinated by the advances of Hector Hushabye, one of the sons-in-law of Captain Shotover and a philanderer. He is the nearest thing to a Socialist that we find in *Heartbreak House*. He has posed as a devotee of that movement and as a veteran of three revolutions. He believes he could save England if he were given a chance to do so, but the society prefers the fraternity of Mangan. And Ellie herself is engaged to marry the millionaire although without enthusiasm for the match. When Ellie learns that Hector has been deceptive, she is shattered and temporarily resolves to go ahead with her loveless marriage to Mangan because of his money. Captain Shotover, the wisest of them all in spite of his occasional insanity and his advanced years, dissuades her. She finally agrees to a spiritual marriage with him, which is tantamount to renunciation of contemporary civilization.

Aside from the transformation and disillusionment of Ellie, Hector's is the most interesting personal conversion in the play. In the beginning, he is only another of the restless but purposeless residents of *Heartbreak House*, albeit with some sensitive perceptions. Near the end, he becomes more desperate.

Early in Act III, Hector utters the often-heard Shavian warning. There has been a strange drumming in the air which the residents of Heartbreak House cannot—or are not willing to—identify. Asked what it can have been, Hector responds:

HECTOR. Heaven's threatening growl of disgust at us useless futile creatures. (Fiercely) I tell you, one of two things must happen. Either out of that darkness some new creation will come to supplant us as we have supplanted the animals, or the heavens will fall in thunder and destroy us.[1]

Here is an echo of the warning that Shaw had put into the mouth of Caesar nearly twenty years earlier and which he had repeated often in the interim. Now there seemed to be more reason than ever to anticipate the destruction of society. In fact the main preoccupation of Shotover is his cache of dynamite and his quest for the 'seventh degree of concentration' which would enable him to touch off an explosion that would kill men of Mangan's type, and in the final scene Mangan is destroyed along with a common criminal when bombs from an airship fall on Shotover's cellar.

Hector's awakening before the finale amounts to an acceptance of destructive anarchism. 'Think of the powers of destruction that

[1] Shaw, *Collected Works*, Vol. XV, p. 130.

Mangan and his mutual admiration gang wield!' he exclaims. 'It's madness: it's like giving a torpedo to a badly brought up child to play at earthquakes with.' He has the impulse to do something to avoid the cataclysm, but he has no programme, and Mazzini Dunn tells him there is no solution. In the grip of this despair, Hector rises to activism when disaster seems imminent. When word arrives that the bombs are falling and that the house must be darkened for safety, Hector rushes inside to turn on the lights and to tear down the curtains. Ellie passionately suggests that he burn the house, and Hector seems to yearn for the cleansing fire. But events do not proceed that far. The aerial machine moves on without having completed its work; it has been very selective in its victims, killing the most contemptible but sparing the rest. Ellie—the person who symbolizes aspiration—closes the play with the 'radiant' hope that the airships will return the next night to complete their work.

In the ending of this play, there is no expression of the optimism that one finds in such earlier works as *Man and Superman* and *Major Barbara*. Not only has Socialism failed as a healing agent, but the whole of society may be incapable of redemption. It was the most thoroughly despondent of any of Shaw's works and the one that he was least disposed to subject to his own interpretation.

Yet the pessimism is not absolute; the end of the play does not bring Armageddon, and the doomsday urge of Ellie and Hector is not fulfilled. It may be soon enough but in the end Captain Shotover says, 'Turn in, all hands. The ship is safe.' There may still be time for Hector to learn his 'business as an Englishman', as the Captain has admonished him to do:

HECTOR. And what may my business as an Englishman be, pray?
CAPTAIN SHOTOVER. Navigation. Learn it and live; or leave it and be damned.

The old alternatives still exist. Men must learn to manage their affairs—to navigate—or they risk chaos and possible extinction. Shaw could see little evidence that his Fabian-style essays had any effect during the war; perhaps that is why he produced a play that contemplated destruction. Several later plays contained similar speculations on the break-up of civilization as an alternative to improved programmes of social management.

Heartbreak House is the work of a near-desperate man who

ardently wanted a formula for human rejuvenation. Of course he frequently asserted in his provocative prose that he had the reasonable solutions to all social and political problems, if only those in responsible positions would heed his wisdom, but one of the messages of this play is that society seems to lack the will or the energy to cure itself with the obvious remedies. This is the most frustrated —and most frustrating—of Shaw's great plays.

BOLSHEVISM AND CREATIVE EVOLUTION

More than thirty years of life and much vitality remained to the Socialist playwright after *Heartbreak House* and the ending of the war. The passage of events and his own energetic optimism did not allow him to remain for long in the mood that this play suggests. A new revolutionary experiment on the opposite side of Europe provoked his interest and eventually his enthusiasm, and additional speculations on the Life Force led him to write the play that he regarded as his most important work.

Shaw wrote *Back to Methuselah* immediately after the war, before his political hopes had been revived by the Russian experiment. Taking up his earlier notion that a better society must be the result of slow, evolutionary development rather than contemporary social adjustment, he tried to make a contribution to the literature of the new religion of Creative Evolution and to the mythology that would have to accompany man's tedious transformation. At approximately the same time that Kropotkin was trying to complete his *Ethics* at Dmitrov outside Moscow, his Irish admirer at Ayot St. Lawrence near London was working on the beginnings of a new Bible, and for much the same reason. Shaw, too, recognized that there must be new doctrines for the new order.

In the case of *Back to Methuselah*, the long Preface is more helpful and more to the point than usual. One of Shaw's objectives was to challenge the neo-Darwinism and the Marxism that the twentieth century had inherited from the nineteenth, and in this, also, his work paralleled that of Kropotkin. Some of Shaw's Lamarckian ideas about the possibility of inheriting the acquired characteristics might well have been suggested by Kropotkin, who had published a series of articles on the subject in *The Nineteenth Century and After* in 1910.

There is little evidence that Shaw had been interested in biological theory before the war, but the failure of political institutions and his speculations on the superman led him to it. The experience of the war, he wrote in the Preface, 'confirmed a doubt which had grown steadily in my mind during my forty years public work as a Socialist: namely, whether the human animal, as he exists at present, is capable of solving the social problems raised by his own aggregation, or, as he calls it, his civilization'.[1] After one of his typical tirades about the inadequacy of contemporary institutions and the stupidity of contemporary governments—emphasizing the futility of hoping for short-term reforms by conventional means—he unfolded a metabiological solution.

Although he thought of the play as a classic, most critics have not shared his enthusiasm, and few theatres have been able to cope with the length and complexity of *Back to Methuselah*. It is five plays in one, requiring more than a single evening for production. To make the point that men must have a longer life span if they are to gain the requisite wisdom to manage their affairs well, Shaw showed man in several stages, beginning with creation and ending in A.D. 31,920. He represented first the Garden of Eden, where death was invented and where Adam and Eve made some elementary decisions about the life span. This initial play is gentle and imaginative, with some comic touches that echo earlier, less bitter periods of his dramatic career.

The second play of the cycle, entitled *The Gospel of the Brothers Barnabas*, is almost strangled by political satire aimed at contemporary figures. The subject is British politics in 1920. Shaw was especially contemptuous of the Liberal leaders David Lloyd George and H. H. Asquith, and he portrayed them with only slightly disguised names as pompous, ineffectual buffoons, inferior to nearly everyone else in the play. When these politicians learn of the theory of the scholarly Barnabas brothers which holds that man's life span can be extended to three hundred years by an act of will, they can only consider the doctrine for its short-range electoral significance.

A Socialist appears at this point of the play-sequence; she is a young girl nicknamed 'Savvy' because she is regarded by her academic elders as a savage in manners. She has canvassed the Strand for the Socialists in a recent election, and she is intellectu-

[1] Shaw, *Collected Works*, Vol. 16, pp. xi–xii.

ally far superior to the politicians. She has studied and rejected
not only the liberal-bourgeois rationale but also the economics of
Marx and the biology of Darwin. When the politician Lubin
(Asquith) lectures her on the fixed scientific laws of economics, she
says it is like hearing a man talk of the Garden of Eden. She—like
her creator—has obviously transcended Socialism, but he has no
positive programme or theory to supersede it. She is not moved or
excited by the Liberals who are now ready to embrace Socialist
concepts for their own ends. But she is not one of the people who
is destined to achieve the three-hundred-year life span that her
elders have conceived. This privilege—and thus the biological
triumph—goes to secondary characters, the clergyman Haslam
and to the parlourmaid, apparently by a kind of accident. They do
not expect it or consciously will it for themselves, but it happens.

The third play is entitled *The Thing Happens*. We are trans-
ported two hundred and fifty years into the future, at which time
we encounter a descendant of the two politicians still playing at
government in an age when wise Chinese men and Negro women
have taken over the real work of administration in Britain. Members of parliament are recruited from a lunatic asylum because
it has long since been recognized that they have no serious function
to perform. The former cleric and the one-time parlourmaid, who
by this time have lived nearly three centuries and have acquired
the superior wisdom necessary for responsible leadership, have
each held high office several times. They are recognized as the
biological types who will prevail in the future. Their achievements
and their promise are in no way related to economic or political
programmes, and there is no indication that Socialism has had
any part in their success. It is simply that two extra centuries of
adult experience have endowed them with superior common sense.

The last two plays were the most ambitious fantasies that Shaw's
inventive mind had created to date. The creatures of the future—
first the 'long-livers' of A.D. 3000 and finally the Ancients of thirty
thousand years hence—are increasingly wise, efficient, and
humourless, and progressively unlike the twentieth-century Englishmen with whom they are repeatedly compared. With each
subsequent play and each stage of evolution, such institutions as
political government, the church, marriage, property—all the
targets of the Socialists and anarchists—recede further into the
superstitious and barbaric past. The 'long-livers' who are the

advanced post-humans of their era are subject to no outside restrictions; 'there are no limits to their power except the limits they set themselves'.[1] Those who are endowed with superior wisdom at each stage must still cope with their short-lived inferiors, but the final hope is that eventually even the remarkably wise and serene Ancients will become disembodied vortices of thought, and presumably all the encumbrances of physical existence and social life will end.

Shaw's image of the future is so fanciful in the last portions of *Back to Methuselah* that it reveals little to those studying his socialism. Attempts have been made to interpret this work as an indication of his Marxist tendencies,[2] but this is hardly more worthwhile or convincing than trying to prove that Morris was putting a Socialist message into his later prose romances. One could use the same evidence to represent Shaw as an anarchist. He still had a didactic purpose, but he did not at this time embrace a narrow political or economic formula. One recurring theme is that the superior creatures at each stage have the right and the duty to eliminate their inferiors who are dangerous or intolerably troublesome, a conclusion that enabled him to defend the Bolsheviks later when they suppressed their opponents by means of Cheka and O.G.P.U.

There was little evidence, in the fifty years after Shaw wrote *Back to Methuselah*, that anyone seriously regarded it as the beginning of a new Old Testament or that Creative Evolution was being widely embraced as the new religion. Perhaps T. S. Eliot offered the typical reaction of his generation to the new Pentateuch that Shaw had offered to the world. Writing shortly after reading the play in 1921, he said:

I should say—for it is amusing, if unsafe, to prophesy—that we shall demand from our next leaders a purer intellect, more scientific, more logical, more rigorous. Shaw's mind is a free and easy mind: every idea, no matter how irrelevant, is welcome.[3]

Shaw's 'book', in Eliot's view, could be taken 'for a moment' as the last word of a century, 'perhaps of two centuries'. It was a

[1] Shaw, *Collected Works*, Vol. 16, p. 164.
[2] See, for example, Paul A. Hummert, 'Bernard Shaw's Marxist Utopias', *The Shaw Review*, Vol. II, No. 9 (September 1959), pp. 7–26.
[3] The article appears initially as a 'London Letter' in *Dial* and is reproduced in *A Dial Miscellany*, edited by William Wasserstrom (Syracuse, 1963), p. 49.

bold experiment, but an untidy and unfruitful one, and it offered
no programme for the activist. For most men motivated by conscience or fascinated by politics, it is not enough to sit and wait
for nature to take its evolutionary course.

And so Shaw, despite the fact that he spoke more favourably
of this particular play than of his others, was not content to wait.
He wanted to see definitive evidence of progress in his own time,
and he became more desperate as the years passed. Instinctively,
he wanted the revolution as much as he and his contemporaries of
the early 1880s had done, but intellectually he was suspicious of
any institutional attempt to achieve it. This dichotomy helps to
explain his admiration for some of the totalitarian rulers of the
1920s and 1930s and those variegated, politically-oriented plays
of the 1930s.

The most spectacular revolutionary sequence of his era occurred
while he was writing *Back to Methuselah*, but apparently it did not
affect the play. In fact, the awesome events in Russia in the period
1917–20 did not even draw substantial comment from him immediately. For some time after November 1917, he had very little
to say about the Bolsheviks' experiment. Such reticence was
unusual for one of such catholic interests. He declined an opportunity to visit Russia shortly after the war, and only gradually did
he become an outspoken defender of the Russian Communists.
When he finally did so in the early 1920s, it was in the context of
controversies with his old British foes. He convinced himself that
the Bolsheviks, in embracing the New Economic Programme of
1921, were becoming Fabians. He admired their efforts to trans-
form Russian society and morality drastically, but he felt better
about it when they embraced a gradualist principle.[1]

As of January 1918, the evidence of a Bolshevik victory seems
to have frightened him. He called it 'formidable' and added:

Yet here again I must sorrowfully dispel the illusion that the Russian
Revolution makes for peace. Our patriots, always seizing the wrong
end of the stick, are in full cry against 'a separate peace' by Russia.
What they would dread if they had any grasp of the situation is a
separate war by Russia: a fight to a finish not only with the German
throne, but with all thrones; a war that will go on when the rest of the

---

[1] For an informative article on the subject, see Katharine L. Auchincloss,
'Shaw and the Commissars: The Lenin Years, 1917–1924', *The Shaw Review*,
VI (May 1963), pp. 51–9.

belligerents want to stop; a war that may develop into a blaze of civil wars in England, France, and Italy, with the Foreign Offices and Courts and Capitalists fighting to restore the Tsar, and the 'proletarians of all lands' fighting to reproduce the Russian Revolution in their own country. What has happened so far is a very old thing: the world has many times before seen the kings of the earth rise up and the rulers take counsel together. But when peoples with new Bibles and new Jewish prophets do the same, there will be no more use for the middle class ignorance that deals with such a danger by a refusal of passports to those who alone understand it. There is a war to be averted ten times more terrible than that war which we are told to get on with by fools who imagine that we have any choice in the matter, and flick their little whips at the earth to make it go round the sun. Which of us would not stop the war tomorrow if he could? Which of us can?[1]

Shaw obviously did not yearn to experience cataclysm as much as some of his characters did. The record at this point, however, suggests a kind of split personality. While as an essayist he was alarmed by the prospects of the Bolshevik Revolution in 1918, as a playwright he was dabbling intellectually with its dramatic possibilities. In January, scarcely two months after Lenin and his cohorts had seized power, Shaw issued one of his 'bravura' playlets under the title *Annajanska, The Bolshevik Empress*. The setting is a chaotic east European country where insurgency has left an imperial general utterly confused about his responsibilities. Suddenly he is confronted by the grand duchess Annajanska, who has joined the revolution in spite of her noble ancestry. She has become convinced that the cause of the Revolution is more worthy than that of the corrupt court to which she once belonged. She convinces the general that the war—a cause to which he can devote himself unequivocally—will unite the revolutionaries on behalf of the commonwealth. The general accepts this principle but yearns for the man who can provide the necessary leadership. Annajanska startles him, and presumably the audience, by throwing aside her cloak and revealing herself in military attire, ready to take the forces of the Revolution into battle.

This is a queer item from the pen of a man who was almost simultaneously expressing concern about the Bolsheviks, but then Shaw was given to odd diversions in his art. This piece has been given little attention by the critics and biographers, but it is an

---

[1] Shaw, *Collected Works*, Vol. 21, p. 291.

interesting indicator. There is a kind of premonition of his later support for the Bolshevik Revolution, and it also suggests, faintly and crudely, the beginning of the story of Joan of Arc, to which Shaw would turn about four years later. It is worth emphasizing, however, that he had very little to say about the Bolshevik Revolution in the months immediately after it occurred.

More than two years later, as Lenin was moving away from his policy of 'War Communism' with its hasty and damaging social effects, Shaw was ready to come to the defence of Bolshevism in the British press. When his old adversary Hyndman produced his book *The Evolution of Revolution*, he characterized the Russian Revolution as premature, terroristic, and un-Marxian. Shaw denied that it was premature, argued the logic of its executions, and questioned the relevance of its Marxism. Furthermore he had become a fan of Lenin for some of his dictatorial features:

For my part, I cannot understand how anyone who has the most elementary comprehension of Socialism can doubt that compulsory labor and the treatment of parasitic idleness as the sin against the Holy Ghost must be fundamental in Socialist law and religion. If Lenin has abolished idleness in Russia, whilst we, up to our eyes in debt, are not only tolerating it, but heaping luxury upon luxury upon it in the midst of starvation, then I am much more inclined to cry 'Bravo, Lenin!' and 'More fools we!' than to share Mr. Hyndman's apparent horror.[1]

In *Back to Methuselah* Shaw had given the superior creatures of the later plays the right to eliminate their inferior contemporaries; it was consistent with that position that he was willing to excuse the Bolsheviks for similar policies. It was consistent also that he admired Mussolini for the acts of brutality that were associated with his consolidation of power in Italy. Although Soviet Russia and Fascist Italy proclaimed conflicting ideologies, they both represented new experiments in the management of human affairs, and they both repudiated the democratic procedures of the West that had so disillusioned Shaw.

Although he came to regard Lenin as the greatest statesman of the post-war period, this did not mean that the Bolsheviks or the institutions of their making were exempt from Shavian criticism. The old foe of the London Marxists could not embrace all the dogmatism; he did not like the Communist International with its

[1] Shaw, *Collected Works*, Vol. 29, pp. 146–7.

programme of designing and directing a world revolution. He denounced the organization and its chairman, Gregory Zinoviev, in articles in *Izvestia* and *The Daily Herald* in 1924 and was thoroughly criticized in turn by the vitriolic Zinoviev.[1] But the Soviet experiment remained for Shaw the most promising effort at social reconstruction in the world, and his enthusiasm for it became greater as the years passed. Even after Stalin became dictator of Russia, Shaw regularly endorsed him and his Bolshevism, and he retained this loyalty with more tenacity than he did his temporary allegiances to Hitler and Mussolini. After his famous visit to Russia in 1931, he was euphoric in his praise of the Communists. In the last decade of his life he occasionally called himself a 'Fabian Communist'.

Nearly all the plays and Prefaces after *Back to Methuselah* contain extended diatribes against contemporary British politics and society, with proposals for change and threats of disasters. There is one significant exception. It seems that life, or perhaps the Life Force, by guiding Shaw through the disappointments in politics and the experiments in drama, had been preparing him for a special mission.

'SAINT JOAN'

Saint Joan is the highest achievement of Shaw's career as a playwright and his most impressive statement as a revolutionist. It is no accident that he gave himself and his talents to a play about the life of an unconventional militant historical figure at the same time that he was announcing himself an admirer of Lenin and Mussolini. Conventional methods and people—the residents of *Heartbreak House*—had muddled the opportunities of the 1890s and had allowed themselves to drift into a brutal war. The hope of evolutionary improvement that is contained in *Back to Methuselah* can hardly be based on the kind of people found in Captain Shotover's ship. If the race is to achieve its evolutionary progress, it must find those men and women who will rise above contemporary lethargy and incompetence. He yearned for the charismatic miracle worker, and with his well-known preference for dynamic women, he was prepared to accept one of them as his

[1] St. John Ervine, *Bernard Shaw: His Life, Work, and Friends* (New York, 1956), pp. 520–1.

saviour. He wanted an Annajanska, and he found one in the history of the fifteenth-century French maiden from Lorraine who had broken all the rules in achieving her historical destiny:

She is the most notable Warrior Saint in the Christian calendar, and the queerest fish among the eccentric worthies of the Middle Ages. Though a professed and most pious Catholic, and the projector of a Crusade against the Husites, she was in fact one of the first Protestant martyrs. She was also one of the first apostles of Nationalism, and the first French practitioner of Napoleonic realism in warfare as distinguished from the sporting ransom gambling chivalry of her time. She was the pioneer of rational dressing for women, and, like Queen Christina of Sweden two centuries later, to say nothing of Catalina de Erauso and innumerable obscure heroines who have disguised themselves as men to serve as soldiers and sailors, she refused to accept the specific woman's lot, and dressed and fought and lived as men did.[1]

Joan struck Shaw as being a person in the grip of the Life Force. She was an instrument of evolution, and not merely a victim of persecution. 'I tell thee it is God's business we are here to do: not our own,' she tells the dauphin, and she insists on pursuing the course that her heavenly voices have set for her even against the resistance of lords, bishops, monarchs, and the executioner himself. At first she carries all before her. The simple peasants, the military squire of her district, the lords of the court, the generals, and the uncrowned king become her pawns, as she assumes the work of driving the English invaders from her land. She is a realist and an activist, brilliant in her perception and her policies. One might even regard her as a Superman, if by suggesting this one does not rule out some very human qualities such as pride, occasional fear, and doubt. But her career is short. In quick sequence come her trial, her conviction by the Church court that conscientiously tries to save her, and her burning at the stake for heresy, witchcraft, and sorcery. These events are compressed into six of the best scenes in modern British drama, but Shaw was not content to end there. The propagandist had something to say when the play was done, and the controversial Epilogue comments on the fact that twenty-five years later the judgement against Joan was reversed and in 1920 she was canonized as a saint.

In 1923 with this play Shaw surprised and confused the critics more than usual. The most prolific author of theatrical comedy of

[1] Shaw, *Collected Works*, Vol. 17, p. 3.

the age had suddenly written a tragedy—or had he? Previously
Shaw's most notable heroes and heroines who were threatened
with martyrdom—Captain Brassbound, Blanco Posnet, the Christians in *Androcles and the Lion*, Dick Dudgeon in *The Devil's
Disciple* for example—manage to escape their fates by some comic
or melodramatic turn of events. Those who are destroyed are
carried off in a light-hearted manner, and there is usually a kind
of poetic justice to their destruction, as in the case of Boss Magnan
or the inferior characters in the latter plays of *Back to Methuselah*.
Caesar, we infer, is going to his death at the end of *Caesar and
Cleopatra*, but comic elements prevail.

In *Saint Joan*, there are some fine comic scenes and situations
but the prevailing structure is tragic, at least until the Epilogue.
One knows, as in a classic or Renaissance tragedy, that the pro-
tagonist is going to certain death. The heroine is motivated by
pride and is in conflict with forces that must inevitably overwhelm
her.[1] One hears her sentenced to die for her beliefs, and sees the
flicker of the flames from offstage as she is burned.

But there is the Epilogue. In a sense, Shaw redeems the tragedy
here, and turns it back towards comedy, but not all the way.
Bringing Joan back, as a dream, to King Charles VII a quarter-
century after she has been burned to death, and assembling with
her all the figures who have acquiesced in her martyrdom, Shaw
makes his final point. The men who let her die—Warwick the
gentleman-politician, de Stromburger the super-patriot, the mini-
sters of secular and ecclesiastical justice, the king whom she has
crowned, the executioner, and even the spokesman of the Catholic
Church which canonized her in 1920—are generous with their
praise of her work and memory. But when she suggests that she
might return from the dead 'and come back to you a living woman',
she provokes consternation. One by one her admirers leave her,
afraid as all responsible men must be of the saviour-saint and
revolutionist. The bell is striking midnight as she stands on the
stage alone and utters the last, poignant question: 'O God that
madest this beautiful earth, when will it be ready to receive Thy
saints? How long, O Lord, how long?'

[1] See Stanley J. Solomon, 'Saint Joan as Epic Tragedy', in *Modern Drama*,
Vol. 6 (February 1964), pp. 437–49. For a somewhat contrary view, see Don
Austin, 'Comedy Through Tragedy: Dramatic Structure in Saint Joan', *The
Shaw Review*, Vol. 8 (May 1965), pp. 52–62.

Comedy or tragedy? Or something in between? It would seem that many of the critics—including some of the best—have not seen it as Shaw intended it and have not successfully put it into the context of his own experience as a revolutionist. Many of the earliest reviewers indicated that Shaw had spoiled his tragedy by adding the Epilogue with its whimsy, irony, and didactic finale. This reaction was so common that Shaw devoted a paragraph to the subject when he penned the Preface about five months after the initial production:

As to the epilogue, I could hardly be expected to stultify myself by implying that Joan's history in the world ended unhappily with her execution, instead of beginning there. It was necessary by hook or crook to shew the canonized Joan as well as the incinerated one; for many a woman has got herself burnt by carelessly whisking a muslin skirt into the drawing room fireplace, but getting canonized is a different matter, and a more important one. So I am afraid the epilogue must stand.[1]

In spite of Shaw's clear statement as to his purpose—to show that Joan's work had been continued in spite of her death—many critics and biographers have not been content. Even those who have known most about his life, thought, and work have not been willing to accept his statement of purpose. William Irvine felt that he had cluttered the ending of a well constructed drama. 'The gravest fault of the Epilogue is that it is unnecessary', he wrote.[2] His friend St. John Ervine persisted in the idea that it was super- fluous, and Archibald Henderson was even more emphatic in his disapproval. He 'frankly deplored the Epilogue, as a Shavian gloss upon the play, which, for all its beauty and reverence, shattered the historical illusion . . .'[3] When he said this to Shaw, he 'caught a tartar in G.B.S.', who was becoming very impatient with such comment.

Writers of this stature seem to have reached a conclusion so contrary to Shaw's because they were inclined to look at *Saint Joan* as the representative of a theatrical *genre* rather than as the statement of a revolutionist who had used the drama as his weapon. As Shaw had reminded his readers many times, he was a revolu- tionist first and a dramatist second, and he was more interested in

---

[1] Shaw, *Collected Works*, Vol. 17, p. 53.   [2] Irvine, op. cit., p. 324.
[3] Henderson, *George Bernard Shaw: Man of the Century*, p. 600.

showing Joan as the maker of a kind of revolution than he was in having his play conform to a classical form. It is surprising that serious scholars, who recognize this in other phases of Shaw's work, still insist that he could or should have omitted the Epilogue.

What the critics of the Epilogue fail to appreciate, perhaps, is that Shaw in this place had employed the concept and the ethic of the revolutionary martyr in the manner of the nineteenth-century Socialists. As a young man and as a Fabian, he had disliked the romantic, melodramatic stories of self-sacrifice, even though he had tinkered with melodrama in a light-hearted way in some of the early plays. Now, with nearly a half-century of frustrations of his revolutionary (or evolutionary) hopes behind him, without a viable formula for future progress in the Fabian manner, he turned to the *genre* that Stepniak had used in *The Career of a Nihilist* and that Morris had employed in *A Dream of John Ball*. Perhaps without fully recognizing himself what he had done—he was occasionally willing to admit that an author is not always in control of the forces that affect his work—he had embraced the ethics of Socialism as defined by Bax in the previous century, and he had put in dramatic form a message not unlike that which Kropotkin had tried to define at the end of his *Ethics* which he had borrowed from Guyau. This is not to say that Shaw was directly influenced by these men or these works, but it is a suggestion that he had, for the moment, accepted a concept of the revolution and a role for the martyr that had not appealed to him during his most active Fabian days.

Revolutions must achieve their objectives gradually. Shaw knew this as a Fabian, but as social critic, who still remembered his early anarchism, wanted action in the present. As a Fabian he could defend and sympathize with the feudal-religious establishment that had to suppress Joan's heresy in the interest of public order. As a rebel he could now see that Joan's death was a triumph for her cause and the world. The Epilogue reinforces the point that the institutions dedicated to the preservation of society are not likely to be any more receptive to a Joan in the twentieth century than their counterparts were in the fifteenth. And yet it is on this type of person that the hopes of the world rest.

So *Saint Joan* draws upon the ambiguities and the tensions that were built into Shaw's Socialism. Several critics have recognized that Shaw's plays are based upon a conflict between the creative innovator and restrictive institutions. It is worth stressing that this dichotomy permeated his revolutionary thought and helps to account for many of the inconsistencies of his last years. Shaw was both a Revisionist and an anarchist, embracing both ends of the Socialist spectrum, and doing it most successfully in the play that allowed him to be most detached from contemporary subject matter.

THE LATER WORKS

Nothing that Shaw wrote after *Saint Joan* adds anything substantial to his Socialism. Although he was to live another quarter-century and to write dozens of articles, two Socialist books, and another fourteen plays, *Saint Joan* is generally regarded as his last great work. He had made his definitive statement, and although still vigorous, was never again able to reach this level.

Shaw continued, of course, to call himself a Socialist or, especially after 1931, a Communist. He also frequently reminded the world that he was an original Fabian. From time to time he wrapped the mantle of Marx around himself, defending the man and his work as Marxism became less popular in the West in the wake of the Bolshevik revolution. But he said too many careless things and he left the impression that he was rather foolish and inconsistent.

Almost in spite of himself, he had become an institution. He received the Nobel Prize for literature in 1925. Even the most hostile of his critics acknowledged his talents and conceded that he had written some good drama. The animosity that had been directed towards him during the war passed away quickly after the hysteria of those years subsided and he was able to resume his place in English life as a rather fascinating and harmless buffoon. He also returned, after a fashion, to democratic Socialism and in the process he descended from the heights he had achieved in *Saint Joan*.

In 1925, the Labour Party honoured him as one of its founders and he delivered a speech, subsequently titled 'Socialism at Seventy', that revealed some of the illogical thinking that was often characteristic of his last years. He talked partly like a Fabian politician, but he sprinkled the remarks with references to Karl Marx that were at best confusing and inconsistent with his own current attitudes:

Fortunately, I think, we have got good intentions. But that is not enough. We must also not run after great men. Socialism did produce a great man in Karl Marx. Many of us would say that Karl Marx produced socialism. Well, I have read Karl Marx, and I can find nothing in him about socialism. But he did the greatest literary feat a man can do. Marx changed the mind of the world. . . .

Karl Marx made a man of me. Socialism made a man of me. Otherwise I should be like so many of my literary colleagues who have just as much literary ability as I have.[1]

He rambled on about Marx's lack of contact with the working class and about the mistaken attempt to apply some Socialist ideas in Russia. It is perhaps unfair to single out this speech—clearly not one of his best pieces—but it is not inappropriate because it suggests that he had returned in the 1920s to some of the uncertainties of the 1880s. He had never denied his Socialism even though the movement had disappointed him, and it required little stimulus to get him immersed in speculation about it once again.

The next project after *Saint Joan* was his elaborate *The Intelligent Woman's Guide to Socialism and Capitalism*, which is essentially an extended Fabian tract decorated by Shaw's cleverness and burdened by his verbosity. In his effort to prove that Socialism was both feasible and respectable he ranged over much of the ground that he had explored in his plays—from marriage and mating to the society of the future. He warned against the idolatry of a neo-Marxian cult. The hopes that Shaw had for conventional Socialism in the late 1920s, as expressed in his speeches and in *The Intelligent Woman's Guide*, did not last for long. In 1929, after a five-year break from dramatic writing, he issued his play *The Apple Cart* and attached a long Preface on democracy, arguing that this form of government as generally understood could not succeed. The play, as a parody and attack on the British political system, set the pattern for most of his later works. Such works as *Too True to be Good* (1931), *On the Rocks* (1933), *The Simpleton of the Unexpected Isles* (1934), *Geneva* (1938), testified to his continuing contempt for politics and his inability to ignore them. It has been suggested that in these plays Shaw returned to the purposes of the Unpleasant Plays of the 1890s, but he lacked the vigour or the skill that he had possessed at the beginning of his career.[2]

---

[1] Shaw, *The Socialism of Shaw*, edited by James Fuchs (New York, 1926), p. 154.
[2] See the interesting article of Albert H. Silverman, 'Bernard Shaw's Political Extravaganzas', *Drama Survey*, Vol. 5 (Winter 1966–7), pp. 213–22.

On the Rocks is the most interesting of these plays in the present
context because it deals specifically with Socialism and it was
written during the Great Depression, when representative governments seemed paralysed by economic events and after the Labour
Party had twice shared power and failed to act as decisively as
Shaw desired.

This play is again a chastisement of British government and
politics, and this time the ineffectual prime minister was drawn
from the example of Ramsay MacDonald, the Fabian and Socialist
who had become the inert leader of a coalition government at the
end of the 1920s. Shaw's replica in the play, Sir Arthur Chavender,
suffers from an underworked brain until he takes a rest cure during
which he is exposed to the works of Karl Marx. Chavender, inspired by Marxian ideas, resumes his duties with drastic proposals
of Socialist reform, and startles not only the Conservatives but
even the members of the working class, most of whom are unwilling
to gamble on the kind of social reconstruction that is necessary.
Only the character Old Hipney, a relic from the Socialist agitation
of the nineteenth century, who has called Marx to the attention
of Chavender and who yearns for any kind of action or leadership
that will break the impasse, has Shaw's affection. Democracy has
proved to be useless as a political form; reform will never be
achieved by ordinary political processes, he asserts. Old Hipney
is another version of the disenchanted Shaw:

... now I'm for any Napoleon or Mussolini or Lenin or Chavender that
has the stuff in him to take both the people and the spoilers and oppressors by the scruffs of their silly necks and just sling them into the way
they should go with as many kicks as may be needful to make a thorough
job of it.[1]

Prime Minister Chavender, in the final analysis, recognizes that
dictatorial method may be needed; the existing people and institutions are incapable of the necessary action, but he is unwilling to
take the responsibility himself. He prefers retirement to the
challenge that is offered him, and the play ends on a note of despair
and threatened chaos. Once again Shaw had offered the old alternatives—thorough reform within the existing establishment or
violence.

This play, composed in the wake of his journey to Russia and

[1] Shaw, *Complete Plays with Prefaces* (New York, 1962), Vol. 5, p. 605.

during the bleakest period of the Depression, represents a high point in his admiration for Marxism, and it was not long after this that he wrote the line about William Morris being 'on the side of Karl Marx *contra mundum*'. This line, as we have seen, has misled some scholars into concluding that Shaw regarded Morris as a disciple of Marx. On the contrary, Shaw recognized at this time that Morris's Socialism—like his own—was the result of a combination of forces and influences. He would continue to pay tribute to Marx the man to the end of his life, but he could not refrain from occasionally criticizing and laughing at the dogmatism of those—including the Russian Communists—who acted in his name.

And so Shaw's Socialism was an amalgamation of his early admiration of Marx's denunciation of capitalism, his preference for the moderate procedures of the Fabians, and his anarchist yearning for the total transformation of society. Stepniak and Kropotkin moved rather gradually from positions of militance and from support for tactics of violence to dependence on democratic procedures; Bernstein went through a similar transition and remained basically consistent in his final years. Shaw-the-artist, like Morris-the-artist, was not as consistent or as systematic in his ideology, partly because he distrusted ideology. He had borrowed from the whole spectrum of Socialism and anarchism, and until his death he was playing with the ideas he had found. His last full-length play, *Buoyant Billions*, completed in 1948 when he was ninety-two years old, has as its hero a young 'World Betterer' trying to cope with the obstacles—primarily poverty—that restrain his work. Characteristically he finds marriage to a billionaire's daughter the solution to his most pressing problem. In his last Preface, attached to the *Farfetched Fables* that he completed in the year of his death, his 'few speculations as to what may happen in the next million light years' contain reflections on contemporary Marxism and the 'Marxist Church'—as he called the Cominform, on the 'Sham Democracy' that still disgusted him, on 'Bohemian anarchism' that he remembered from his early years, and a dozen other subjects of contemporary relevance. Until his final illness, he remained a jovial Kant to the Socialist movement, preaching as he had done since he discovered the opportunities of London some seventy years earlier.

BIBLIOGRAPHY

In general, the footnotes provide full details of newspaper articles and manuscript collections. These items are not therefore included in the following bibliography of works cited.

ANGEL, Pierre, *Eduard Bernstein et l'évolution du socialisme allemand.* Paris, 1961.

ARNOT, R. Page, *William Morris: the man and the myth.* London, 1964.

AUCHINCLOSS, Katharine L., 'Shaw and the Commissars: The Lenin Years, 1917–1924', *The Shaw Review*, Vol. 6 (May 1963), pp. 51–9.

AUSTIN, Don, 'Comedy Through Tragedy: Dramatic Structure in Saint Joan', *The Shaw Review*, Vol. 8 (May 1965), pp. 52–62.

AVRICH, Paul, *The Russian Anarchists.* Princeton, 1967.

BANHAM, Reyner, 'The Reputation of William Morris', *New Statesman*, Vol. 65 (8 March 1963), pp. 350–1.

BARON, Samuel H., *Plekhanov: The Father of Russian Marxism.* Stanford, 1963.

BAX, Ernest Belfort, *The Ethics of Socialism: Being Further Essays in Modern Socialist Criticism, &c.* Third edition, London, 1893.

——, *Reminiscences and Reflexions of a Mid and Late Victorian.* London, 1918.

BEER, Max, *A History of British Socialism.* Two volumes, London, 1919–20.

BENTLEY, Eric, *Bernard Shaw.* London, 1950.

——, *A Century of Hero-Worship.* New York, Philadelphia, 1944. Revised edition, Boston, 1957.

BERKOVA, K., *S. M. Kravchinskii.* Moscow, 1925.

BERLAU, Abraham Joseph, *The German Social Democratic Party: 1914–1921.* New York, 1949.

BERNERI, Camillo, *Peter Kropotkin: His Federalist Ideas.* London, 1942.

BERNSTEIN, Eduard, *Aus den Jahren meines Exils.* Berlin, 1918.

——, *Cromwell and Communism: Socialism and Democracy in the Great English Revolution.* London, 1930; New York, 1963.

——, *Die deutsche Revolution: Geschichte der Entstehung und ersten Arbeitsperiode der deutschen Republik.* Berlin, 1921.

——, *Die englische Gefahr und das deutsche Volk.* Berlin, 1911.

——, 'Entwicklungsgang eines Sozialisten', *Die Volkswirtschaftslehre der Gegenwart in Selbstdarstellungen, I.* Leipzig, 1924. pp. 1–58.

BERNSTEIN, Eduard, *Evolutionary Socialism: A Criticism and Affirmation.* Translated by Edith C. Harvey. London, 1909; reissued New York, 1930.

——, *Ferdinand Lassalle und seine Bedeutung für die Arbeiterklasse.* Berlin, 1904.

——, *Die Internationale der Arbeiterklasse und der europäische Krieg.* Tübingen, 1916.

——, *My Years of Exile: Reminiscences of a Socialist.* Translated by Bernard Miall. London, 1921.

——, *Die parlamentarische Kontrolle der auswärtigen Politik.* The Hague, 1916.

——, *Der politische Massenstreik und die politische Lage der Sozialdemokratie in Deutschland.* Breslau, 1905.

——, *Sozialismus und Demokratie in der grossen englischen Revolution.* Stuttgart, 1908.

——, *Völkerbund oder Staatenbund: Eine Untersuchung.* Berlin, 1919.

——, *Von 1850 bis 1872: Kindheit und Jugendjahre.* Berlin, 1926.

——, *Die Voraussetzungen des Sozialismus und die Aufgaben der Sozialdemokratie.* Stuttgart, 1899.

——, *Die Wahrheit über die Einkreisung Deutschlands.* Berlin, 1920.

——, *Was ist Sozialismus?* Berlin, 1919.

——, *Wie ist wissenschaftlicher Sozialismus möglich?* Berlin, 1901.

BEVIN, Edwyn, *German Social Democracy During the War.* London, 1918.

BLATCH, Harriot S., 'Stepniak on American Authors', *The Critic.* New York. Vol. XV, 24 January 1891, pp. 48–9.

BLUM, George P., 'German Social Democracy in the Reichstag'. Ph.D. Dissertation, University of Minnesota, 1962.

BOROVOI, A., and LEBEDEV, N., editors. *Sbornik Statei Posviashchennyi Pamiati P. A. Kropotkina.* Moscow, 1922.

BRANDES, Georg, *Correspondance de Georg Brandes.* Two volumes, Copenhagen, 1952–6.

BRINTON, Crane, *English Political Thought in the Nineteenth Century.* Cambridge, Mass., 1949.

BROMBERGER, Frederick Sigmund, 'William Morris's Concepts of Ideal Human Society as Indicated in Public Lectures, 1877–1894; and in Three Prose Romances, 1886–1890'. Ph.D. Dissertation, University of Southern California, 1964.

BRUSTEIN, Robert, *The Theatre of Revolt.* Boston, 1964.

CARPENTER, Edward, *Forecasts of the Coming Century by a Decade of Writers.* Manchester, 1897.

——, *My Days and Dreams: Being Autobiographical Notes.* Third edition, London, 1921.

CARY, Elisabeth Luther, *William Morris: Poet, Craftsman, Socialist*. New York, London, 1902.

CHESTERTON, G. K., *George Bernard Shaw*. London, 1935.

CLAYTON, Joseph, *The Rise and Decline of Socialism in Great Britain: 1884–1924*. London, 1926.

CLUTTON-BROCK, Arthur, *William Morris: His Work and Influence*. London, 1914.

COLE, G. D. H., *A History of Socialist Thought*. Five volumes in seven, London, 1953–60.

COLE, Margaret, 'The Fellowship of William Morris', *Virginia Historical Quarterly*, Vol. 24 (Spring, 1948), pp. 260–77.

——, *The Story of Fabian Socialism*. Stanford, 1961.

——, editor. *The Webbs and Their Work*. London, 1949.

COMPTON-RICKETT, Arthur, *William Morris: A Study in Personality*. New York, 1913.

DAN, Theodore, *The Origins of Bolshevism*. Edited and translated from the Russian by Joel Carmichael. New York, 1964.

DEDIJER, Vladimir, *The Road to Sarajevo*. New York, 1966.

DEICH', Lev', *Sergei Mikhailovich' Kravchinskii-Stepniak': (Baloven' Sud'by)*. Petrograd, 1919.

DRACHKOVITCH, Milorad M., *Les socialismes français et allemand et le problème de la guerre: 1870–1914*. Geneva, 1953.

DRINKWATER, John, *William Morris: A Critical Study*. New York, 1912.

DUKORE, Bernard F., 'Toward an Interpretation of "Major Barbara" ', *The Shaw Review*, VI (May 1963), pp. 62–70.

——, 'The Undershaft Maxims', *Modern Drama*, IX (May 1966). pp. 90–100.

DUTT, R. Palme, 'George Bernard Shaw', *Labour Monthly*, Vol. 32 (December 1950), pp. 529–40.

ELIOT, T. S., 'London Letter', in *A Dial Miscellany* edited by William Wasserstrom. Syracuse, 1963. pp. 47–50.

ELLIS, Havelock, *Kropotkin: A Tribute*. Berkeley Heights, N.J., 1963.

ELLIS, R. W., ed., *Bernard Shaw and Karl Marx: A Symposium, 1884–1889*. New York, 1930.

ELTZBACHER, Paul, *Anarchism*. Translated by Steven T. Byington. New York, 1908.

ENGELS, Friedrich, letters translated in 'Marx and Engels on the British Working-Class Movement: 1879–1895', *The Labour Monthly: A Magazine of International Labour*. London (October and November, 1933).

EPSTEIN, Klaus, 'Three American Studies of German Socialism', *World Politics*, XI (July 1959), pp. 629–51.

ERVINE, St. John, *Bernard Shaw: His Life, Work, and Friends*. New York, 1956.

ESHLEMAN, Lloyd Wendell, *A Victorian Rebel: The Life of William Morris*. New York, 1940.

FAULKNER, Peter, *William Morris and W. B. Yeats*. Dublin, 1962.

FISCHER, George, *Russian Liberalism: From Gentry to Intelligentsia*. Cambridge, Mass., 1958.

FORD, Ford Madox, *The Soul of London: A Survey of a Modern City*. London, 1911.

FREMANTLE, Anne, *This Little Band of Prophets*. London, 1960.

FRITZSCHE, Gustav, *William Morris' Sozialismus und anarchistischer Kommunismus: Darstellung des Systems und Untersuchung der Quellen*. Leipzig, 1927.

GAY, Peter, *The Dilemma of Democratic Socialism: Eduard Bernstein's Challenge to Marx*. New York, 1952.

GLASIER, J. Bruce, *William Morris and the Early Days of the Socialist Movement*. London, New York, 1921.

GNEUSS, Christian, 'Eduard Bernstein', *Soviet Survey*, No. 32 (April–June 1960), pp. 14–20.

——, 'The Precursor: Eduard Bernstein', in Leopold Labedz, ed., *Revisionism: Essays on the History of Marxist Ideas*. New York, 1962.

GOLDMAN, Emma, *My Disillusionment in Russia*. Garden City, New York, 1923.

GRONLUND, Laurence, *The Co-operative Commonwealth*. Edited by G. B. Shaw. Third edition, London, 1892.

GUYAU, Jean Marie, *Esquisse d'une morale sans obligation, ni sanction*. Second edition, Paris, 1890.

HARE, Richard, *Portraits of Russian Personalities Between Reform and Revolution*. London, 1959.

HAYES, Carlton J. H., 'The History of German Socialism Reconsidered', *American Historical Review*, XXIII (October, 1917), pp. 62–101.

HEADLAM, Stewart D., 'A Plea for Peace', *To-Day* (September 1887).

HELMHOLTZ-PHELAN, Anna A. von, *The Social Philosophy of William Morris*. Durham, 1927.

HENDERSON, Archibald, *Bernard Shaw: Playboy and Prophet*. New York, 1932.

——, *George Bernard Shaw: His Life and Works*. Cincinnati, 1911.

——, *George Bernard Shaw: Man of the Century*. New York, 1956.

HENDERSON, Philip, *William Morris: His Life, Work and Friends*. New York, 1967.

HICKS, Granville, *Figures of Transition: A Study of British Literature at the end of the Nineteenth Century*. New York, 1939.

HODGSON, W. Earl, *A Night with a Nihilist*. Cupar-Fife, 1886.

HOWELLS, William Dean, *Life in Letters of William Dean Howells*. Edited by Mildred Howells. Two volumes. Garden City, N.Y., 1928.

HUMMERT, Paul A., 'Bernard Shaw's Marxist Utopias', *The Shaw Review*, Vol. II (September 1959), pp. 7–26.

HURLBERT, William H., 'State Christianity and the French Elections', *The Nineteenth Century*, XVIII (November 1885), pp. 745–62.

HYNDMAN, Henry Mayers, *The Record of an Adventurous Life*. New York, 1911.

IRVINE, William, *The Universe of G.B.S.* New York, 1949.

JACKSON, Holbrook, *Bernard Shaw*. London, 1907.

——, *Dreamers of Dreams: The Rise and Fall of 19th Century Idealism*. New York, n.d. (1948).

——, *The Eighteen Nineties: A Review of Art and Ideas at the Close of the Nineteenth Century*. London, 1913.

——, *William Morris: Craftsman-Socialist*. Revised edition. London, 1926.

JAMES, Henry, *English Hours*. Boston, New York, 1905.

JAURÈS, Jean, *Les origines du socialisme allemand*. Translated from the Latin by Adrien Veber. Paris, 1960.

JOLL, James, *The Anarchists*. Boston, 1964.

——, *The Second International: 1889–1914*. New York, 1956.

JONES, Peter d'A., *The Christian Socialist Revival, 1877–1914: Religion, Class and Social Conscience in Late-Victorian England*. Princeton, 1968.

KAUTSKY, Karl, *Ethik und materialistische Geschichtsauffassung*. Stuttgart, 1906.

KAYE, Julian B., *Bernard Shaw and the Nineteenth-Century Tradition*. Norman, 1958.

KENNAN, George, *Siberia and the Exile System*. Two volumes, New York, 1891.

KENNAN, George and STEPNIAK, S., *George Kennan on Russian Justice and S. Stepniak's Appeal to President Cleveland: 1893*. New York, n.d. (1893?).

KRAVCHINSKII, S. M., see STEPNIAK.

KROPOTKIN, Peter, *Anarchist Morality*. Ninth edition, London, n.d.

——, 'Assez d'illusion', *Les Temps Nouveaux*, Vol. 13 (20 July 1907), pp. 1–2.

——, 'The Coming Anarchy', *The Nineteenth Century*, Vol. 22 (August 1887), pp. 149–64.

KROPOTKIN, Peter, 'The Coming Reign of Plenty', *Nineteenth Century*, Vol. 23 (June 1888), pp. 817–37.

——, *The Conquest of Bread*. London, 1906.

——, *La conquête du pain*. Préface par Élisée Reclus. Twelfth edition, Paris, 1913.

——, 'The Constitutional Agitation in Russia', *The Nineteenth Century*, Vol. 57 (January 1905), pp. 27–45.

——, 'La crise du socialisme', *Les Temps Nouveaux*, I (26 October–1 November), 1895, pp. 1–2.

——, *Ethics: Origin and Development*. Authorized translation from the Russian by Louis S. Friedland and Joseph R. Piroshnikoff. New York, 1924.

——, *Fields, Factories and Workshops, or Industry Combined with Agriculture and Brain Work with Manual Work*. Second Impression, New York, London, 1901.

——, *The Great French Revolution: 1789–1793*. Translated from the French by N. F. Dryhurst. London, 1909.

——, *In Russian and French Prisons*. London, 1887.

——, 'The Industrial Village of the Future', *Nineteenth Century*, Vol. 24 (October 1888), pp. 513–30.

——, *Kropotkin's Revolutionary Pamphlets*. Edited by Roger N. Baldwin. New York, 1927.

——, 'Une lettre inéditée de Pierre Kropotkine à Max Nettlau', *International Review of Social History*, IX. 1964. Part 2, pp. 268–285.

——, *Memoirs of a Revolutionist*. Boston, New York, 1899.

——, *Modern Science and Anarchism*. London, 1912.

——, *Mutual Aid: A Factor of Evolution*. Foreword by Ashley Montagu. Boston, 1955.

——, 'Nashe Otnoshenie k' Krest'ianskim' i Rabochim' Soiuzam'', *Listki 'Khleb' i Volia*' (14 November 1906), pp. 3–5.

——, 'On the Present Condition of Russia', *The Outlook*, vol. 58 (8 January 1898), pp. 113–17.

——, *Paroles d'un révolté*. Edited by Élisée Reclus. Paris, 1885.

——, 'The Present Condition of Russia', *The Nineteenth Century*, vol. 38 (September 1895), pp. 519–35.

——, 'The Present Crisis in Russia', *North American Review*, Vol. 172 (May 1901), pp. 711–23.

——, 'Revoliutsiia Politicheskaia i Ekonomicheskaia', *Listki 'Khleb' i Volia*' (30 October 1906).

——, 'The Revolution in Russia', *The Nineteenth Century*, Vol. 58 (December 1905), pp. 865–83.

——, *Russian Literature*. New York, 1905.

KROPOTKIN, Peter, 'Russian Schools and the Holy Synod', *North American Review*, Vol. 174 (April 1902), pp. 518–27.

——, 'Syndicalisme et parlementarisme', *Les Temps Nouveaux*. Vol. 12 (13 October 1906), pp. 1–2.

——, *The Terror in Russia: An Appeal to the British Nation*. London, 1909.

LABEDZ, Leopold, ed., *Revisionism: Essays on the History of Marxist Ideas*. New York, 1962.

LANDAUER, Carl, *European Socialism: A History of Ideas and Movements*. Two volumes. Berkeley, 1959.

LANSBURY, George, *What I Saw in Russia*. London, 1920.

LASSALLE, Ferdinand, *Ferd. Lassalle's Reden und Schriften: Neue Gesammtausgabe*. Mit einer biographischen Einleitung herausgegeben von Ed. Bernstein. Three volumes. Berlin, 1904.

LEMIRE, Eugene Dennis, 'The Unpublished Lectures of William Morris: A Critical Edition, Including an Introductory Survey and a Calendar and Bibliography of Morris's Public Speeches'. Ph.D. Dissertation, Wayne State University, 1962.

LEWIS, C. S., *Rehabilitations and Other Essays*. London, 1939.

LIDTKE, Vernon L., *The Outlawed Party: Social Democracy in Germany, 1878–1890*. Princeton, 1966.

MCBRIAR, A. M., *Fabian Socialism and English Politics: 1884–1918*. Cambridge, England, 1962.

MACKAIL, J. W., *The Life of William Morris*. Two volumes, London, 1899.

MAITRON, Jean, *Histoire du mouvement anarchiste en France (1880–1914)*. Paris, 1951.

MARTIN, James J., *Men Against the State: The Expositors of Individualist Anarchism in America, 1827–1908*. De Kalb, Illinois, 1953.

MASARYK, Thomas Garrigue, *The Spirit of Russia: Studies in History, Literature, and Philosophy*. Translated from the German by Eden and Cedar Paul. Two volumes, London, New York, 1919. Second edition, 1955.

MATTHIAS, Erich, 'Ideologie et pratique: Le faux débat Bernstein-Kautsky', *Annales: Économies, Sociétés, Civilisations*, 19(1), 1964, pp. 19–30.

MAVOR, James, *My Windows on the Street of the World*. Two volumes, London, 1923.

MAXIMOV, G. P., *Internatsional'nyi Sbornik Posviashcennyi Desiatoi Godovshchine Smerti P. A. Kropotkina*. Chicago, 1931.

MAYER, Gustav, *Friedrich Engels: A Biography*. London, 1936.

MEHRING, Franz, *Geschichte der deutschen Sozialdemokratie*. Two volumes, Berlin, 1960. .

MORRIS, May, *William Morris: Artist, Writer, Socialist.* Oxford, 1936. Reissued 1966.

MORRIS, William, *Chants for Socialists.* London, 1885.

——, *The Collected Works of William Morris.* Twenty-four volumes, London, 1910–15. Reissued 1966.

——, *The Letters of William Morris to His Family and Friends.* Edited by Philip Henderson. London, 1950.

——, 'The Society of the Future', *The Commonweal*, Volume Five. (30 March 1889, pp. 98–9; 6 April 1889, pp. 108–9; and 13 April 1889, pp. 114–15.)

——, 'Where Are We Now?' *The Commonweal.* (15 November 1890), p. 361.

MORRIS, William and BELFORT BAX, E., *Socialism: Its Growth and Outcome.* Second edition, London, 1896.

MOSER, Charles A., 'A Nihilist's Career: S. M. Stepniak-Kravchinskij', *The American Slavic and East European Review*, XX, No. 1 (February 1961), pp. 55–71.

NETHERCOT, Arthur H., *The First Five Lives of Annie Besant.* Chicago, 1960.

——, *Men and Supermen: The Shavian Portrait Gallery.* Cambridge, Mass., 1954.

NETTL, J. P., *Rosa Luxemburg.* Oxford, 1966.

N. (NETTLAU, MAX?), 'German Social Democracy and Edward Bernstein', Freedom Pamphlets, No. 12. London, 1900.

NETTLAU, Max, *Ocherki po istorii anarkhicheskikh idei i stat'i po raznym sotsial'nym voprosam.* Detroit, 1951.

NOVAK, David, 'The Place of Anarchism in the History of Political Thought', *The Review of Politics*, XX (July 1958), pp. 307–29.

OSTERGAARD, Geoffrey, 'G.B.S.—Anarchist', *The New Statesman and Nation*, Vol. 46 (21 November 1953), p. 628.

OZY, 'The Dramatist's Dilemma: an Interpretation of Major Barbara', *The Shaw Bulletin*, Vol. 2 (January 1958), pp. 18–24.

PEASE, E. R., *The History of the Fabian Society.* Third edition, London, 1963.

PELLING, Henry, *The Origins of the Labour Party: 1880–1900.* Second edition, London, 1965.

PLANCHE, Fernand and Jean Delphy, *Kropotkine*, Descendant des Grands Princes de Smolensk, Page de l'Empereur, Savant illustre, Révolutionnaire international, Vulgarisateur de la Pensée anarchiste. Paris, 1948.

POBEDONOSTSEV, Constantine, 'Russia and Popular Education', *North American Review*, Vol. 173 (September 1901), pp. 349–54.

PRAGER, Eugen, *Die Geschichte der U.S.P.D. Entstehung und Entwick-*

lung der Unabhängigen Sozialdemokratischen Partei Deutschlands.
Second edition, Berlin, 1922.

RUSSELL, Bertrand, *German Social Democracy.* London, 1896; New York, 1965.

——, *Proposed Roads to Freedom.* New York, 1919.

SALT, Henry S., *Company I have Kept.* London, 1930.

SANDERS, Wm. Stephen, *Early Socialist Days.* London, 1927.

SCHORSKE, Carl E., *German Social Democracy: 1905-1917.* Cambridge, Mass., 1955.

SHAW, George Bernard, *Collected Letters: 1874-1897.* Edited by Dan H. Laurence. New York, 1965.

——, *The Collected Works of Bernard Shaw.* Ayot St. Lawrence edition, New York, 1930. Thirty volumes.

——, *Complete Plays With Prefaces.* Six volumes. New York, 1962.

——, Editor, *Fabian Essays.* Jubilee edition, London, 1948.

——, *The Fabian Society: What it has Done & How it has Done It.* Fabian Tract No. 41. London, 1892.

——, 'The Jevonian Criticism of Marx', *To-Day*, No. 13 (January 1885).

——, *Selected Non-Dramatic Writings of Bernard Shaw.* Edited by Dan H. Laurence. Boston, 1965.

——, 'Socialism at the International Congress', *Cosmopolis: An International Review,* III (September 1896), pp. 658-73.

——, *The Socialism of Shaw.* Edited by James Fuchs. New York, 1926.

——, 'A Word About Stepniak', *To-Morrow: A Monthly Review,* No. 2 (February 1896), pp. 99-107.

——, 'A Word for War', *To-Day* (September 1887).

SHISHKO, L. E., *Sergei Mikhailovich' Kravchinskii i Kruzhok' Chaikovtsev'.* St. Petersburg, 1906.

SHORT, Clarice, 'William Morris and Keats', *PMLA* 59 (June 1944), pp. 513-23.

SHUB, David, 'Kropotkin and Lenin', *The Russian Review,* XII (October 1953), pp. 227-34.

SILVERMAN, Albert H., 'Bernard Shaw's Political Extravaganzas', *Drama Survey,* Vol. V (Winter, 1966-7), pp. 213-22.

SMITH, Henry Nash, and William M. Gibson, editors, *Mark Twain-Howells Letters: The Correspondence of Samuel L. Clemens and William D. Howells, 1872-1910.* Cambridge, Mass., 1960.

SMITH, Percy J., *The Unrepentant Pilgrim: A Study of the Development of Bernard Shaw.* Boston, 1965.

SOLOMON, Stanley J., '*Saint Joan* as Epic Tragedy', *Modern Drama,* Vol. 6 (February 1964), pp. 437-49.

Sozialdemokratische Partei Deutschlands, *Protokoll über die Verhand-*

lungen des Parteitags der Sozialdemokratischen Partei Deutschlands, 1919. Berlin, 1919.

STEPNIAK, S. (S. M. KRAVCHINSKII), 'The Actual Position of Russia', *Commonweal*, I (March 1885), pp. 10–11.

——, *The Career of a Nihilist: A Novel.* Second edition, London, n.d. (1901?).

——, *King Stork and King Log: A Study of Modern Russia.* Two volumes, London, 1896.

——, *The New Convert: A Drama in Four Acts.* Translated from the Russian by Thomas B. Eyges. Boston, 1917.

——, *Nihilism as It Is.* London, n.d. (1894).

——, *Russia Under the Tzars.* Rendered into English by William Westall. New York, 1885.

——, *The Russian Peasantry: Their Agrarian Condition, Social Life and Religion.* New York, 1888.

——, 'Russian Political Prisons', *To-Day*, I (June 1884), pp. 401–15; and II (July 1884), pp. 1–19.

——, *The Russian Storm-Cloud; or Russia in her Relations to Neighbouring Countries.* London, 1886.

——, *Shtundist' Pavel' Rudenko.* Geneva, 1900.

——, *Smert' za smert' (Ubiistvo Mezentseva),* Introduction by V. Petrovskii. Reprinted from the 1878 edition, Petrograd, 1920.

——, *Sobranie Sochinenii.* Six volumes. St. Petersburg, 1907–8.

——, *Sochineniia v Dvukh Tomakh*, Moscow, 1958.

——, *Underground Russia: Revolutionary Profiles and Sketches from Life.* With a Preface by Peter Lavroff. Translated from the Italian. London, 1883.

——, 'What Americans Can Do for Russia', *The North American Review*, Vol. 153 (November 1891), pp. 596–609.

STOKES, E. E., Jr., 'Morris and Bernard Shaw', *The Journal of the William Morris Society*, Vol. I (Winter 1961), pp. 13–18.

——, 'Shaw and William Morris', *The Shaw Bulletin*, No. 4 (Summer 1953), pp. 16–19.

——, 'William Morris and Bernard Shaw: A Socialist-Artistic Relationship', Ph.D. Dissertation, University of Texas, 1951.

STRAUSS, E., *Bernard Shaw: Art and Socialism.* London, 1942.

STRETTON, Hesba, and ******, *The Highway of Sorrow.* New York, 1894.

THOMPSON, E. P., *William Morris: Romantic to Revolutionary.* New York, 1961.

THOMPSON, Paul, *The Work of William Morris.* New York, 1967.

THUN, A., *Geschichte der revolutionären Bewegungen in Russland.* Leipzig, 1883.

TIKHOMIROV, L., *Russia: Political and Social*. Translated from the French by Edward Aveling. Second edition, London, 1892.

TSUZUKI, Chushichi, *H. M. Hyndman and British Socialism*. London, 1961.

TUCHMAN, Barbara, *The Proud Tower: A Portrait of the World Before the War: 1890–1914*. New York, 1966.

ULAM, Adam B., *Philosophical Foundations of English Socialism*. New York, 1964.

VALLANCE, Aylmer, *William Morris: His Art, His Writings and His Public Life*. London, 1897.

VENTURI, Franco, *Roots of Revolution: A History of the Populist and Socialist Movements in Nineteenth Century Russia*. Translated from the Italian by Frances Haskell. New York, 1960.

VOYNICH, E. L. (translator)., *The Humour of Russia*. With an introduction by Stepniak. London, 1895.

WALL, Bernard, 'William Morris and Karl Marx', *The Dublin Review*, Vol. 202 (January 1938), pp. 39–47.

WALLACE, Donald Mackenzie, *Russia*. London, 1877.

WEST, Alick, *A Good Man Fallen Among Fabians*. London, 1950.

WINSTEN, Stephen, *Days With Bernard Shaw*. London, n.d. (1919).

WOODCOCK, George and Ivan Avakumović, *The Anarchist Prince: A Biographical Study of Peter Kropotkin*. London, New York, 1950.

YARMOLINSKY, Avrahm, *Road to Revolution: A Century of Russian Radicalism*. London, 1957.

INDEX

INDEX

other writings, 18, 111–15, 127–9, 136–7, 193–5, 199–200, 206, 218, 225–8; Shaw and anarchism, 114–115, 118–21, 198, 205; and Fabianism, 18–19, 114–18, 193–5, 226; and Marxism, 18, 111–14, 136–7, 225–8; and Bernstein, 152–3 f.; and Kropotkin, 53, 76, 115, 118–22, 192, 204, 208–9; and Morris, 77–9, 106–7, 110, 113, 117, 120, 122–30, 193, 200, 204, 205, 224, 228; and Stepniak, 30, 40, 48–9, 132, 135–6, 208, 224

Smith, Adam, 79

Social Democratic Federation (British), 15–16, 21, 79, 81, 85 ff., 106 f., 113 ff., 124, 129, 140

Social Democratic Party (German), 11–14, 44, 45, 136–7, 138–65, 167, 174

Socialism, Marxian, in England, 10, 14–17, 23, in 1880s, 11–13; Erfurt Programme, 14–17; Stepniak on, 38–40, 44, 50; Kropotkin on, 62, 73–4, 166–7, 174, 176, 179; Morris's, 19–21, 77 ff., 105 ff.; Shaw's, 17–19, 111–22, 130–7, 192–228 passim; Bernstein's, 138–65; see also Marx, Engels, Fabianism

Socialist League, 16, 85–105 passim; 114 ff., 124–5, 129, 140

Society of the Friends of Russian Freedom, 43; American Branch, 47

Sophists, 187–8

Sorge, F. A., 92

Sozialdemokrat, 11, 12, 140, 143

Sozialistische Monatshefte, 160

Sparticists, 163

SPD, see Social Democratic Party (German)

Spencer, Herbert, 189

Spinoza, Baruch de, 188

Stalin, Joseph, 220

Stepniak, S. M., 7–9, 22–4, 29–52; bibliographical notes, 25; narodnik, 7–8; terrorist and exile, 8–9, 29–30; Underground Russia, 9, 16, 31–4, 41; Smert' za Smert', 8, 31–3; Russia Under the Tsars, 35–7; Sochinennia (1958), 25, 36; The Russian Storm-Cloud, 37; The Russian Peasantry, 37–9; The Career of a Nihilist, 41–4, 51–2; Nihilism As It Is, 44 n.; King Stork and King Log, 49–50; other

writings, 34–5, 47–9, 50–1, 73; Free Russia movement, 43–7, 71; in America, 30, 45–7; and Bernstein, 29–30, 45, 143, 144; and Kropotkin, 7–9, 53–5, 71, 73, 75, 169, 174; and Morris, 21, 33–4, 40, 79–80, 82, 92, 109; and Shaw, 30, 40, 48–9, 132, 135–6, 208, 224

Stokes, E. E., 122 n., 127

Stolypin, P. A., 174

Storm, The, 47

Strauss, Emil, 199, 201

Stretton, Hesba, 47–8

Stundists, 38, 47–8

Temps Nouveaux, Les, 166, 167

Terror, Stepniak's justification of, 8–9, 29–33; Kropotkin on, 7, 73; Shaw on, 205

Theatre, see Drama

Theatre of Revolt, The, 192

Third Section, 8

Thompson, E. P., 27, 78, 103

Thompson, Paul, 27, 78 n.

Thunderstorm, The, 47

Times (London), 3, 34, 35, 161, 181

To-Day, 34, 113, 122, 124

Tolstoy, Leo, 46, 137, 168, 208

Tory Gold scandal, 115

Trepov, F. F., 8

Tucker, Benjamin, 93, 118, 128

Turgenev, Ivan, 6, 41, 47, 208

Tyler, Wat, 84

Unabhängige Sozialdemokratische Partei Deutschlands, 162–3

Versailles Treaty, 164

Voinich, E. L., 47

Volkhovsky, Felix, 8 n.

Voltaire, F. M. A. de, 1, 2, 188

Vperiod, 6

Wagner, Richard, 128

Wallace, Donald M., 36

Wallas, Graham, 115, 116, 158 n.

Watson, Robert Spence, 43

Webb, Sidney, 113, 115, 126, 155

Weber, Max, 152

West, Alick, 201

Whittier, John Greenleaf, 47

William II, Kaiser, 14, 157, 158

Wilson, Charlotte, 54, 114

Wilson, Woodrow, 162, 207, 209